D0747233

Practical Lessons from the Experience of Israel

F. C. Gilbert

TEACH Services, Inc.
P U B L I S H I N G
www.TEACHServices.com • (800) 367-1844

World rights reserved. This book or any portion thereof may not be copied or reproduced in any form or manner whatever, except as provided by law, without the written permission of the publisher, except by a reviewer who may quote brief passages in a review.

The author assumes full responsibility for the accuracy of all facts and quotations as cited in this book. The opinions expressed in this book are the author's personal views and interpretations, and do not necessarily reflect those of the publisher.

This book is provided with the understanding that the publisher is not engaged in giving spiritual, legal, medical, or other professional advice. If authoritative advice is needed, the reader should seek the counsel of a competent professional.

Facsimile Reproduction

As this book played a formative role in the development of Christian thought and the publisher feels that this book, with its candor and depth, still holds significance for the church today. Therefore the publisher has chosen to reproduce this historical classic from an original copy. Frequent variations in the quality of the print are unavoidable due to the condition of the original. Thus the print may look darker or lighter or appear to be missing detail, more in some places than in others.

Copyright © 2017 TEACH Services, Inc.
ISBN-13: 978-1-4796-0812-6 (Paperback)
Library of Congress Control Number: 2017906038

TEACH Services, Inc.
PUBLISHING
www.TEACHServices.com • (800) 367-1844

PRACTICAL LESSONS

FROM THE

EXPERIENCE OF ISRAEL

FOR THE

CHURCH OF TO-DAY.

BY F. C. GILBERT,

A CONVERTED HEBREW.

PUBLISHED BY THE AUTHOR.

Press of
South Lancaster Printing Company,
South Lancaster, Mass.

Entered, according to Act of Congress, in the year 1902, by
F. C. GILBERT,
In the Office of the Librarian of Congress, Washington, D. C.
All Rights Reserved.

"For whatsoever things were written aforetime were written for *our learning*, that we through patience and comfort of the scriptures might have hope." Romans 15 :4.

" Moreover, brethren, I would not that ye should be ignorant, how that all our fathers were under the cloud, and all passed through the sea; and were all baptized unto Moses in the cloud and in the sea; and did all eat the same spiritual meat; and did all drink the same spiritual drink : for they drank of that spiritual Rock that followed them : and that Rock was Christ. But with many of them God was not well pleased : for they were overthrown in the wilderness. *Now these things were our examples,* to the intent we should not lust after evil things, as they also lusted. Neither be ye idolaters, as were some of them; as it is written, The people sat down to eat and drink, and rose up to play. Neither let us commit fornication, as some of them committed, and fell in one day three and twenty thousand. Neither let us tempt Christ as some of them also tempted, and were destroyed of serpents. Neither murmur ye, as some of them also murmured, and were destroyed of the destroyer. Now all these things happened unto them *for ensamples ;* and they are written for *our admonition, upon whom the ends of the world are come.* Wherefore let him that thinketh he standeth take heed lest he fall." 1 Cor. 10 : 1–12.

"So we see that they could not enter in because of unbelief. Let us therefore fear, lest, a promise being left us of entering into His rest, any of you should seem to come short of it. . . . Let us labor, therefore, to enter into that rest, lest any man fall after the same example of unbelief." Hebrews 3 : 19 ; 4 : 1–11.

" The history of the children of Israel is written for the instruction and admonition of all Christians. When the Israelites were overtaken by dangers and difficulties, and their way seemed hedged up, their faith forsook them, and they murmured against the leader whom God had appointed for them."

" The example of ancient Israel is given as a warning to the people of God, that they may avoid unbelief and escape His wrath. If the iniquities of the Hebrews had been omitted from the sacred record, and only their virtues recounted, *their history would fail to teach us the lesson that it does.*"

" With the history of the children of Israel before us, let us take heed, and not be found committing the same sins, following in the same way of unbelief and rebellion."

—White.

INTRODUCTION.

A PEOPLE without a home, a race without a country, such is the orthodox Jew of to-day; and such he has been for nearly two thousand years. No people ever had so many promises offered them as the Jews, no people ever had such bright and cheering prospects. They were originally set apart for a particular purpose which meant then, and still to-day means, much to the people and church of God. Israel was to be a lesson for the church.

Their refusal to comply with the wishes of God led them to become a forsaken people; and the Savior said to them just before the close of His earthly ministry:

"The kingdom of God shall be taken from you, and given to a nation bringing forth the fruits thereof." [1]

During these many years their sufferings and persecutions have been a faithful witness to the truth of the Savior's words. Still God offered them salvation, and does even to this present day. His work, however, did not cease; for what if some of them did not believe? Shall their unbelief make void the promise of God? God forbid.

The work of the Gospel of the grace of God continued, even though the Jews remained in unbelief; and it does continue till this day. However, it should be remembered that the experience of the Jews has many valuable and profitable lessons for the church of all ages; for history repeats itself.

It has been the purpose of the author to present some of the practical lessons from the experiences of Israel for the church of to-day. Disobedience to God's commands resulted in great loss to the Jewish people; obedience always brought to them many blessings. As the Apostle Paul says:

"Be not deceived; God is not mocked: for whatsoever a man soweth, that shall he also reap." [2]

[1] Matt. 21:43.   [2] Gal. 6:7.

Thus it always has been, and thus it is at the present time.

It is the wish of the author that all the profits which may accrue from this work be devoted to the advancement of the gospel among his kinsmen in the flesh ; for this reason he has also supervised its publication.

And now this work is commended to those who desire to become better acquainted with the ways of Him who dealeth after the counsels of his own will,—with the prayer that the Holy Spirit shall use the feeble efforts to encourage, strengthen, comfort, and enlighten those who desire to see the purpose of God for the church of to-day, as revealed through Jesus Christ and His ancient people Israel.

F. C. G.

South Lancaster, Mass., July, 1902.

NOTE TO THE READER.

THE author has designed to make this work helpful, simple, and practical in all its phases. Because of the simplicity of the Master's teachings, the common people heard Him gladly. No effort, therefore, has been spared to bring this work within the comprehension of all.

Paragraphs throughout the entire work are numbered, and sub-headings are frequently placed in the chapters. The small figures in the body of the work are an index to the scriptures found at the foot of the page.

The alphabetical letters signify explanatory notes at the end of the chapter. The Appendix was inserted to give other laws of the Jews not found in the body of the work.

Many of the Jewish laws quoted have no reference given; this is because the names would not be of any special service to the reader. The authorities are mostly translated, when selected from the Talmudic writings.

In addition to the Bible, the writer has consulted such works as Geikie, Edersheim, Pick, McCall, and others. Most of the Talmudical quotations are taken from the Talmud direct, or from translations of the same.

This work is now committed to the hands of all, and the author must ask the reader to manifest that large charity which hides a multitude of errors. "Abhor that which is evil; cleave to that which is good." Romans 12 : 9.

F. C. G.

" The Lord bless thee, and keep thee ;"

" The Lord make his face shine upon thee, and be gracious unto thee :"

" The Lord lift up his countenance upon thee, and give thee peace."

—Numbers 6 : 24–26.

PRACTICAL LESSONS.

CHAPTER I.

God's Purpose with the Jews.

"But Israel shall be saved in the Lord with an everlasting salvation."
Isa. 45:11.

THE JEWS AS A DISTINCT PEOPLE.

IN all the annals of history during the past four thousand years, no people have stood so prominently yet distinctively alone, separated from all other peoples yet mingled with them, as have the Jews. There is neither country, nor clime, nor race, nor city, where the Jew is not found. He may be an English Jew, an American Jew, a German Jew, a Russian Jew, a French Jew, a Karaite Jew, an African Jew; still he is a Jew, in every case bearing the distinctive characteristics of the race. Why is this? What reasons can be offered that, amid all these opposing circumstances, this racial individuality is preserved?

2. In nearly every large city a colony of these people can be found, the colonization usually being styled "The Ghetto." They have their own peculiar customs, ceremonies, feasts, fasts, rites, in which no other people participate. But the remarkable thing of it all, is that most of the customs and distinctive features of the Jew can be traced back to the days of Bible record, and have as their basis a " Thus saith the Lord."

A PECULIAR MISSION.

3. When we consider them as a race from this standpoint, it is not difficult to believe that in the mind of God a specific mission must have been theirs in the history of the world. This purpose is very clearly portrayed in the word of God, and a

large part of the Bible is occupied with its explanation. Particularly is this evident when we come to the New Testament, and read the Savior's conversation with the woman at the well of Samaria [1] concerning the purpose of God with the Jews. We can then readily see why, till the advent of Christ, they were kept as a peculiar people. He said:

"Ye worship ye know not what: we know what we worship: for salvation is of the Jews." [2]

4. The world was lost through sin; [3] all mankind had become involved in this terrible condition; [4] the race was unable to lift itself to its original exalted position. It must be redeemed; it must be brought back by redemption; it must be purchased again from the usurper. [5] By man or by nations of men this could not be done. [6] It must be accomplished by One who was set apart for this particular work, chosen purposely of God. [7] In other words, it was to be carried out by One who must be *anointed* [8] for this work; set apart, set off, separated, from every other person.

THE CHOSEN ONE.

5. This particular One was Jesus Christ; He was the chosen of God: He was the Anointed One. Hence He himself said, when in His home town, one Sabbath day in the synagogue:

"The Spirit of the Lord is upon me, because he hath anointed me to preach the gospel to the poor." [9]

And of Him the Apostle Peter said later:

"How God anointed Jesus of Nazareth with the Holy Ghost and with power." [10]

6. On another occasion when a large number of the followers of Christ were gathered together, after the release of the apostles Peter and John from prison, in their prayer to God, they said:

"For of a truth against thy holy child Jesus, whom thou hast

[1] John 4:7–10.　[2] John 4:22.　[3] Rom. 3:19.　[4] Rom. 6:23.　[5] Isa. 52:3.
[6] Ps. 49:7.　[7] Isa. 43:10.　[8] Ps. 2:7, margin.　[9] Luke 4:18.　[10] Acts 10:38.

Abraham Leaving Home.

anointed, both Herod, and Pontius Pilate, with the Gentiles, and the people of Israel, were gathered together, for to do whatsoever thy hand and thy counsel determined before to be done." [11]

Again the Savior said to the Jews in another place:

"Is it not written in your law, I said, Ye are gods? If he called them gods unto whom the word of God came, and the Scripture cannot be broken; say ye of him, whom the Father hath sanctified, and sent into the world, Thou blasphemest, because I said, I am the Son of God." [12]

THE JEWS TO REVEAL THE MESSIAH.

7. It is thus clear from the word of God that the "Anointed," "Sanctified," "Separated" One whom God chose to carry on this work was Jesus (Helper, Savior) Christ (Hebrew, Messiah, Anointed). But that the world might be prepared for Him; that the world might learn concerning Him and His great work for the lost and sinful race, God chose the Jewish people as a nation. Through this nation the world was to be enlightened concerning the truth of the true God. From this nation the Messiah was to come. With this nation God was to illustrate both to them and to the world what would be done with the Messiah when He should come into the world. This nation was to serve as an object lesson of the great and wonderful blessings and benefits that should come by truth and loyalty to God.

8. So, when the Lord called the father of this race, He said:

"Get thee out of thy country, and from thy kindred, and from thy father's house, unto a land that I will shew thee: and I will make of thee a great nation, and I will bless thee, and make thy name great; and thou shalt be a blessing: and I will bless them that bless thee, and curse him that curseth thee: and in thee shall all the families of the earth be blessed." [13]

A little later the Lord made the following promise to Abraham:

"And, behold, the word of the Lord came unto him, saying, This shall not be thine heir; but he that shall come forth out of thine own bowels

11 Acts 4:27, 28.   12 John 10:34-36.   13 Gen. 12:1-3.

shall be thine heir. And he brought him forth abroad and said, Look now toward heaven, and tell the stars, if thou be able to number them : and he said unto him, So shall thy seed be. . . . And he said unto Abram, Know of a surety that thy seed shall be a stranger in a land that is not theirs, and shall serve them; and they shall afflict them four hundred years; and also that nation, whom they shall serve, will I judge: and afterward shall they come out with great substance. And thou shalt go to thy fathers in peace; thou shalt be buried in a good old age. But in the fourth generation they shall come hither again. . . . In the same day the Lord made a covenant with Abram, saying, Unto thy seed have I given this land, from the river of Egypt unto the great river, the river Euphrates." [14]

DOUBLE APPLICATION OF PROMISE.

9. All these promises which God made to Abraham had a double application. First, they were to receive a partial ful-fillment in the Jews as a nation; second, to have their complete fulfillment in Jesus Christ. That this latter statement is true is evident from many scriptures; but perhaps one will be suffi-cient as proof:

"Now to Abraham and his seed were the promises made. He saith not, And to seeds, as of many; but as of one, And to thy seed, which is Christ." [15]

ISRAEL A PECULIAR PEOPLE.

10. For this reason the Lord, when He brought the Israel-ites from Egypt, made them a separate, distinct, and peculiar people, and made the following prediction concerning them:

"Lo, the people shall dwell alone, and shall not be reckoned among the nations." [16]

When He brought them to Sinai, He made a covenant with them, a part of which is the following:

"Now therefore, if ye will obey my voice indeed, and keep my cove-nant, then ye shall be a peculiar treasure unto me above all people: for all the earth is mine: and ye shall be unto me a kingdom of priests, and an holy nation." [17]

WHY HE GAVE THEM THE LAWS.

11. In order to preserve them a separate and distinct peo-

[14] Gen. 15: 4–18.   [15] Gal. 3: 16.   [16] Num. 23: 9.   [17] Ex. 19: 5, 6.

ple, the Lord gave to them special laws, ordinances, feasts, festivals, ceremonies, fasts, and rites. These services were designed also to teach them, and through them the world, great lessons of truth concerning the Deliverer, the Redeemer, the Messiah, who was to come. *Everything* had a meaning; *nothing* was devoid of significance; all were designed as signs; precious lessons were intended by them all. In other words, they were to be a great typical people, typifying in and through them what should be realized in its fullness when the Messiah would appear. The objects they were to have in their worship and in their services were to be God's kindergarten methods of teaching the lessons of salvation from sin, and the power to be kept from sinning, through the Messiah who was to come.

WHAT WAS NOT INTENDED BY THESE LAWS.

12. These laws and regulations *in* and *of themselves* had no virtue; no efficacy was placed in these objects. Neither help, nor benefit, nor grace, nor goodness, nor strength, could be obtained or granted by the mere performance of these various commands and observances. In everything: in every lesson, in every board, in every garment, in every feast, in every rite, God intended the people to see some great truth concerning the Messiah. In other words, these institutions and laws were God's means to a great end. If the lesson were not learned, or if the meaning were lost, then the whole economy of itself was of no use. (*a*) If rightly understood and recognized in the light of the Holy Spirit, these objects meant everything.

13. If the reader will notice these facts as they have been presented, he will be better prepared for what will follow; and will more clearly perceive many of the truths as they shall be presented from the word of God. He will the better understand the great purpose of God concerning Israel. He will furthermore see where the Jews failed, why they failed, and why they did not appreciate Jesus when He came into the world.

A TYPICAL MODEL.

14. To keep ever before them the thought that they were a separated people, God built for them also a sanctuary, and afterwards a temple. These subjects will be considered in later chapters. But everything connected therewith must be consecrated,˙ must be set off, must be set apart, must be anointed, [18] must be kept clean. By these means God sought to teach them also the significance of distinction and separation, that they might not have mingled with them and with their worship anything that was impure or unclean, a fit type or symbol of sin.

WHY EVERYTHING WAS SET APART.

15. When a priest was to be prepared for service, he must be anointed; [19] when his children were devoted to service they must be anointed. [20] When a man was to act as the king of the people, he was to be anointed. [21] So it was with everything; the idea of separation, of distinctiveness, of peculiar aloneness was to characterize the people always and everywhere. If the people would only be true to their purpose and their grand and sacredly solemn mission, what a mighty revelation they would give to the world. How the professed people of God and the world would learn wonderful truths concerning the Messiah of God, the One anointed for the people's deliverance.

ONLY PARTLY FULFILLED THEIR MISSION.

16. In a measure the Jews fulfilled their mission. For nearly two thousand years they were kept a separate people, but not wholly in harmony with God's intention. As a separate people, from a genealogical standpoint their records were perfectly accurate; for whenever a child was born his name, his family, was immediately recorded with his tribal ancestry. [22] In order to lay claim to any inheritance, his genealogy must be proved beyond any shadow of doubt. [23]

[18] Ex. 40:9-11. [19] Ex. 28:3; 40:13. [20] Ex. 28:40, 41; 40:14, 15. [21] 1Sam. 9:16; 15:17; 16:12; 1 Kings 1:39. [22] 1 Chron. 5:17; 9:11; Neh. 7:5. [23] Ezra 2:61, 62.

THE ERECTION OF THE SANCTUARY.

[15]

LINEAGE OF JESUS.

17. For this reason when Jesus was born, the people at the time never questioned his lineage; they all knew He belonged to the family of David, [24] to the tribe of Judah. [25]   About twenty times in the New Testament it is recorded that He was the Son of David. [26]   From the days of Abraham to the times of Jesus every member of every family, *especially* the males, was recorded in the genealogical record; and the Jews were extremely particular that this was attended to with the greatest of care.   Of all the tribes, however, who manifested this extreme loyalty the tribe of Judah stood first.   The ten tribes were scattered everywhere; the two were in Babylon and in the lands of the Persians.   Still the latter sought to preserve their register correct.   In this phase of their mission the Jews were true. (*b*)

THE PEOPLE FAITHLESS.

18. But their relation to the other parts of their mission was very far from God's purpose.   Never were a people more rebellious to God's will than were the Jews. [27]   Never were a people who committed greater sins than they did; [28] never were a people more faithless in God than they were; [29] never were a people more disobedient than they; yet never were a people who professed to love God more than they did.   Rather than deny or sacrifice what they believed to be right, they would give up life; yet the real purpose of their mission in all its fullness they never realized.

19. They did give birth to the Savior of the world; they did preserve the word of God for the world; they did give floods of light to the world, in the sacred pages that God gave to them; they did bring salvation to the world. [30]   Still they themselves never gained what God desired they should.

[24] Matt. 1:1. [25] Heb. 7:14; Rev. 5:5. [26] Matt. 1:1, 20; 9:27; 12:23; 15:22; 20:30, 31; 21:9, 15; 22:42; Mark 10:47, 48; 12:35, etc. [27] Eze. 2:3-8; Num. 17:10; Dan. 9:5, 9; Lam. 3:42; Jer. 5:23; Acts 7:51, 52. [28] Isa. 1:4; 59:2; 2 Chron. 33:2, 9; 36:14. [29] Deut. 32:20; Matt. 17:17; Heb. 4:2. [30] John 4:22

ISRAEL'S STUMBLING.

20. The reader may perhaps be a little perplexed at this condition of the people, and what could have brought them to such a state? He will understand this when he learns that the cause of all their troubles and difficulties was in taking these laws, ordinances, feasts, and ceremonies, as the *ends* of their national existence, hoping to secure virtue from these things rather than in the words of the living God, and in the great Messiah, to whom they pointed. They built up a great wall [31] around them; fenced themselves within it; excluded everybody outside of it; completely covered themselves with it, until no ray of light from God could pierce their souls, as a nation.

21. As a result, it is said, " He came unto His own, and His own received Him not." [32] The central truth that God gave them in all these objects, which was the Messiah,—the suffering, the afflicted, the enduring, the lowly, the crucified, the humble Messiah,—they lost sight of; and they gloried in the observance of these objects. Instead of finding their righteousness in the Christ, the Righteous One, they thought they received it by the carrying out of these observances. [33] So while God brought the Messiah to save the world through the Jews, they fell [34] from their exalted position and mission in not receiving Him.

22. This state was due to the great heap of traditions, maxims, and writings of rabbis, sages, philosophers, and wise men. Through these means, the people were led to look at the men, [35] instead of looking at the Christ.

THEIR PRESENT SEPARATION.

23. More upon the subject of traditions will be given in successive chapters, but now the reader's attention is called to the *cause* of their condition. This will also explain why the Jews have been kept separate for two thousand years this side of Christ.

31 Eph. 2:14.   32 John 1:11.   33 Luke 16:15.   34 Matt. 21:33, 46.
35 1 Sam. 16: 7 ; Acts 4:12.

2

24. Before the Savior came, they were kept as a separated people to preserve the word of God, and to bring salvation to the world in Jesus. Since that time they have been preserved as a witness to the truthfulness of God's word; to the integrity of the holy Scriptures; to the results of not performing God's will; to the great bond which human tradition has bound around them. They are in a measure greater slaves to the iron fetters of human tradition than their fathers were to the rulers of Egypt; and the reader will better appreciate as he follows these pages the significance of the Savior's words, when He said to the Jews, "If the Son, therefore, shall make you free, ye shall be free indeed." [36]

25. It also vividly portrays the awful condition a people can reach who have once known God, and turned from Him to obey the traditions [37] of men; while at the same time it clearly shows us the blessed and glorious experience of liberty and freedom that the Lord Jesus Christ can give to the soul, if the heart will only turn [38] to Him as does the flower to the sun.

HOW WE SHOULD REGARD THE JEWS.

26. While the Jews did crucify the Savior and murder the Prince of Life [39] they should be regarded much more with tenderness and sympathy than with condemnation. [40] It is evident that if they had only known the Lord of glory, they would never have crucified Him; [41] and what they did to Him, they did because of ignorance. [42] The church of the present time should learn a profitable lesson from their experience, that it may not repeat the sad failure of Israel, [43] and be cast away even as they were. The church should learn there is danger in following the maxims of men; in the word of the Lord God only is found safety and security. The church of God will then accomplish the true purpose which the Lord has for it. If they do, they will surely remember the Jews, their purpose and their mission; they will do all in their power to open the

[36] John 8: 36.   [37] Matt. 15: 1-9 ; Mark 7: 1-4.   [38] 2 Cor. 3: 16-18.
[39] Acts 3: 13-15.   [40] Matt. 23: 37.   [41] 1 Cor. 2: 8.   [42] Acts 3: 17.   [43] 1 Cor. 10: 11.

eyes of the blind, to restore sight [44] to those who do not see. They also will remember that the Lord Jesus was a Jew, who said that "salvation is of the Jews." [45] (*c*)

[44] Luke 4:18.   [45] John 4:22.

EXPLANATORY NOTES.

Paragraph 12.

(*a*) Some of the rabbis themselves claim that all these sacrifices and ceremonies would cease when the Messiah came. One rabbi says: "All sacrifices shall end in the days of the Messiah." Another says: "In the days of Messiah there shall be no remembrance of the deliverance from Egypt. . . . And if the deliverance from Egypt is no more remembered, surely those ceremonies . . . will be done away.—*Ben Zoma*.

Paragraph 17.

(*b*) Since the temple was destroyed by the Romans in A. D. 70, no genealogical record has been faithfully preserved by the Jews. Certain classes have a traditional record, as those of the tribe of Levi, but this is only traditional. This idea might be suggestive concerning the literal restoration of the Jews as a nation.

Paragraph 25.

(*c*) Whenever any people have taken interest in the conversion of the Jews to Christ it has always brought great blessings to the church. It has led the people to study God's word, and to learn more of God's plan concerning them. It will do the same at the present time.

CHAPTER II.

The Talmudic Writings. Their Origin.

" To the law and to the testimony; if they speak not according to this word, it is because there is no light in them." Isa. 8:20.

NO doubt every lover of the word of God, especially the student of the New Testament, has often wondered what the Savior meant when He rebuked the Pharisees and other teachers of His time for holding certain traditions; or, what Paul had reference to where he mentions certain persons obeying the laws and ordinances of men. For instance, in Matthew[1] we find the Jewish leaders condemning the disciples of Jesus for not washing their hands according to the traditions of the elders; and Jesus in turn condemning them for frustrating the commandment of God, in order to observe their own tradition. In several other places in the teachings of the Savior, we find this thought mentioned,[2] also a number of times in the epistles.

2. In Colossians we find this statement:

" Beware lest any man spoil you through philosophy and vain deceit, after the tradition of men, after the rudiments of the world, and not after Christ."[3]

And again another statement:

" Touch not; taste not; handle not; which all are to perish with the using, after the commandments and doctrines of men."[4]

Again, in writing to Timothy, Paul says:

" Of these things put them in remembrance, charging them before the Lord that they strive not about words to no profit, but to the subverting of the hearers."[5]

Again, in writing to Titus, the same apostle says:

[1] Matt. 15:1-9; Mark 7:1-13. [2] Matt. 9:14. [3] Col. 2:8. [4] Col 2:20-23.
[5] 2 Tim. 2:14.

[20]

"Not giving heed to Jewish fables, and commandments of men, that turn from the truth."[6]

3. Similar statements,[7] too numerous to mention, abound in the teachings of the Savior and of the Apostles, and have awakened inquiry in the minds of every thoughtful reader of the word of the Lord. This is especially true of those who are not familiar with the teachings and writings of the Jewish rabbis. To gain an intelligent idea of these scriptures, and the reason for the Master's statement of them, is the purpose of this chapter concerning the writings of the Talmud.

THE TALMUD A COMPENDIUM.

4. The Talmud is not the writings of one man, nor of a mere set of men; it was not formed in a day, in a month, nor in a year. It was a growth and a development of the sayings of the supposedly great teachers, covering a period of many centuries. The Talmud was begun soon after the return of the Jews from the Babylonian captivity several centuries before Christ, and was completed about the middle of the fourth century after Christ. The Talmud consists of two great general divisions: the "Mishna," a commentary or text on the Old Testament Scriptures, containing nearly five thousand "mishnaioth," sections, or traditions; and the "Gemara," the commentary of the Mishna, containing hundreds and thousands of laws, illustrations, allegories, commentaries, and a lot of other definable and indefinable sayings on anything and everything. As Milman, the church historian, says of the Talmud: "That wonderful monument of human industry, human wisdom, and human folly!"

TWO TALMUDS.

5. There are two Talmuds, known as the "Talmud Je-ru-shalmi," or Jerusalem Talmud; "Talmud Bo-vel," or Babylonian Talmud, so-called because the men who commented on the Mishna dwelt at Jerusalem and at Babylon. It may be of

6 Titus 1:14. 7 2 Peter 2:1-3, 12-18; 3:16; 2 John 7; 3 John 9, 10; Acts 20::28-31.

interest to the reader to follow the development of the Mishna, since this was what constituted the basis of the Jewish traditions at the time of Christ.

6. The Jews on account of their sins were sent into Babylonian captivity.[8]   Here they remained in exile for seventy years.[9]   While in this state of captivity the Scriptures were little known among them. They had very little of the word of God, occasionally a roll of the Scriptures having been laid up by some very godly man.[10]   By the study of the books of Nehemiah and Ezra,[11] it will be seen that the people in general had greatly departed from the word of God in their captivity, and had lost sight of their worship of God. Ezra, Nehemiah, Mordecai, and other men of God, sought to bring about a restoration of the word of God to the people, and associated with them men who would teach the people the pure word of God.

7. In the days of these leaders, the truth was held up before the people, and much good was accomplished; but after their decease a new generation, as it were, arose, and these followed not in the ways of their predecessors. Of the men who sought to bring about a reformation, the Talmud says:

"As soon as the men of the Great Synagogue met together, they restored the law to its pristine glory." [12]

THE GREAT SYNAGOGUE.

8. These men who were the successors of Ezra and his associates, were formed into a sort of college, called " K-Nes-Seth Hagdola," "the Great Synagogue," or Synod, the last member of this order being " Simon the Just " who died about the second century before Christ. The one great object of these men seemed to be so to protect the law, or to make a fence or hedge about it, that it should be impossible for the people ever to depart from it. It can easily be understood that

[8] Dan. 1: 1, 2; 2 Chron. 36: 14–21. [9] Jer. 29: 10; 25: 11, 12. [10] See Dan. 9: 2.
[11] Ezra 10; Neh. 10, 13.
[12] As quoted in " The Talmud ; What it is," by Bernard Pick.

when the teachings of any people were left to the minds of just a few, who were to regulate their every mode of living, even to the least detail and minutia, the religion of the people would soon dwindle into a mere formalism; their piety would consist in the observance outwardly of the legal enactments of these teachers; and at the same time would be built up a sort of spiritual despotism, with these men as the ecclesiastical despots. This is but a logical conclusion of such religion. And this exactly happened with the Jews; so that when Christ came, the people were bound with the fetters of human tradition, and were enslaved by the spiritual despots, otherwise known as rabbis. ·That this really was so will be made more evident as we continue.

THE SCRIBES.

9. After the last one of the Great Synagogue passed away, the leaders of the people, who were the learned men of the Jews, took the name of "Sophrim," or scribes, (*a*) because their business was to teach the people the contents of the "Books of the Law," and to be the expositors of the Scriptures. Their great burden seemed to be to make a hedge about the law; so to circumscribe the word of God, according to their ideas of it, that the people should be fenced in by what they said, and hence their teaching came to be regarded as of equal importance with the word of God. Yes, in fact they regarded their teachings above the word of God.

THE ORAL LAW.

10. In the book, "Ethics of the Fathers," we find this statement concerning the purpose of these men:

"They said three things: 'Be deliberate in judgment; train up many disciples; and make a fence for the law.'"—*Chapter 1.*

11. This they did, and did it well. These sayings of the teachers were not written in a book, but were handed down from one to another; and hence received the name, "To-rah

Shel Ba-peh," the law of the mouth, or "the oral law." The Bible, or the Scriptures, were called, "To-rah Sh-bek-thav," or "the written law." While there were many of these "scribes" or teachers, there was always a great leader, who had the general supervision of the period in which he lived. When one man passed away, he was succeeded by another. Thus after Simon the Just, Antigonos of Socho, who was a disciple of this Simon, became the great leader. Every one of these leaders had disciples; sometimes they had many; and from among these disciples the successor was appointed. Thus of Hillel, the great teacher, it is said that he had eighty disciples. Thirty of them were worthy to have the glory of God rest upon them as it did upon Moses. Thirty, that the sun should stand still at their command as it did for Joshua; twenty were only moderately learned. The greatest of these eighty disciples was Joshua, son of Uziel, of whom it is said, that when he studied the law, every bird that flew over his head was at once burned up.

12. This Antigonos received the oral law from Simon; and one of the things he said was: " Be not like servants who serve their master for the sake of receiving a reward; but be like servants who serve their master without receiving a reward, and let the fear of heaven be upon you." [13] Thus one rabbi after another would leave certain sayings which would be handed down to his successors; and these were preserved. Then if any teacher made a statement that some of the people doubted, all that would be necessary for him to say would be: " I heard such and such a rabbi say it;" and this would end the discussion.

THE RABBI TO BE FEARED.

13. As a result of these methods, the oral law kept increasing, and regulations kept multiplying. The words of the rabbis became law to the people; and in studying the

[13] " Ethics of the Fathers," chap. 1.

A Typical Rabbi.

Scripture it must be interpreted only in the light of the rabbis. As a result, the rabbi came to be looked upon as a sort of deity; and was to be feared even as God. A few illustrations may be to the point:

"As a man is commanded to honor and fear his father, so he is bound to honor and fear his Rabbi more than his father."

"If a man should see his father lose something, and his Rabbi lose something, he is first to return what his Rabbi has lost, then to return that which his father has lost."

"If his father and his Rabbi be oppressed with a load, he is first to help his Rabbi down, then assist his father."

"If his father and his Rabbi be in captivity, he is first to ransom his Rabbi, after that his father, unless his father be the disciple of a wise (or learned) man."

"Thou must consider no honor greater than the honor of the Rabbi, and no fear greater than the fear of the Rabbi. The wise men have said 'The fear of thy Rabbi is as the fear of God.'"

And the rabbi who first introduced this last saying is Rabbi Eleazer, son of Shamuang, which saying is found in "Ethics of the Fathers," chapter 4.

Again: "It is forbidden to a disciple to call his Rabbi by name, even when he is not in his presence."

"Neither is he to salute his Rabbi, neither to return his salutation in the same manner that salutations are given or returned among friends. On the contrary he is to bow down before the Rabbi, and say to him with reverence and honor, 'Peace be to thee, Rabbi.'"

14. The reader will no doubt see a new meaning in these words of the Savior in the light of the above statements:

"And greetings in the market-places, and to be called of men, Rabbi, Rabbi. Be not ye called Rabbi; for One is your Master, even Christ; and all ye are brethren." [14]

TEACHINGS OF RABBIS PLACED ABOVE GOD'S WORD.

15. They were putting themselves in the place of God to the people; their sayings were placed upon equality with God's teachings. Hence we read that the written law was like water;

[14] Matt. 23: 7, 8.

but the oral law, Mishna, was like wine : the Gemara, like
spiced wine.   Some went as far as to say that the words of the
scribes are lovely above the words of the law (meaning the written law), for the words of the written law are weighty and light ;
but the words of the scribes are all weighty.   One, Rabbi
Judah, son of Tamai, said : "A child at five years should study
the Bible, at ten the Mishna, at fifteen the Gemara."

From this last statement it can be seen that three times as
much value is placed upon the words of men as upon the words
of God.   The person as he comes to years of maturity should
regard the words of the Scripture only one-third as much as he
does the words of the rabbis.   Yes, they go so far as to say :

"Yea, though they should tell thee that thy right hand is the left, and
the left hand that it is the right, it must be believed."

It is not surprising, then, that the Savior condemned those
teachers for making void the word of God by their tradition.
By their multiplicity of maxims they enslaved the man; they
put the word of God aside, in order that their words might be
highly esteemed.

CONTEMPORARY LEADERS.

16. There were times when there were several leaders, and
frequently they would disagree as to their ideas of the Scriptures,
or Scriptural exposition.   Which is right was often the question,
as the people were only to understand the law interpreted and
expounded by these men.   The common people were never
supposed to understand the Scriptures *themselves;* this is why,
no doubt, we find the following statement:

"But this people who knoweth not the law are cursed." "They
answered and said unto him, thou wast altogether born in sins, and dost
thou teach us ? And they cast him out." [15]

17. It was only the wise and educated who were expected to
know the Scriptures ; whatever these men said must be final.
An appeal to any other source meant excommunication.[16]   No
doubt this is why Nicodemus came to Christ *at night.*[17]   This

[15] John 7: 49.   [16] John 9: 22; 12: 42.   [17] John 3: 1-10.

will also explain why more of the people did not receive Jesus.

HILLEL AND SHAMMI.

18. Two of the most noted contemporary teachers were Hillel and Shammi, who flourished about the time of Christ's advent. Each represented a different school of theology, and frequently were engaged in strong arguments. On one occasion there arose a heated discussion about a hen that laid her eggs on the Sabbath,—whether or not it was lawful to eat such egg or eggs. As a result of this strong debate, an entire treatise, called " Bet-za " (egg), is written on this subject. Hillel stuck to his legal decision, and what he claimed would be the position of the other great rabbis, namely, that the egg was not to be eaten. Shammi, however, who was of the more lenient class, claimed that it could be. What was to be done? Both of these men were held in great esteem. Their disciples were sitting by and awaiting the outcome. The whole structure of their interpretation of Scripture might crumble should either admit defeat.

19, Finally one of the company raised his voice, and shouted, " Bath-kol " (literally, the daughter of a voice). This was their substitute for " the spirit of prophecy." They claimed this is the way God revealed Himself to them. When some person said " Bath-kol " a hush fell upon the entire company. " What said the Bath-kol concerning the point under discussion ?" This was the reply :

" *Both* are the words of the living God, yet the rule of the school of Hillel should be followed."—*Tractate Eruvin.*

20. Is it to be wondered at that the Savior said they strained at a gnat, and swallowed a camel? Can we not see why the Savior condemned them and their teachings, and why the Apostles warned the people against listening to them ?

DISTORTING SCRIPTURE.

21. As a result of such misinterpretation of Scripture, we can the better understand what the Apostle Peter meant when he

said there were some who wrested the Scripture to their own damnation.[18] The word of God was made of none effect through such twisting and distorting. The people were taught to believe anything and everything; and whatever came from these men to them must be the word of God.

LOOSE INTERPRETATION.

22. It was not difficult for these teachers, in view of such license and arrogancy, to claim that the word of God had more than one interpretation, and, whichever way the Scripture was interpreted, was lawful. As a result it was claimed that every passage of Scripture had at least four different interpretations, to which were given the following names: "Peshat," or the simple way (This is taking the text as it reads); "Derush," or the spiritual way; "Remez," the allegorical or parabolical way; "Sod," or the secret way. From the first four letters of Peshat, Remez, Derush, Sod, the acrostic PaRDes was formed; hence the word "Paradise."

It having been established that Scripture could be interpreted, it was found that *four* ways were not sufficient; hence this Hillel formed what was known as the seven rules of interpretation. This method was followed for a time until Rabbi Ishmael raised it to thirteen rules, and finally one, Rabbi Jose of Galilee, (*b*) introduced what is known as the "Thirty-two Rules of Interpretation." And the Talmud itself says that the law can be interpreted in forty-nine different modes. From the foregoing, we can the better understand why the Savior said on one occasion:

"Ye do err, not knowing the Scriptures, nor the power of God."[19]

23. Scores, hundreds, even thousands of laws and interpretations were made from the Scriptures; they surely succeeded in making a fence for the law; but the law and the Scripture had dwindled into a mere form of words.[20] They had the shell, but did not taste the sweetness of the nut within.

[18] 2 Pet. 3: 16.   [19] Matt. 22: 29.   [20] Rom. 2: 20.

A VOLUMINOUS MASS.

24. To say nothing of the Gemara, the commentary of the Mishna, the latter alone contains sixty-three tractates, divided into five hundred and twenty-five chapters, consisting of nearly five thousand separate sections, or traditions. Nearly all these were in vogue in the days of the Savior, and these were the *special* laws. There were a vast number of others which, while perhaps more secondary, were nevertheless to be observed and obeyed. It should be further remembered that all these thousands of laws were not written at the time of Christ, they were simply handed down from mouth to mouth. During the second century after Christ, they were collected in volumes by a very learned rabbi called " Rabbi Juda, the Na-si, or Prince." (*c*) He gathered these sayings which had been handed down for nearly six centuries, and classified them under six great heads, or divisions, giving them the name of " Sederim," or Orders. (*d*) This voluminous work, the Mishna, was the basis for all study of the law. The Bible itself, if studied, must be understood in the light of the Mishna. Of course the people had the scrolls; they read them some, but if they wanted to know their meaning they must ascertain what the rabbis said concerning them. If two or more disagreed upon any point, they were to believe what all the teachers said. They durst not ask many questions; if they did they were liable to excommunication. It was further claimed that these expositions of the rabbis were in direct succession from Moses, because it is written in " The Ethics of the Fathers " that

" Moses received the law from Sinai, and delivered it to Joshua, and Joshua to the elders, and the elders to the prophets, and the prophets to the men of the Great Synagogue."

IT IS CLAIMED MOSES RECEIVED THESE TRADITIONS.

25. Tradition goes even farther and says that Moses received these teachings and explanations of the Scriptures from the Lord himself; and, instead of committing them to writing, he

spake them orally to Aaron, to his sons, to the seventy elders, and to all the people; each class having heard him repeat them four times. Still another passage in the Talmud tries, by a perverted interpretation of the following passage of Scripture, to prove conclusively that "the oral law" was given to Moses:

"'And I will give thee tables of stone, and a law, and commandments which I have written; that thou mayest teach them.' Ex. 24:12. Rabbi Levi argues that 'the tables of stone' are the ten commandments. The 'law' is the written law in the five books of Moses. The 'commandments' are the Mishna; 'which I have written' refers to the prophets and the Scriptures: while the words 'that thou mayest teach them,' point to the Gemara. From this we learn that all was given to Moses on Sinai." [21]

26. In view of the above, we should not be surprised that the Jews reviled the blind man, as recorded in John 9, and said: "Thou art His disciple; but we are Moses' disciples. We know that God spake unto Moses: as for this fellow, we know not from whence he is." [22] But ah! did they only know and understand Moses and the prophets, they would have understood Him; for Moses wrote of Him. [23] In Moses' writings were contained scriptures which were fulfilled in Him, [24] and which they would have seen had they only studied them in the light of the Spirit instead of in the darkness of their tradition.

IMPOSSIBLE TO FORM CORRECT ESTIMATE.

27. It would be absolutely impossible to give the reader any fair or comprehensive idea of the voluminous mass that forms the Talmud. Its origin we have traced; its composition in part we have seen; its intent we have learned; its results can be better appreciated.

The people left the Fountain of Living Water, [25] and hewed for themselves cisterns, broken ones at that, which could hold no water. Surely, then, we ought to appreciate more the purity of the word of the Lord as revealed by Jesus Christ, made plain by the Holy Spirit. We can also see more clearly, I trust,

---

[21] Talmud, Berachoth, chapter 5.   [22] John 9:28, 29.   [23] John 5:46, 47.
[24] Luke 24:44.   [25] Jer. 2:12, 13.

many sayings which hitherto have seemed hard to understand, that our love for the word of God may become more intensified.

EXPLANATORY NOTES.

Paragraph 9.

(*a*) The title of " scribe " was not first introduced at this period, as there had for centuries been certain persons whose business it was to write and transcribe the Scriptures. But this period developed a distinct class who abused the original design of the scribe to gain self-emolument.

Paragraph 22.

(*b*) This Rabbi Jose, of Galilee, lived about the middle of the second century after Christ.

Paragraph 24.

(*c*) Rabbi Juda was pre-eminently called " the Rabbi." No other Rabbi did so much to hold the Jews together as a people as he did. He was a great scholar, very pious, had accumulated great wealth which he lavished freely; was quite ambitious to build up a permanent ecclesiasticism among the Jews, with which plan he succeeded well. The time, labor, and means expended to gather the mass of traditions which had accumulated for nearly five centuries must have been tremendous; nevertheless he accomplished this before his death. The influence of his work has been so powerful that, like Romanism, it has succeeded in keeping the Jews together as a separate people with their peculiar customs, nearly seventeen hundred years.

(*d*) The following are the names of the six great divisions of the Mishna:

1. Zeraim, or Seeds. This division contains eleven tractates.

2. Moed, or Festivals. This division has twelve tractates. Most all the laws and traditions concerning the Sabbath come under this order.

3. Nashim, or Women. This division has seven tractates, and is devoted to the female sex, from infancy to death.

4. Nezekim, Damages, containing ten tractates.

5. K-do-shim, or Consecration, containing eleven tractates. These tracts deal largely with the sacrificial system.

6. T-ho-roth, or Purifications, containing twelve tractates.

CHAPTER III.

The Different Sects of Jews, and Their Belief.

"Not every one that saith unto Me, Lord, Lord, shall enter into the kingdom of heaven; but he that doeth the will of My Father which is in heaven." Matt. 7:21.

CHRIST'S PRAYER FOR UNITY.

THE burden of the prayer of Christ, as recorded in John 17, was for unity and harmony. He longed and hoped and prayed for oneness. He said:

"Neither pray I for these alone, but for them also which shall believe on Me through their word; that they all may be one; as Thou Father, art in Me, and I in Thee, that they also may be one in Us; that the world may believe that Thou hast sent Me. And the glory which Thou gavest Me I have given them; that they may be one, even as We are one: I in them, and Thou in Me, that they may be made perfect in one; that the world may know that Thou hast sent Me, and hast loved them, as Thou hast loved Me." [1]

2. Not only in this chapter do we have Him breathing these sentiments, but all through His life's experience we find the same truth taught and lived. For instance, in another place, He says:

"I and My Father are one." [2]

3. When the Jewish teachers came to Him, on one occasion, seeking for information upon the subject of divorce, he referred them to the oneness between man and wife, the plan of God in the beginning. [3] There was to be the same relation between people as between Christ and God; and this bond of unity was designed of God to bind every person in Jesus Christ. Thus

[1] John 17:20–23.   [2] John 10:30.   [3] Matt. 19:3–6.

would be fulfilled that prayer of the Apostle Paul, as recorded in Ephesians :

" For this cause I bow my knees unto the Father of our Lord Jesus Christ, of whom the whole family in heaven and earth is named." [4]

4. Hence Paul made that statement which we find recorded in another place in Ephesians :

" That in the dispensation of the fullness of times He might gather together in *one* all things in Christ, both which are in heaven, and which are on earth ; even in Him." [5]

5. After the Savior went away, the same thought of oneness was ever kept before the church of Christ by His Apostles, in teaching, in preaching, and in writing.

WHY GOD WISHED UNITY AMONG THE PEOPLE.

6. The Lord sought to keep the Jews together as a people, in order to impress them with the thought of unity, that the true God was *one*, [6] and that He desired that same unity to exist between Himself and His people, as well as among the people themselves. This was to be an object lesson both to the Jews, and to the world through them, of the harmony which was to be brought about through the blessed Messiah.

7. This oneness and harmony could only be maintained by strict obedience to the word of God,—in always following the truth as God gave it. It is a fact familiar to every reader of the Bible that the Jews were most united when they strictly followed the word of God ; [7] when they failed to comply with His wishes, there followed division, diversion, confusion.

CAUSE FOR DIVISION.

8. It can easily be understood why there existed so many different beliefs and sects among the Jews when Christ came to earth. It was because of so *many* traditions, opinions, " hala-chath " (laws), " haggodoth " (discussions), and other fanciful notions of the Scriptures. Every teacher had the opportunity

[4] Eph. 3 : 14, 15. [5] Eph. 1 : 10. [6] Deut. 6 : 4 ; Zech. 14 : 9. [7] Ps. 81 : 13 ; Isa. 48 : 18

3

of hearing the "Bath-kol," the substitute for the spirit of prophecy; while if several learned men held opposite views, they could all be easily reconciled by this poor substitution. Their decisions and legal maxims became law; even should another person or set of men arise, and speak altogether contrary to their predecessors. Still these decisions must also be respected as the word of God. So that at the time of Christ there existed various classes of thought ; each claiming supreme authority; each claiming to be right and true; each claiming that its laws and statutes must be followed; and yet no two of them agreeing. It is but natural then that the Savior should make the following statement concerning the people :

"And Jesus, when He came out, saw much people, and was moved with compassion toward them, because they were as sheep not having a shepherd: and He began to teach them many things." [8]

SECTS AMONG THE JEWS.

9. Of the ten classes of religionists that existed at the time of Christ, entirely or in part Jewish, four different distinct sects will cover them all. Three of the sects are mentioned in the New Testament. These are the Sadducees, the Pharisees, the Samaritans. The other is mentioned by Josephus, [9] the Essenes. While there were other classes or parties, in matter of belief and religious views they held to some one of the four sects mentioned. It might be well to notice them for the information of the reader: the Galileans, the Nazarites, the Proselytes, the Publicans, the Herodians, the Scribes.

THE GALILEANS.

10. Of the Galileans the New Testament says but little, though Josephus gives us slightly more information. They are mentioned but twice in the New Testament; [10] and from the inferences drawn from these scriptures, it might appear that they were considered a turbulent and seditious people. Josephus

---

[8] Mark 6: 34.   [9] Josephus, "Antiquities of the Jews." book 13, chap. 5.
[10] Luke 13: 1; Acts 5: 37.

conveys the idea that nearly all the troubles that came to the Jews were due to them. From Luke 13:1, it would seem that the Jews in general thought them a very wicked and sinful class, because of Pilate's treatment of them. The Savior, in His reply, recognized that they were sinners;[11] though He said they were no worse than others who did not believe God. In their flourishing period they had for a leader one Judas,[12] who drew a great following after him, especially from among the Pharisees. They were soon scattered, and came to nought. Their religious belief was similar to the Pharisees, though they offered sacrifices by themselves. They claimed that civil governments had nothing whatever to do with religion, and they would not concede any rights to any foreign power.

THE NAZARITES.

11. The Nazarites had been in existence for many centuries, though they could not exactly be termed a sect. There were two divisions even of this class. The term " Nazar," separated, was given to those people who were to be especially separated to God. The origin of the people is found in the laws given to Moses, recorded in Numbers.[13]

12. The one class were dedicated to God from the birth. Such were Samson, Samuel, and John the Baptist.[14] Three things especially were to be observed by this class : they must not drink wine, must not eat any unclean food, and must shave the head. The other class were those who devoted themselves to God for a certain period, during which time they made vows which they must perform; they also shaved their heads. We find an illustration of this class in Paul, also in Paul with four other men.[15] In essential belief they were classed with the Pharisees.

THE PROSELYTES.

13. The term " proselyte " is used in the New Testament

---

[11] Luke 13:2, 3. [12] Acts 5:37. [13] Num. 6:1-21. [14] Judges 13:1-7; 1 Sam. 1:11; Luke 1:15. [15] Acts 18:18; 21:23-26.

only four times.[16] It is derived from a Hebrew word, " Ger," which means a stranger. It was the coming over of a person who formerly was a Gentile into the Jewish faith. The Jews were not desirous to have people of other nationalities come over and join themselves to them, though the Lord had repeatedly said in the Old Testament that He made special provisions if the stranger wished to join himself to the people of God, and be one with them.[17] When a Gentile, however, did wish to become a proselyte, the Jews caused him to pass through some severe experiences, among which were circumcision, a mode of dipping or baptism, the acceptation of all the Mosaic laws, with many other rites. However, they were generally informed that they could not become true Israelites or Jews, or ever think to share in the fullness of the promise to Abraham. How different are the teachings of the Savior, when he declares that there shall be one Shepherd and one fold.[18] Paul, also, in his epistle to the Galatians, plainly states that if we are Christ's, we *are* Abraham's seed, and heirs according to the promise.[19]

14. When the Pharisees succeeded in gaining a " Ger," a proselyte, they often made him ten times worse than he was before, as he was apt to be taught many of their vices, as well as their supposed virtues. This is evident from the following words of the Savior: " Woe unto you, scribes and Pharisees, hypocrites! for ye compass sea and land to make one proselyte, and when he is made, ye make him two-fold more the child of hell than yourselves."[20] However, there were many proselytes who were good men, men of God, who longed to be free from much of the form and tradition that surrounded their teaching, and to understand the pure truth. This is clear from the following scripture:

" Now when the congregation was broken up, many of the Jews and religious proselytes followed Paul and Barnabas: who, speaking to them, persuaded them to continue in the grace of God."[21]

[16] Matt. 23: 15; Acts 2: 10; 6: 5; 13: 43. [17] Ex. 12: 48, 49; Num. 9: 14, 15; Lev. 19: 33, 34; Isa. 56: 3. [18] John 10: 16. [19] Gal. 3: 29, 7-9; Rom. 4: 11-13. [20] Matt. 23: 15. [21] Acts 13: 43.

THE PENITENT PUBLICAN.

One of the proselytes became a member of the deacons [22] chosen in the early church. In belief they generally followed the Pharisees.

THE PUBLICANS.

15. The publicans were a class of Jews who were social outcasts. They were not considered a sect, neither had they any special belief. What religious views they held leaned toward the Pharisees, though the latter regarded them with a terrible hatred. This class, however, is frequently spoken of in the New Testament, and the cause of their being so lightly esteemed is, in brief, as follows:

HOW THIS CLASS ORIGINATED AMONG THE JEWS.

16. After Palestine and other Jewish territory came under Roman jurisdiction, the country was divided into districts, and the right to gather taxes upon all taxable goods was sold to the highest bidder. These rights were generally bought by the Roman senators, who in turn sub-sold them to another class. The latter were generally non-Jews, who resided in districts away from the Jewish quarters. Hence these, in turn, sub-sold their rights to the Jews, who followed as a profession the gathering of taxes from their fellow countrymen. The reader will perhaps better appreciate why this contempt by their fellow men, when he considers that the Romans were regarded as extremely hostile to the Jews, and their most-to-be-dreaded foes. This being true of the Romans, how much more terrible must it have been for these Jews to become willing tools in the hands of Rome. They were therefore looked upon as the vile, the refuse, the outcast; they were associated with the lowest classes of people, with the heathen and with the sinners.[23] The Pharisee, therefore, thought he had a right, when going to the temple, to thank God he was not like the publican.[24]

17. The publicans were apt to take advantage of their countrymen because of this deep-seated hatred, and would nat-

22 Acts 6 : 5. 23 Matt. 9 : 10; 11 : 19; 18 : 17; 21:32; Luke 18 : 11. 24 Luke 18 : 11.

urally extort money unjustly, by charging an exorbitant amount per tax. Rome, however, generally sympathized with the publicans, when complaints were offered by the Jews, because of the surplus the law-makers received as a lion's share.

18. Being ostracised by their fellow countrymen, they were naturally led to form a social order among themselves. In this social familiarity they were very strong, and were highly esteemed by each other.   This is no doubt why the Lord made the mention He did in the following text: "And if ye salute your brethren only, what do ye more than others? do not even the *publicans* so?" [25]

HOW THE PHARISEES REGARDED THE PUBLICANS.

19. We find, however, that these people were strongly drawn toward John the Baptist [26] and toward Jesus.[27]   Not having the social comforts of the Jewish religion; not having permission to attend any of the religious services; not being even privileged to attend the temple service, or to contribute toward the support of the worship of God; not being allowed any of the society of the Jews with their families,—it can readily be seen why they would welcome the teachings of the Baptizer and of Jesus. The Pharisees, on the other hand, not only refused to associate with them, but anathematized every one who had *any* dealings with them.   They went so far as to teach that it was impossible for a publican to be saved, or to have any share in the world to come. They would not even give him a Jewish burial in order to keep him from defiling Jewish soil.   This naturally in the estimation of the pious Jew would exclude him from a resurrection, as only those Jews would be revived in the last day who were laid in sacred soil. (*a*)

They *were susceptible* to religious truth.   They realized that they were sinners; [28] if they could secure any other occupation, many were ready to accept it.

[25] Matt. 5 : 46, 47.   [26] Luke 3: 12; 7:29.
[27] Matt. 9: 10.   [28] Luke 18:13.

The Call of Matthew.

MANY PUBLICANS RECEIVED THE MESSAGE OF JOHN AND JESUS.

20. Large numbers of them were baptized by John, and believed his message; consequently when Jesus came, they were prepared to receive him. Jesus saw in them honest souls, hungry for His truth, ready to follow Him. While their business was naturally a profitable one, thus giving many of them great wealth, there were those among them who were prepared at the call of Jesus to leave their post, cast aside their garment, and follow him. Hence Matthew, [29] the publican, was one of the twelve, the writer of the wonderful Gospel by that name. Then we find Zacchæus, [30] another wealthy person of the same class, who received the Savior very cordially, and was prepared to devote at least half of his wealth to the cause of Christ. To him Jesus brought salvation, which he eagerly and gladly accepted.

PHARISEES ANGRY BECAUSE JESUS ATE WITH PUBLICANS.

21. Frequently the Savior would receive invitations to dine with them, and attend other social gatherings.[31] Jesus nearly always accepted the invitation; for he knew it would be a grand opportunity to feed them with the bread of life, while they supplied his physical needs. This, however, angered the Pharisees and the scribes, and led them to conclude that Jesus could not be sent of God. If He were, they reasoned, He never would associate with such a class. Jesus understood the needs of this people, and this no doubt explains why He answered the Pharisees as he did.[32] As a result of the life, the teaching, the labors of Jesus and the disciples, a large number of this class [33] were firm and devoted followers of Christ.

THE HERODIANS.

22. This class of people received their name from Herod, the king, the father of the house of that name. He was the one who reigned when Jesus was born, and to whom the wise men came, and inquired for the location of Jesus' birthplace.[34] The

29 Luke 5: 27.   30 Luke 19: 5-10.   31 Matt. 9: 10, 11.   32 Matt. 9: 12.   33 Luke 15: 1.
34 Matt. 2: 1-3.

Herodians were a sort of political party, though their faith was Jewish. They, however, had no special regard for the laws of Moses nor for the traditions of the Fathers; 'yet they were always prepared to adopt them when, by so doing, their ends could be best served. They had strong hope that Herod would found so great and powerful a dynasty that the Jews would eventually be brought under the permanent rule of the Herod family.

23. They mingled the heathen practices of Rome with their politico-religious ideas of the Jews. Every opportunity they had they would introduce some evil practice among the Jews, and thus lower the religious tone of the people. By so doing they hoped to gain in favor and in power with those whom they so influenced. They would gladly unite with any class of the Jews in any plot, in order to accomplish their purpose for gaining prestige. Thus we find them uniting with the Pharisees in a plot for Christ's death.[35] At another time we find them used as willing spies for the Pharisees and Sadducees to entrap[36] the Savior. Jesus, however, knew their design, and he sternly rebuked them. They had not a very long existence after the rule of the Herods. Like other religio-political parties their own hypocrisy helped to bring about their destruction.

THE SCRIBES.

24. These people were not an independent sect, but were a branch of the Pharisees. The term "scribe," is from the Hebrew word "Sofer," meaning "one who writes," or "transcribes."[37] This is why the term is applied to this class. As a party they began to flourish after the passing away of Ezra, and were prominent for several centuries in influencing the people by their writings and teachings. Having so great an advantage by virtue of their position, they used it largely for self-aggrandizement. Instead of being true teachers and writers, imparting the knowledge of God and His law, they

---

35 Mark 3: 6.   36 Matt. 22: 15, 16.   37 Ezra 7: 6, 11; Esther 3: 12; Jer. 8: 8.

were denounced by the Savior as hypocrites.[38] They were inclined toward strong Pharisaical tendencies, and were feared, reverenced, and highly esteemed by the people. With this class can also be reckoned the lawyers. More will be said concerning them when describing the sect of the Pharisees.

THE ESSENES.

25. Of this sect of the Jews nothing is said directly in the Scriptures; but Dr. Ginsburg, in "Kitto's Encyclopedia," thinks that this is the class referred to by the Savior in Matt. 19 : 12. They disbelieved in marriage, and placed very little confidence in womankind. They would take the children of different classes of Jews at an early age, and instruct them in their teachings, which prolonged the life of the sect. Their main teaching was piety, holy living, and a low regard for wealth. Josephus gives a lengthy description of them in his "Second Book of Jewish Wars," (*b*) as a result of which some are inclined to think that he leaned in that direction himself. They believed very much as did the Pharisees concerning the Scriptures and the laws of Moses; but they rejected absolutely the traditions and maxims of the rabbis. They did not have a very long existence, and never became very influential among the Jews.

THE SADDUCEES.

26. This class is frequently mentioned in the New Testament, and they often came in contact with the Savior and with the Apostles. They were a large and powerful faction, though they did not have the following of the masses. They were very wealthy and quite influential, but were strongly inclined toward infidelity. They held a similar relation to the Pharisees of the time as do the so-called "higher critics" to the orthodoxy of the present, who not only discard many of the popular theological errors, but also seek to undermine faith in the word of God.

[38] Matt. 23 : 13, 14, 15, 23, 25, 27, 29.

27. Of their origin nothing definite can be determined, though it is claimed by some they were the offspring of one Zadok, which means " righteousness," a disciple of Antigonos of Socho. He succeeded Simon, the Just, the last member of the Great Synagogue, who lived about the middle of the second century before Christ. While like the Pharisees they claimed to be closely following the word of God, they in fact thrust aside many of the fundamental truths of the Bible. They claimed to teach and interpret the law of Moses according to the strict letter; and took the position from their standpoint that many of the beliefs the Pharisees held could not be proved from the Scriptures. True the Pharisees did adhere to views which were anti-scriptural and man-made only. Nevertheless there were many things they did believe which the Sadducees rejected, that were in harmony with the word of God. The idea of the resurrection of the literal body from the dead they ridiculed; [39] and thought it almost preposterous to think that when a person once was dead he could again rise with a material body. Being rather extreme literalists on much of the letter of the Bible, they reasoned that such a view was neither philosophical nor logical.

CHRIST SILENCING SADDUCEES, WHO DISBELIEVED IN RESUR-
RECTION.

28. The Pharisees, however, regarded this doctrine of the resurrection as a fundamental belief, without which they considered they could not have hope in God. [40] (c) This view of things will explain many passages of Scripture, showing why the Sadducees came to Christ as they did. At one time, be it remembered, they came to Christ, and thought they would cite an instance which came under their observation, to show him the utter fallacy of the doctrine of the resurrection of the dead, if He did believe in it as did the Pharisees. [41] The Savior revealed to them their ignorance and put them to silence.

[39] Acts 23 : 8.　[40] Acts 23 : 6.　[41] Matt. 22 : 23-31.

PAUL TAKING ADVANTAGE OF SADDUCEES.

29. On another occasion when Paul was before the Sanhedrin, the Jewish council or tribunal to determine law cases among the Jews, which was composed of both Pharisees and Sadducees, he noticed that there was a discussion going on among themselves on this very point. He seized the opportunity to declare himself on the side of the Pharisees; this of course gave him a great advantage for the time being, as there was constant and bitter hatred between the Pharisees and Sadducees.

THEY NEITHER BELIEVED IN SPIRITUAL BEINGS.

30. Not believing in the resurrection of the dead, it is easy to see why they should not believe in angelic ministrations or in spiritual beings of any kind; hence their belief on this point can be readily known whenever the subject would come under consideration. For this reason we read the following:

"For the Sadducees say that there is no resurrection, neither angel, nor spirit." [42]

OPPOSED TO ALL TRADITIONS.

31. Against traditions of every kind they were bitterly and relentlessly opposed. They claimed that it was sufficient to believe the teachings of Moses as they were, without adding any further burden; though these teachings were not regarded by the Sadducees from their truly inspired standpoint. They considered the Pharisees hypocrites, ridiculing them, constantly seeking to sow strife and discord among them; pulling their believers from them at every opportunity. They would often say and do things against the Pharisees which were very bitter and foul. They used every means in their possession to cause the rivalry between these two sects to continue. So the Savior warned the people of His time of the leaven or malice of the Sadducees, [43] and of imbibing their teachings or their spirit.

[42] Acts 23: 8.　　　[43] Matt. 16: 6.

SADDUCEES WOULD UNITE WITH PHARISEES TO OPPOSE JESUS.

32. While it is true they were bitterly opposed to the other religious sect, whenever the common cause of opposing Christ gave opportunity, they would always join with the Pharisees. For the Savior made bare their iniquities, and showed their true character before the people. Jesus would read their hearts and open their real condition as religious leaders and teachers. This angered them greatly, and they would stoop to almost anything to get revenge. And so we find them joining hands with the Pharisees in tempting Christ,[44] and also taking part in condemning him to death.

33. We find them later persecuting the Apostles by imprisoning them, forbidding them to preach the gospel of Christ, and especially condemning them for preaching about the resurrection of the dead.[45] In nothing concerning religious belief were they as strict as the Pharisees, though claiming to be the proper kind of Jews, and the true idealists of the worshipers of God. However, sad to say, they had very little use for the blessed Savior, because his life was so pure and holy, as contrasted with their pompous, outward show, and their laxity of morals. While they assisted in the crucifying of the Christ and the persecution of the Apostles, the truth of the gospel continued just the same, with the power of the Spirit accompanying it, and many believing in the Lord Jesus through the preaching of the risen Savior from the dead.

OF SHORT DURATION.

34. They did not last very long after the early church began to flourish, though they did all in their power to stop its progress. Sad to say, however, Sadduceeism, or non-resurrectionism, is in a measure extant at the present time; but the same power of the Christ that conquered error then, will again do likewise.

44 Matt. 16:1. 45 Acts 4:1, 2. 46 John 8:44.

THE PHARISEES.

35. The greatest, most powerful, most influential, most scrupulous, most religious sect of the times, and the most bitter to the gospel of Christ, was the Pharisees. In fact from the opening of the New Testament, the beginning of the work of John the Baptist, till the close of the earthly ministrations of Christ, continuing through to the work of the early church, even when it was quite well advanced, we constantly meet with this class of Jews. While claiming to be the true children of God, the Savior said they were the children of the devil.[46] While professing to be leaders of the religious thought of the day, their lives and conduct, when compared with their profession, showed them to be the most irreligious.

36. The subject is one of importance and deserves much attention, especially since they were the chief actors against the work of the Savior and the early church. Many of the traditions, customs, and ceremonies of the Jewish people at the time of Christ originated with them, by an understanding of which we can better appreciate the sayings of Christ. We shall therefore consider them, their belief, their teachings, and some of their customs, in a chapter by itself.

EXPLANATORY NOTES.

Paragraph 19.

(a) The rabbis taught that all soil outside of Palestine was unclean and defiling. They would permit plants to be brought from other soil; but before the person could bring the plant into the city, he was obliged to shake off every bit of the soil attached to it. To do otherwise would be accounted sinful. This thought lends force to the Savior's exhortation to the disciples when they were sent to preach the gospel. He said: "And whosoever shall not receive you, nor hear you, when ye depart thence, *shake off the dust under your feet*, for a testimony against them." Mark 6:11. See also Acts 13:51.

When this was done, the Jew would learn that he was regarded as unworthy of being put in Jewish soil. To him it would also mean he would not sleep with his fathers, nor have any resurrection in the last day. In other words, it would be to him practically the loss of the world to come.

At the present time the orthodox Jews have special, consecrated soil, as being the nearest they can have to the original, the blessing upon it being substituted for the holy city in location.

Paragraph 25.

(*b*) In chapter eight of the "Second Book of Wars," Josephus gives quite a lengthy description of this class. The reader is referred to this chapter should he wish an extended knowledge of this sect.

Paragraph 28.

(*c*) Even to the present day the orthodox Jew confesses his firm faith in the resurrection of the dead. Their prayer-books abound with the idea. Frequently we find this thought closely associated with the coming of the Messiah. As for instance, on the first page of the daily service we find the following: "At the end of the days He will send our Messiah, to redeem those who hope to the end for salvation. God will raise the dead according to his abundant mercy. Blessed be the name of His praise to all eternity."—*Daily Prayer-book.*

CHAPTER IV.

The Sect of the Pharisees.

"And have put on the new man, which is renewed in knowledge after the image of Him that created him: where there is neither Greek nor Jew, circumcision nor uncircumcision, Barbarian, Scythian, bond nor free: but Christ is all, and in all." Col. 3:10, 11.

THAT the Pharisees were regarded a sect, and a strict one, is evident from the following words of Paul:

"That after the most straitest sect of our religion I lived a Pharisee."[1]

2. Possibly the reader may have wondered why the Savior had so much to say about the Pharisees, and why such scathing denunciations should ever have come from His lips. Especially is this thought forcible when viewed in the light of Matthew 23.[2] No less than nine woes are there pronounced, as well as a prophecy of the most dire punishment meted out to any people since the days of Adam.[3] This, however, will be made plain as we trace their history.

3. The word "Pharisee," from the Hebrew "Parash," separate, was applied to these people because of their attempt to separate themselves from all other classes, as the particularly favored ones of heaven, the especially chosen of God. This is evident from the manner in which the Pharisee offered his prayer:

"God, I thank thee, that I am not as other men are, extortioners, unjust, adulterers, or even as this publican."[4]

4. They professed to trace their history to the times of Ezra, and regarded with great pride their ancestry. It is no doubt known that when the children of Israel returned from Babylon, there were many of the people who had intermarried with the

[1] Acts 26:5. [2] Matt. 23:13-16, 23-29. [3] Matt. 23:34-38. [4] Luke 18:11.

[47]

heathen, during their sojourn in captivity. At their return Ezra
read to them from the law of Moses that they ought not to have
committed so grievous a sin; and so many of the people immediately separated themselves from their wives. They then
entered into a covenant with God, and with one another, that
they would follow strictly the law of Moses, and ever after keep
themselves from being defiled and made impure by contamina-
tion with strangers.[5]

REFORMATION OF THE JEWS.

5. It was mentioned in Chapter II. that after the restoration
of the Jews from Babylonian captivity, several of the leaders
brought about a reformation, hoping so to impress them with the
truth of the word of God that they would never commit the same
sins again. The reformation was made upon several points,
among which were the following in particular : the observance of the Sabbath ;[6] separation from heathen women,[7] and
from strangers of all classes who were not Jews ;[8] and the payment of the tithes for the support of the priesthood.[9] The
purpose of these men of God in bringing about this reformation
was certainly noble, inspiring, God-like ; and the Jews certainly
needed the work done. But like every other truth, the devil
took these very means which should have been a blessing to the
whole race, and should have prepared them for the coming
Messiah, and hid the truth under the great mass of traditions,
until they lost sight of the true knowledge of God.

6. While these people claimed to be the successors, in
name, of those reformers of Ezra's period, they were far from
having the same spirit of love and truth. As these teachers
increased in power and influence, their methods of action and
association increased accordingly. It thus became necessary
to explain to the people the extent of the meaning of these
customs and reforms, as they asserted the Scriptures intended.
As a result these religious teachers, and those people who

5 Ezra 9; Neh. 13: 23-27.   6 Neh. 13: 15-22.   7 Ezra 10: 9-17.   8 Neh. 13: 1-3.
9 Neh. 13: 10-14.

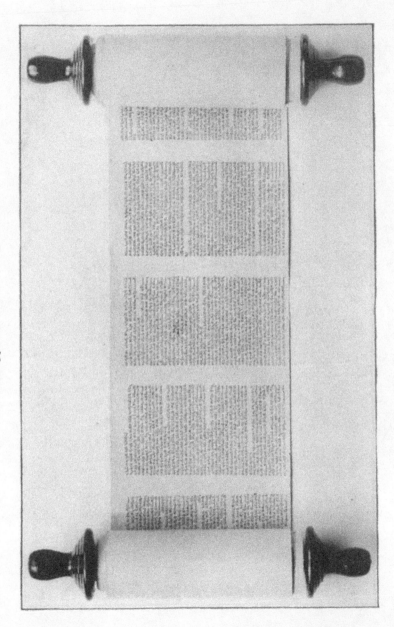

THE PENTATEUCH IN MINIATURE.

accepted their teachings, formed themselves into a sort of community or fraternity, known as the "Che-voorah." The way this was brought about was as follows:

ORIGIN OF "CHE-VOORAH," OR FRATERNITY.

7. After Haggai and Malachi, the last two prophets, passed away, the "spirit of prophecy" ceased from among the Jews. Having no one to instruct them directly from God, apostasy naturally soon followed. Some of the leading theologians, instead of seeking God ever to teach the people right ways and true statutes, spent much of their time in discussing theology, and making additional outward observances for the people; hoping these would keep the people in a spiritual state, as well as reform them, where reformation was needed. A commission was appointed to go through the land, to ascertain to what degree the people were complying with the statutes and laws, especially those pertaining to the tithing, and to the separation from the heathen. It was found that the offerings which belonged to the priests were devoted; but the second tithes and those for the poor, were not observed. It was then found necessary to enforce certain laws which should decide who would be loyal to the law. Therefore decrees were issued calling upon those people everywhere who would pay these various tithes, as well as follow the other teachings and observances of these leaders, to form associations, or companies. Everybody who would not tithe all that came to him, or everything he raised, before he used any portion of it, was to be excluded from the fraternity. These people were to buy and sell to one another; were to associate only among themselves; were exempt from certain taxes and imposts that other Jews were not who did not belong to the "Che-voorah." Of course this gave these Jews great advantage over all others; and, in view of these facts, no doubt there is much meaning in the statement of the Savior when He said:

" The scribes and the Pharisees sit in Moses' seat: all therefore what-

4

soever they bid you observe, that observe and do; but do not ye after their works : for they say, and do not. For they bind *heavy burdens and grievous* to be borne, and lay them on *men's shoulders ; but they themselves will not move them with one of their fingers.*" [10]

8. It can readily be seen what great hardship such laws would work on the people who were in the minority, who did not belong to this fraternity, yet were dependent to secure their necessities from these people. They would have to pay more for those things they needed in their worship ; they would be obliged to conform to many observances in which they had no faith ; they would be heavily burdened in various ways. So the Savior just informed the people all about their actions.

HOW THE PHARISEES EXALTED SELF.

9. Having become the teachers, the law-makers, the writers or scribes of the people, it was but natural they should feel themselves above the masses, and especially superior to those who did not agree with them. They came to believe they were highly favored above everybody, were not to mingle with the ordinary classes; that no one but an educated person was worthy of consideration. (*a*)   Some of the characteristics of this sect are well described by the Savior :

" And He spake this parable unto certain which trusted in themselves that they were righteous, and despised others." [11]

"And the Pharisees also, who were covetous, heard these things : and they derided Him." [12]

"And He said unto them, Ye are they which justify yourselves before men ; but God knoweth your hearts : for that which is highly esteemed among men is abomination in the sight of God." [13]

"Woe unto you, scribes and Pharisees, hypocrites ! for ye devour widows' houses, and for a pretense make long prayers : therefore ye shall receive the greater damnation." [14]

"And it came to pass, as Jesus sat at meat in the house, behold many publicans and sinners came and sat down with Him and His disciples. And when the Pharisees saw it, they said unto His disciples, Why eateth your Master with publicans and sinners ?" [15]

[10] Matt. 23 : 2-5.   [11] Luke 18 : 9.   [12] Luke 16 : 14.   [13] Luke 16 : 15.
[14] Matt. 23 : 14.   [15] Matt. 9 : 10, 11.

THE PROUD PHARISEE. [51]

"Now when the Pharisee which had bidden him saw it, he spake within himself, saying, This man, if he were a prophet, would have known who and what manner of woman this is that toucheth him: for she is a sinner." [16]

PAUL INFORMED OF THE PLOT TO KILL HIM.

10. Being a fraternity, they would be obliged to communicate many of their plans and purposes to their fellows or "chaverim," as they were called. No doubt this explains how Paul's nephew learned of the plot the forty had formed to neither eat nor drink till they had killed him.[17] It should be remembered that Paul cried out before the council that he was not only a Pharisee, but the son of a Pharisee.[18] It is but natural, therefore, to conclude that all of the family belonged to the guild. This is further shown from Philippians.[19]

11. The day after the dissension in the council when the Pharisees came to their senses, and really considered who and what Paul was, they concluded that, according to their organization and their principles which controlled them, he was not only unworthy of favor, but that he ought to be put out of the way. So they decided after an assembly, to carry their thought into execution. A number of them, therefore, made a vow that they would neither eat nor drink till they had killed him. Paul's nephew, being a member of the fraternity, heard the conversation; he, therefore, immediately went to the guardhouse, and informed the captain of their plot. Thus Providence interposed, and Paul was saved. (*b*) The Pharisees, however, were very punctilious when they made an oath of execration, as they were *bound* to fulfil it. The question might arise, therefore, "How did they ever free themselves from this dilemma?" The following incident from the Talmud will probably answer such a question:

"If a man makes a vow to abstain from food, woe to him if he eateth, and woe to him if he does not eat. If he eateth, he sinneth against his vow; if he does not eat, he sinneth against his life. What then must he do? Let him go before 'the sages,' and they will absolve him from his vow."— *Edersheim, "Sketches of Jewish Life."*

[16] Luke 7: 39.　[17] Acts 23: 12-17.　[18] Acts 23: 6.　[19] Phil. 3: 5.

PHARISEES VERY STRICT.

12. While the Pharisees were a very strict class, they carried their scruples to an extreme. Not only were they separated from the heathen and Gentiles around them, but there existed a separation even among themselves. As a result they became divided into four separate classes, each class being nearly as distinct from the other as these were from the Gentiles around them. Certain restrictions were removed, thus allowing them to eat and drink together; but as to social standing and piety they had nothing in common. Possibly this idea might throw some light on the statement of Paul when he says:

"For ye have heard of my conversation in time past in the Jews' religion, how that beyond measure I persecuted the church of God, and wasted it: and profited in the Jews' religion above many my equals in mine own nation, being more exceedingly zealous of the traditions of my fathers."[20]

And again another expression:

"Though I might also have confidence in the flesh. If any other man thinketh that he hath whereof he might trust in the flesh, I more: circumcised the eighth day, of the stock of Israel, of the tribe of Benjamin, an Hebrew of the Hebrews; as touching the law, a Pharisee."[21]

THEIR FOUNDATION OF FAITH.

13. For the basis of their belief, they claimed Moses and the prophets. They heralded far and wide that they were the children of God, and that they were the only true believers in God; anybody who did not believe with them, and accept their interpretation of Scripture could not be saved. Just a few illustrations will here be cited, touching certain of their points of belief, which perhaps may make some passages of Scripture more clear.

PHARISAICAL LAWS OF SEPARATION.

14. Before we consider some of these laws concerning the question of separation, we might with profit notice a certain scripture which will perhaps enable us better to understand its

[20] Gal. 1: 13, 14.   [21] Phil. 3: 4, 5.

significance as we consider these rabbinical laws. This passage is found in Acts 10 :

"And he [Peter] said unto them, Ye know how that it is an *unlawful* thing for a man that is a Jew to keep company or come unto one of another nation; but God hath shown me that I should not call any man common or unclean." [22]

15. Possibly some may have thought that the unlawfulness here referred to originated with God, and at some time was commanded to the Jews; and, therefore, Peter had this in mind when he said, "Ye know how that it is an unlawful thing." Such an idea is erroneous. God had nothing whatever to do with any such law; He never had commanded it in any such term or spirit. The *Pharisees taught* that not under any circumstance was a Jew allowed to have any dealing with a Gentile.

SYNOPSIS OF LAWS.

If a Jew were compelled to transact *any* business with a Gentile, he was obliged to cleanse himself both before and after the meeting.

If a Gentile were invited into the home of a Jew, the Gentile must not be left alone in the house during any portion of the time of his visit; if he were, then all the food in the house became unclean; and everything connected with the rooms through which the Gentile passed was defiled.

If a Jew were obliged to purchase any article of clothing, furniture, or any other utensil for domestic purposes from a Gentile, after he brought it to his house, he first had to wash his hands, because of his defilement in touching the object. Then the article itself would have to be cleansed, scoured, and thoroughly renovated.

If any Gentile lived in the same community with a Jew, and peradventure the Gentile was to have some festal celebration, for at least three days before this festal occasion, the Jew

[22] Acts 10 : 28.

should have no transaction with the Gentile. If the Jew should have any intercourse with him during this time, he would be considered as assisting the Gentile in preparing his festivities.

If Gentiles were celebrating any heathen festivity, the Jew, if it were possible, should not pass through the city at this time, for fear that some bit of uncleanness might adhere to him.

It was forbidden to the Jew under most any circumstance, to do anything for a non-Jew. A Jewess was forbidden to assist a Gentile woman when giving birth to a child; she was not permitted to feed a child of another nationality, because then it would not only be defiling the Jewess, but would at the same time, by lengthening the life of the infant, encourage idolatry.

If a Gentile met with a disaster, such as having his house destroyed by fire, it was permissible for the Jew to assist him only in extreme cases; and these extreme cases had so many limitations and modifications, that the poor Gentile might have his house reduced to ashes and everything in it destroyed before he could receive any assistance.

A Jew must not have any part in the erection of any dwelling for a Gentile; this would be a defilement, and would cause him to become unclean. In the construction of no buildings was he permitted to have part.

A Jew must not sell, lease, or permit the use of any lands, houses, or real estate to a Gentile; for, after the Gentile had touched it, especially if he had used the house or land, all was unclean and defiled.

If a Gentile brought anything to a Jew as a gift, or for any other purpose, the Jew must not permit him to bring it into the house. Should the non-Jew succeed in bringing it into the house, the goods must be destroyed, and the house cleansed.

16. And so the list of laws might be continued indefinitely. The reader can better appreciate the thought when he is informed

there is a tractate, entitled, "Abodah-Zorah," or "Idolatry," which treats of the relation between the Jew and the Gentile, containing five chapters, and no less than fifty sections. These are exclusively devoted to this one subject, and do not include scores of other laws scattered throughout the rabbinical writings. Can we not, then, appreciate the meaning of that text which Peter used when he came to Cornelius, in saying that it was *unlawful* for a man that is a Jew to come unto, or to keep company with, one who is not a Jew? But thank the blessed Lord, God revealed to him that there was *no man* common or unclean.

PHARISAICAL LAWS OF TITHING.

17. It was mentioned in the previous part of this chapter that some of the peculiar laws that the Pharisees made were those relating to tithing. On this subject of "Terumah," "heave offerings," the first tithe, and the second tithe, almost an endless set of laws, definitions, explanations, suggestions, and rules were laid down. There are three tractates, containing over two hundred sections, especially devoted to these laws. (*c*) They treat upon the objects which ought to be tithed; how these should be tithed, and how they should not be tithed; where they should tithe them, and where they should not tithe them; the kinds of fruits, and other foodstuffs which may be tithed, also the exceptions to these rules. The laws also were laid down what to do with the people who did not tithe, and who did not strictly adhere to the letter of the Pharisaical commands. The sentence was hard, cruel, and often mingled with severe flogging. It was not surprising, in view of these conditions, to hear the following from the lips of the Savior:

"Woe unto you, scribes and Pharisees, hypocrites! for ye pay tithe of mint and anise and cummin, and have *omitted* the weightier matters of the law, judgment, mercy, and faith: these ought ye to have done, and not to leave the other undone." [23]

18. The Pharisees did not know what mercy meant; this

[23] Matt. 23: 23.

CHRIST QUESTIONING THE RABBIS.

we shall prove later. They were hard, austere, rigorous, exacting, proud, yes, even cruel; ever seeking to satisfy their own ambitious ends, which they did by clothing their laws and their teachings with the Scripture. The Savior knew full well the meaning of those words He uttered:

"Woe unto you, scribes and Pharisees, hypocrites! for ye are like unto whited sepulchres, which indeed appear beautiful outward, but are within full of dead men's bones, and of all uncleanness. Even so ye also outwardly appear righteous unto men, but within ye are full of hypocrisy and iniquity." [24]

PHARISAICAL LAWS OF EATING.

19. Many readers of the Bible have noted with interest the experience that Paul and Peter had on one occasion at Antioch, [25] and the cause of this difficulty. It was a strong controversy, involving three leading Apostles, [26] affecting the central church of Gentile influence, and causing Paul to administer to Peter a very sharp rebuke. [27] The basis for the whole difficulty was the separation of Peter from eating with Gentile Christians. [28] He had eaten with the Gentiles on several occasions, and it was right that he should. This Peter knew; but there were certain Jews who came to him, followers of the Lord Jesus, who had not fully overcome their Pharisaical ideas. They found Peter eating with these Gentiles. They then declared they would withdraw their fellowship from him if he persisted in eating with them. Then Peter withdrew himself from these Gentiles, refused to eat with them any more, and separated himself from them on this account. The reason for his actions, the Scripture says, was that he feared them of the circumcision. [29]

DIFFICULT FOR CONVERTS TO OVERCOME TRADITION.

20. It would seem that the experience which he had some fifteen years prior, when he received a special vision upon this subject of the relation between Jew and Gentile, [30] would have been sufficient to forever save Peter from falling into this very

[24] Matt. 23:27. [25] Gal. 2:11. [26] Gal. 2:13. [27] Gal. 2:14. [28] Gal. 2:12.
[29] Gal. 2:12. [30] Acts 10:9-16.

serious difficulty. For when he went to visit Cornelius, he took with him six Jewish brethren, expecting on his return from this trip that he would be accused by the Jews of going in unto Gentiles, and possibly of having eaten with them.[31] When the accusation was brought against him, he rehearsed the whole story from the beginning, how God made the matter plain.[32] Still it was difficult for the Jews and even for Peter, though all believed in Christ, to overcome those teachings which had been from earliest infancy so deeply rooted in their lives.

SYNOPSIS OF LAWS ON EATING.

No Jew was permitted to sit at the same table with a Gentile and to eat with him under any circumstances.

If an animal were set apart to be slaughtered for Gentile use, it was permissible to kill the animal for Jewish use. But if the animal had passed into the hands of the Gentile, or had been touched by him, the Jew must neither touch nor eat the animal under any consideration.

If the Jew were to plant seed in his field for his own personal use, if the seed had been handled by a Gentile, it was unlawful to be used.

If a cow were milked by a Gentile, her milk must not be drunk by any Jew; the milk was unclean, because it had been handled by an unclean man.

If the Gentiles lived in the land where the Jews were, any bread they baked, or oil they prepared, or any other food they handled might be sold to Gentiles; but it must not be sold to the Jews.

There was nothing, *absolutely* nothing, that a Gentile prepared personally for food, raised in his own garden, or touched with his own hands, that a Pharisee was permitted to either touch, taste, or handle.

THEY SHOW NO MERCY.

21. Possibly some might inquire if there was nothing in the

---

[31] Acts 10: 23.   [32] Acts 11: 1–18.

writings of these rabbis which might indicate that they did have some fellow-feeling for the Gentiles, and that under *some* circumstances they would be permitted to feed them, and to show them some kindliness in this direction? As a reply to this, we cite one or two statements from a rabbinical work, entitled, "Hilchoth Accum," as follows:

"The poor of the idolaters [Gentiles] are to be fed with the poor of Israel, because of the ways of peace. They are also allowed to have part of the gleaning, the forgotten sheaf, and the corner of the field, for the sake of the ways of peace. It is also permissible to ask after their health, even on their feast-day, because of the ways of peace."

This passage would seem almost like a contradiction of some of the laws cited above; but if the entire section be read, the true position of Pharisaism will be evident.

"All these things are said of Israel only during the time when she is in captivity to the Gentile nations, or when the hands of the Gentiles are strong upon her. But when the hand of Israel is strong upon them [that is, upon the Gentiles] we are forbidden to suffer an idolater [Gentile] amongst us, even so much as to sojourn incidentally, or to pass from place to place."

Is it any wonder, then, that the Savior should pronounce such punishments upon those who could be so harsh and relentless?

THE SAMARITANS.

22. In future chapters we shall touch upon other laws, teachings, and traditions of the Pharisees, sufficient having been given to illustrate them and their belief. Before we close this chapter, it may be in place to give a brief account of another class of religionists at the time of Christ, mentioned in the previous chapter; and these are the Samaritans. This sect also play a prominent part in the early experience of New Testament history, especially in the days of Christ.

THEIR ORIGIN.

23. As to the origin of these people, writers, even among Jews, are not agreed. The best information, however, that can

be gained concerning their origin, is that they were descendants of the Cuthites, whom the king of Babylon brought to
Samaria, after he had conquered the ten tribes of Israel, and
transplanted them into the cities of the Medes. These people,
however, had no knowledge of the true God. Soon after their
advent into Samaria the Lord sent lions among them, which
destroyed many of the people. They informed the king of
Babylon that they were unacquainted with the gods of the land;
therefore the deities were angry, and sent these wild beasts to
devour them. The king then sent to them one of the priests
of Israel, who was to teach them the laws of his God, and
how they were to worship the God of Israel. A full account
of this experience will be found in 2 Kings 17.

24. With the worship of the true God they mingled their
heathen customs. They perverted the ways of truth by following many of their former idolatrous habits. Gradually the
two modes of worship were combined; so that they had a
measure of faith in the law of God, and especially in the
writings of Moses. [33] After the return of the Jews from their
captivity in Babylon to Jerusalem, these people wished to unite
with them in the building of the temple, [34] and in the worship
of the true God. But the Jews refused. As a result the
Samaritans became their bitter enemies. This is evident by
reading Ezra 4, especially verses 9, 10. This enmity continued for centuries, and increased in intensity with the lapse
of time.

HYPOCRITICAL IN THEIR PROFESSIONS.

25. Whenever they had opportunity to further their *own*
ends, and gain any advantage, they claimed to be Jews, and used
the Jews as a tool to this end. To do this, they freqently re-
sorted to deception. Thus, for instance, in the days of Alexander
the Great, when the Jews were in favor with the king, they
claimed to be descendants of Manasseh and Ephraim. They

[33] 2 Kings 17: 32-34.   [34] Ezra 4: 1, 2.

asked to be excused from doing certain work on the Sabbath, and during the Sabbatic year. Then at other times, when the Jews were in trouble, they refused to have anything to do with them, and claimed they were Sidonians, or Medes and Persians. This was especially manifest when King Antiochus entered Jerusalem, and spoiled the sanctuary and its vessels.

DEFILED THE TEMPLE AT JERUSALEM.

26. They built a temple on Mount Gerizim, and here they carried on their worship. Whenever they could, it is said, they would go to Jerusalem and harass the Jews in their worship. Josephus tells of an incident where the Samaritans once entered into Jerusalem and defiled the temple at the Passover. It was the custom of the priests to open the gates of the temple soon after midnight of the Passover, and other festal days. Certain of the Samaritans secured some dead bodies, and secretly entered the temple on a Passover night, scattering the corpses all over the sacred place. This so enraged the Jews that they never after permitted a Samaritan to enter the temple.

PHARISEES DESPISED THEM.

27. Though the Samaritans professed faith in much of the Scriptures, as did the Pharisees, the latter hated them most bitterly. Among the writings of the rabbis against them, we find the following:

" There be two manner of nations, which my heart abhorreth, and the third is no nation; they that sit upon the mountain of Samaria, and they that dwell among the Philistines, and the foolish people that dwell among Shechem."—*Ben Sirach, in Ecclus. 1:25, 26.*

28. The Pharisees would have nothing whatever to do with them. If they saw a Samaritan dying, and they could assist him to life, if it were only a little water that was needed, it would be refused. We can thus see why the woman at the well was so surprised when the Savior asked her for a drink.

'" How is it that thou, being a Jew, askest drink of me, which am a woman of Samaria? for the Jews have no dealings with the Samaritans." [35]

[35] John 4:9.

29. In the temple and in the synagogue services, the Samaritan was cursed by the Pharisees. A Samaritan would never be accepted as a witness by the Jews. He was regarded as a vile sinner, and an associate of Satan. Thus we can see why the Jews, in accusing Christ as a Samaritan, classed him with the devil.

"Say we not well that thou art a Samaritan and hast a devil ? [36]

THEIR WORSHIP A MIXTURE OF JUDAISM AND HEATHENISM.

30. They regarded Moses as a very great man, and esteemed the Pentateuch with great veneration. It is said there exists an original copy of the five books of Moses, in a scroll, preserved by the few Samaritans of the present time. These claim this scroll was handed down since the days when the priest of Israel was among them, and taught them this law. They also had certain vague ideas concerning the Messiah, but did not believe in any of the traditions of the Pharisees. All things considered, their worship was a mixture of ideas inexplicable ; and no doubt because of this the Savior said to the woman : " Ye worship ye know not what." [37]

MANY ACCEPT CHRIST.

31. There were many of them, however, who were kindly disposed to their enemies, the Jews, as is seen in the parable of the good Samaritan. [38] They were also quite susceptible to the teachings of the Savior. The power of the gospel of Christ finally broke down the wall that was built up by both these classes. This was begun in Christ's own day. It is true it was hard for the Jews to believe that the Samaritans could be saved, or that Christ could love them. This was forcibly illustrated by the feelings of the disciples when they wanted to bring down fire from heaven to have them consumed, because they refused to receive the Savior. [39] But Jesus showed them by the parable there were some of that class who had fully as

[36] John 8:48.   [37] John 4:22.   [38] Luke 10:30-37.   [39] Luke 9:51-55.

much love for their fellow men as did the Jews; and that they sometimes appreciated acts of kindness more than the Jews, is seen in the healing of the ten lepers.[40] All were Jews save one; he was a Samaritan, and the only one to return and express his gratitude for the kindness the Savior had bestowed upon him.

32. A very fruitful field was opened among them for gospel work by the disciples a few years after the ascension, and large numbers of them were converted to Christ.[41] It is said that there are about one hundred Samaritans at the present time who live in a community by themselves at Nablous (formerly Shechem), and that the only scriptural writings they have, is this copy of the Pentateuch. They observe several of the Mosaic laws, among which is the Passover.

[40] Luke 17: 11–19.   [41] Acts 8: 5–25.

EXPLANATORY NOTES.

Paragraph 9.

(a) The following quotations will give an idea of how the Pharisees regarded the illiterate and uneducated:

" Said Rabbi Eleazer, It is permissible to split the nostrils of an illiterate man on the Day of Atonement which occurs on the Sabbath. His disciples said unto him, " Rabbi, better say he may be slaughtered." He replied, " That would need a blessing; but the other would not."—*Talmud, Pesachim.*

" Our rabbis have advocated: A man should sell all his possessions, and marry the daughter of an educated person. If he cannot find such a person, let him take the daughter of one of the great men of the time. . . . If he cannot find such a person, let him marry the daughter of an almoner. If he cannot find such a person, let him marry the daughter of a school-master. But *let him not marry the daughter of the unlearned, for they are an abomination,* and their wives are vermin; and of their daughters it is said, Cursed is he that lieth with any beast."—*Abbreviated from " The Old Paths."* These statements mark a strong contrast with what the Lord says through his servant Paul, in 1 Cor. 1 : 25–31.

Paragraph II.

(b) Dr. Edersheim states the fact that very shortly after this experience of the forty had happened, there were three enactments passed by a son of Gamaliel, Paul's teacher.

1. The first of these repealed the statute which permitted children, who had not been personally accepted, to be part of the fraternity.

2. That before a person should be admitted into the fraternity, his previous conduct should be investigated.

3. If a person who once had belonged to the Che-voora apostatized, he should never be permitted to come back.

All this simply demonstrates beyond a doubt the truthfulness of this experience of Paul.

Paragraph 17.

(c) The three tractates are in the first great division, or seder, of the Mishna, and are entitled, " Terumoth ; " " Maa-seroth," or tithes ; " Maa-ser Shani," or second tithe.

CHRIST TEACHING THE PEOPLE.

CHAPTER V.

The Teachings of Christ Versus the Teachings of the Rabbis.

"I will raise them up a Prophet from among their brethren, like unto thee, and will put My words in His mouth; and He shall speak unto them all that I shall command Him. And it shall come to pass, that whosoever will not hearken unto My words which He shall speak in My name, I will require it of him." Deut. 18:18, 19.

CHRIST THE TEACHER OF TRUTH.

CHRIST came into the world to teach the truth;[1] His mission was to lead men into truth; His purpose was to reveal its beauties. On the other hand the work of the rabbis was to pervert the truth; to mingle fables with the truth;[2] and to place their ideas before men as the true idea of righteousness. For instance, the rabbis taught:

"To be against the words of the scribes is more punishable than to be against the words of the Bible."

"The voice of the rabbi is as the voice of God."

"He who transgresses the word of the scribes throws away his life."

"Whosoever transgresses the words of the wise men, is to be beaten without number and without consideration. Why is this called the flogging of rebellion? Because he has transgressed against the words of the law and against the words of the scribes."

2. Jesus Christ, however, came to teach men what *God* said;[3] what God wanted men to say. He came to reveal to the people the value and the truth of the word of God.[4] He came not to reveal Himself; He came to reveal God. This, however, He could do only as in His life and teaching He upheld the words of the living God.[5] The Pharisees also claimed to teach the

---

[1] John 18:37.   [2] 1 Tim. 6:4.   [3] John 3:11; 7:16; 8:28; 12:49.
[4] John 1:18; 10:36; Matt. 11:27.   [5] Deut. 18:18-22.

words of the Bible, the words of the living God. They advocated that all. *their* teachings were based on Moses and the
prophets; they further said they had no desire other than to
teach in harmony with Moses and the prophets. Of course
they maintained before the people that they were the expositors
of the Scriptures; their lives and their teachings being a reflection of the writers of the Bible, and of the truths which the
prophets uttered. From the foregoing it is evident that between
the Pharisees and the Savior there could be neither harmony
nor co-operation, because His life and teachings were so different
from theirs. Hence they always feared that Christ would gain
greater power over the people than they had, and would in the
end lead the masses after Him. No doubt this is why Caiaphas
gave vent to his feelings in the following expression:

"If we let Him thus alone, all men will believe on Him: and the
Romans will come and take away both our place and nation." [6]

Shortly after this the Pharisees were compelled to acknowledge that they could not prevail against Him, for the world was
following Him.[7]

THE FULFILLMENT OF THE SCRIPTURES.

3. In His teaching, Christ claimed *He* was the fulfillment
of the law,[8] Moses, and the prophets.[9] He was a profound
believer in the Patriarchs.[10] He always appealed to the Old
Testament as His authority;[11] and ever recognized the Jews as
the chosen people of God.[12] At the same time His teaching
was bitterly opposed to that of the rabbis. They too claimed
to believe Moses and the prophets; they professed to be the
disciples of Moses;[13] they claimed that they were the children
of Abraham;[14] and boasted that they taught nothing only
what they could prove either directly or by inference from
Moses and the prophets. Illustrations of this latter method
will be given later.

[6] John 11:48. [7] John 12:19. [8] Matt. 5:17. [9] Luke 24:26, 27, 44.
[10] Mark 12:26. [11] Matt. 4:4, 7, 10; 5:21, 27, 33. [12] John 4:22; 8:37.
[13] John 9:28. [14] John 8:33, 39.

4. It will be well, therefore, to consider certain of the Savior's teachings from Moses and the prophets, and compare them with those of the Pharisees. When the devil came to Christ on the mount of temptation, the Savior met him with three different scriptures.[15] He did not stop to argue with Satan; He simply quoted the words of God, without any comment or explanation. When John the Baptist sent two of his disciples to Jesus, to inquire if he were the Messiah, the Savior selected from the crowds that thronged him, some who were blind, others who were deaf, those who were dumb, and many suffering with various ailments.[16] Then he healed them all. He instructed these disciples to tell John what they had seen and heard. He then added:

"Blessed is he, whosoever shall not be offended in Me." [17]

Why did the Savior act thus in answering John's question? Because John knew that the Messiah must fulfil the scriptures of Isaiah,[18] particularly those referring to the performance of these mighty works, and the preaching of the gospel to the poor. John's own message was based on this book; [19] the Messiah's works must follow him, for He was the forerunner. Hence the Savior knew that this would be the most convincing way to satisfy John's mind, that Christ was the One that was to come, because He was doing exactly as the Scriptures predicted should be done by the Messiah.

CHRIST QUOTING SCRIPTURE.

5. When the Savior accepted the invitation of Matthew to dine at his home, there were a *number of publicans* who also received invitations [20] to be guests for the occasion. The Pharisees were angered to see a man who claimed to believe in the Scriptures and to be an expounder of the law, associate with such a class of men. They finally raised the question to His disciples:

[15] Luke 4:4, 8, 12.　　[16] Luke 7:21, 22.　　[17] Matt. 11:6.　　[18] Isa. 35:5, 6.
[19] Isa. 40:3, 4.　　[20] Luke 5:29.

"Why eateth your Master with publicans and sinners?"[21]

It was not only disbelieving what they considered that the Scriptures taught, but it was also denying them as true teachers, because He was defiling Himself, as well as encouraging this custom among the Jews. The Savior finally answered them:

"Go ye and learn what that meaneth, I will have mercy and not sacrifice."[22]

Here the Savior meets them on their own ground, with the words of the prophet. By this means He sought to have them see that they did not know the truth of the Bible, nor did they believe in the teachings of the inspired men of God.

6. It is evident from their own writings that they did not know what mercy meant, for here is a passage from the Talmud to the point:

"Although a wise man has power to excommunicate on account of his honor, yet it is not to be praised in the disciple of a wise man who does so. . . . . The greatest of the wise men used to glory in their good deeds, and say, that they had never excommunicated nor anathematized any man on account of their honor, and this is the way the disciples of the wise men ought to walk. In what case is this to be applied?—When they have been despised or reviled in secret. But if the disciple of a wise man be despised or reviled publicly, it is *unlawful for him to forgive any affront to his honor ; and if he forgive, he is to be punished,* for this is a contempt of the law. *He is on the contrary to avenge and keep the thing in mind, like a serpent, until the offender entreat to be forgiven.*"

Did they need to learn to have mercy? From these statements can we not also see what the Savior evidently intended when he told the people to pray:

"Forgive us our trespasses, as we forgive those who trespass against us." And also these words: "For if ye forgive men their trespasses, your Heavenly Father will also forgive you: but if ye forgive not men their trespasses, neither will your Father forgive your trespasses."[23]

7. When the leper came to Him for healing, He told him to go and see the priest, and to carry out the instructions Moses commanded.[24] When He wanted the Pharisees and the people

---

[21] Matt. 9:11.   [22] Matt. 9:13.   [23] Matt. 6:14, 15.   [24] Matt. 8:2-4.

to know the authority the Baptist had for his commission, He referred them to Isaiah and to Malachi. [25]

8. When the Pharisees accused Him of violating the law of the Sabbath, He proved by the experience of David that what He did was in accordance with the law of the Sabbath,[26] though it might nor be in harmony with their view of the Scriptures. Thus He again showed them to be wrong in their teaching. On another occasion, when He healed a man on the Sabbath, who had a withered hand, and they sought to condemn Him for the act, He appealed to their own traditions which they acknowledged to be in harmony with the law.[27]

9. When the Pharisees came to the Savior, asking Him for a sign that His power and authority were from heaven, He appealed to the Prophet Jonah as a witness;[28] and, from the experience of this prophet, He convinced them that He was working in harmony with the word of God.

There was scarcely a prophet in whom they professed to have faith but that He quoted in support of His mission. He also showed that these prophets were witnesses to their iniquity. [29]

THE GROUND OF CHRIST'S DEFENSE.

10. Finding that they could not condemn Him from the Scriptures, they sought to class Him with themselves in exalting Himself, and holding Himself up before the people. This Jesus refuted from Moses and the prophets:

" Do not think that I will accuse you to the Father : there is one that accuseth you, even Moses, in whom ye trust. For had ye believed Moses, ye would have believed Me : for he wrote of Me. But if ye believe not His writings, how shall ye believe My words." [30]

"Abraham saith unto him, They have Moses and the prophets ; let them hear them. . . . And he said unto him, If they hear not Moses and the prophets, neither will they be persuaded, though one rose from the dead." [31]

" Jesus answered them, Many good works have I showed you from

25 Matt. 11: 10, 14.   26 Matt. 12: 3, 4.   27 Matt. 12: 10–12.   28 Matt. 12: 38-40.
29 Matt. 13: 14, 15.   30 John 5: 45–47.   31 Luke 16: 29-31.

My Father; for which of those works do ye stone Me? The Jews answered Him, saying, For a good work we stone Thee not; but for blasphemy , and because that Thou, being a man, makest Thyself God. Jesus answered them, Is it not written in your law, I said, Ye are gods? If He called them gods, unto whom the word of God came, and the Scripture cannot be broken; say ye of Him, whom the Father hath sanctified, and sent into the world, Thou blasphemest; because I said, I am the Son of God." [32]

CHRIST'S METHOD OF APPLYING SCRIPTURE.

11. Another peculiar feature of His teaching, so different from rabbinical exposition of Scripture, was the method He used in the application of the Scriptures directly to the people, instead of using such generalities. For instance: When the Savior quoted the scripture of Isaiah 5, [33] concerning the vineyard, as recorded in Matthew 21, [34] He made the application of that scripture to those very men; and then proved that they were the ones referred to by quoting from the Psalms. [35] This greatly angered the Pharisees, [36] for it led the people to believe that instead of their being the expositors of the word of God, they were really the perverters of the Scripture. This is no doubt why the Savior warned His disciples and the people to beware of the leaven of the Pharisees, for it was hypocrisy. [37]

12. This direct method of application of Scripture was no doubt what led the common people to hear Him gladly. [38] Doubtless it was this method that led the officers who were sent to arrest Jesus, to return without Him, and to say: " Never man spake as this man." [39] It was no doubt because of this method of application that many hung upon His words. He knew when, where, and how, to apply the word of God.

CHRIST THE TRUE TEACHER.

13. Yes, the Scriptures were His stay, staff, and support; He ever appealed to them; He always quoted them; He always referred to them. And the time came when it was

[32] John 10:32-36. [33] Isa. 5:1, 2. [34] Matt. 21:33-41. [35] Matt. 21:42; Psa. 118:23-27.
[36] Luke 20:19. [37] Matt. 16:6. [38] Mark 12:37. [39] John 7:32, 45, 46.

"The Common People Hear Him Gladly."

manifest before all the people that He taught the truth, and
that the Pharisees *were perverters of the truth*. This was illustrated in a forcible manner. The instance is recorded in John,
chapter eight. [40] It was at a time when the temple was packed
with worshipers, many having gathered to hear Him. The
Pharisees had just found a case which would prove them to be
the true expositors of the Bible; for whichever way He would
answer them, they thought evidence could be brought from the
Sacred Writings that He was in error. So burning in their
hearts with revenge, while full of glee at the same time, they
came into His presence with this woman who had violated the
law of God. Now, they asserted, Moses in the law commanded
that such a person should be stoned: [41] but what do *You* say?
It was practically a challenge, as well as defiance. It was
claiming, Now we believe Moses; we teach Moses; if we were
going to follow out the precepts of Moses, we would know what
course to pursue. And why?—Because Moses told us. Yes;
we teach the people truthfully what Moses commanded. *You*
have claimed that *You* believe in Moses; that if *we believed in
Moses we should have believed You*. We do believe in Moses,
and have practically confessed this before all the people in this
temple assembled; and we quote to You the very scripture from
Moses that declares what should be done with such a person.
Oh what a challenge! Oh what defiance!! Oh what an apparent victory!!! The sixth verse of this chapter in John will
show that all this was in the minds of these Pharisees at this
time.

14. Jesus apparently took little notice of what they said.
He wrote upon the ground. He never uttered a word. Ah,
thought these Pharisees, of course He keeps silent; why should
He not? He has nothing to say; He is baffled. But how
different the Savior must have felt in His soul toward these
poor people. No doubt, while He knew what was taking place
in their hearts, He was sad to think He should have to expose

[40] John 8: 3-10.   [41] Lev. 20: 10; Deut. 22: 22.

them so completely. So after they repeatedly asked Him for a reply, He gently raised Himself, and quietly said: " *He that is without sin among you, let him first cast a stone at her.*" And without another word, He stooped again, and continued writing. Oh! Oh! what a defeat! How vanquished and crestfallen! How completely foiled and baffled! How entirely overthrown! He never denied what Moses said; He simply added what they left unsaid, and what they *knew* Moses also declared. (*a*) Jesus was left before the people as the *true* expositor of the word of God; as the *true* Teacher of the Bible; as the proper Guide of Moses and the prophets.

TEACHING THE SCRIPTURE BY INFERENCE.

15. While it is true that the Pharisees taught the Scriptures, they used them largely to fit their own reasonings. For instance: They would introduce certain allegories, parables, fables, which the Bible neither countenanced nor sanctioned; then they would introduce some portion of Moses and the prophets to substantiate their conclusions. Many illustrations might be cited showing the force of this idea, but we will mention a few:

" Rabbi Hannania, son of Akashya, said, it pleased the Almighty to exonerate Israel [or cause them to have a special merit]; therefore, he *multiplied* unto them laws and commandments."—" *Ethics of the Fathers*," *chapter 1.*

This is the general way of the teaching of this rabbi, though it is evident from the word of God that He has no favorites, because with God there is no respect of persons.[42] But from this saying of the rabbi, the Jews were to conclude that they *were* especially favored of God, because this rabbi had so declared. For fear that his authority and conclusion might be questioned, he proves both premise and conclusion by the following scripture:

" For it is said: ' The Lord is well pleased for His righteousness' sake; He will *magnify* the law, [literally, יַגְדִּיל - " Yog-dil," to enlarge, to make

---

[42] Deut. 10: 17, 18; Job 34: 19; Acts 10: 34; Rom. 2: 11.

great, to broaden, to make excellent, to exalt], and make it honorable.'"
Isa. 42:21.

FALSE INTERPRETATION OF SCRIPTURE.

16. This scripture is used to prove that, because of the special favor which has been bestowed on Israel, the Lord gave them *a great many laws and commandments*. In other words, He expanded the law so that it may be divided into fragments. (*b*) They, therefore, say that when Moses received the law on Sinai, he also received the expansion of it, which comprehended some six hundred thirteen commandments.

17. Another illustration : In the introduction to the " Ethics of the Fathers," one of the tractates of the Mishna, it is said :

" *All Israel* have a share in the world to come."

Of course by " all Israel," here is meant, all Jews. Hence they do not consider that any non-Jews will have a share in the future world. Some of the Jews might question such a statement, if it had no Scripture to prove it. Hence they say :

" It is said, ' Thy people also shall be *all* righteous : they shall inherit the land forever, the branch of My planting, the work of My hands, that I may be glorified.' " [43]

18. Other incidents might now be given to show their style of explaining and teaching the Scriptures. These, however, will be shown in another chapter, when we come to the various objects used in their worship. In view of these facts, it is not difficult to understand the following statements from Paul :

" Study to show thyself approved unto God, a workman that needeth not to be ashamed, *rightly dividing* the word of truth." [44]

It is one thing to divide the word of truth ; another altogether to *rightly divide it*. And again :

" Behold, thou art called a Jew, and restest in the law, and makest thy boast of God, and knowest His will, and approvest the things that are most excellent, being instructed out of the law ; and art confident that thou thyself art a guide of the blind, a light of them which are in darkness, an

[43] Isa. 60: 21.   [44] 2 Tim. 2: 15.

instructor of the foolish, a teacher of babes, which hast the *form of knowl-edge* and of the truth in the law." [45]

Or this statement from Peter :

"As also in all his epistles, speaking in them of these things ; in which are some things hard to be understood, which they that are unlearned and unstable wrest, as they do also the other Scriptures, unto their own destruction." [46]

CHRIST TEACHING WITH AUTHORITY.

19. Before this chapter closes, there is another point of interest which should be considered, while contrasting the teachings of Christ with those of the Pharisees. It is said in a number of places in Scripture that *Christ did not teach as did the scribes and the Pharisees ; but rather He taught as one having authority.* Many passages might be quoted, but perhaps one will suffice :

"And it came to pass, when Jesus had ended these sayings, the people were astonished at His doctrine : for He taught them as one having author-ity, and not as the scribes." [47]

20. Some no doubt have asked, "What does it mean that He taught as one having authority, and not as the scribes? Where was the difference ? " If the reader will notice the say-ings of Jesus, he will perceive that the Master was very positive in His expressions.[48] Whenever He uttered a saying, He talked as one who was sure that He knew what He said, could say nothing else, had nothing to say only that which was necessary to be said on that point, and felt certain that His statements would bear all the investigations His hearers wished to pursue. Fur-thermore, He never said one thing to-day, which He would repent of to-morrow.[49] What he said, He *always* proclaimed without fear or favor. In other words, He brought salvation to the world ; and His message would decide a man's destiny for either weal or woe, as the hearer believed or rejected it.[50]

[45] Rom. 2: 17-20.   [46] 2 Peter 3: 16.   [47] Matt. 7: 28, 29; Mark 1: 22; Luke 4: 36.
[48] John 3: 11.   [49] Heb. 13: 8.   [50] John 12: 48, 49.

THE DISAGREEMENT OF THE RABBIS.

21. With the scribes and Pharisees, however, the method of teaching was very different. For instance: a man might teach a certain thing to day; to-morrow it might be refuted. Both sayings, however, would have to be believed. As the case of Hillel and Shammi about the question of the egg which was laid on the Sabbath; (c) one said it might be eaten; the other opposed this idea. It was claimed that both were the words of the living God. (d) That had forever to settle the question.

22. While they compelled the people to believe what they said, there was nothing positive about their teaching. They largely declared what they heard from other wise men, and would quote what *they* said as proof of their own teachings. For instance: Two great teachers, Abtalion and Shemaiah, (e) died; and left their seats to two sons of one Bethera. These men were discussing the subject of the Passover; and their discussions caused much perplexity. Finally some one inquired if there was not a disciple present who had heard the two great wise men, Shemaiah and Abtalion, give their opinion on this subject. To this, Hillel, (f) afterward one of the leading men in the Sanhedrin, replied; but the teachers refused to accept his opinion. Then he remarked: "Thus have I heard from my masters, Shemaiah and Abtalion." Nothing further was needed.

23. Then another way they had of teaching was to make certain statements in the name of some other person; as for instance: "Rabbi Dosethai, the son of Jonah, in the name of Rabbi Myer, said . . ." "Rabbi Simeon, son of Judah, in the name of Rabbi Simeon, son of Jocheai, said . . ." etc.

DISSECTING THE BIBLE.

24. In their method of teaching, they would also spend hours, days, and sometimes weeks, in discussing one particular

point about the Scripture. Then after they had analyzed and dissected the statement,they would divide the words, the phrase, the sentence, and sometimes the letters. Naturally all this was very dry and spiritless to the people. The masses only believed their sayings because they were compelled to, for fear of ostracism; not, however, because they loved to. This is evident from many of the scriptures. [51]

CHRIST'S WORDS, LIFE.

25. When the Savior taught the people, the teaching had spirit and life in it. It burned in their hearts. The multitude longed for more. They would stay hours to listen; it was so interesting; it had so much comfort and helpfulness; it was water to the thirsty soul. How wonderfully the words of Jeremiah were thus fulfilled:

"Be astonished, O ye heavens, at this, and be horribly afraid, be ye very desolate, saith the Lord. For My people have committed two evils; they have forsaken Me the fountain of living waters, and hewed them out cisterns, broken cisterns, that can hold no water." [52]

26. The reader can the better understand why it is said He spake as one having authority and not as the scribes. Can we not, however, learn a forcible lesson from this? Is it not true that as a result of much of the theology, people at the present time are beginning to feel that Christianity has little in it for them? It is simply discussion and exposition. Therefore, feed the people with the word of God. The Great Teacher desires to open the Scripture to the understanding of *every* person, [53] if he will only sit at His feet and learn of Him. [54] Then the heart will burn to-day when the word of God is revealed in the light of the Spirit, even as the hearts of men burned in the days of the Savior. [55]

"Who teacheth like Him?" [56]

[51] John 9: 22, 34; 12: 42.   [52] Jer. 2: 12, 13.   [53] John 6: 45.   [54] Matt. 11: 28, 29.
[55] Luke 24: 32.   [56] Job 36: 22.

EXPLANATORY NOTES.

Paragraph 14.

(a) To the casual observer it might seem from this experience of Christ and the Pharisees, that He told them the person who had no sin of any kind, was to be the first to cast the stone. But by close observation of this scripture, it must be apparent that He intended to have all the on-lookers know that these very persons who were accusing this poor soul, were guilty of the *very same* sins. It was practically saying: If any one of you here has not committed the *same sin*, he has a right to cast the first stone. They were so convicted of their own guilt, as they saw *their* sins made bare on the sand, that rapidly they departed from His presence, feeling no doubt thankful that Christ did not expose them publicly.

Paragraph 16.

(b) The rabbis claimed that no one person could carry out all of the commands. Evidently not, when we remember the abundance of their own that they added. Still they claimed that though a person did not perform them all, if his intentions were only agreeable, the deeds would be supplied some other way. Thus for instance: If a man was very wealthy and carried on a large business, it would hardly be expected he could devote sufficient time to fulfil all his religious obligations each day. Therefore, they allowed that if such a person would contribute largely of his means, those of the people who were less blessed in this world's goods, but had more piety, would impart of their piety to those who contributed the means. In this way, they taught that all righteousness in Israel would be divided, so that each one would have sufficient to carry him through.

As a result of such teaching, the very term "righteousness," became perverted, and was used in an erroneous manner. It became a synonym for money or alms. This is clear from Matt. 6:1, where the word "alms" in the text, is given in the margin, "righteousness;" and to this day the Jews, when speaking of giving charity or philanthropy, use the word "ts-da-ka," literally, "righteousness."

Thus the word of God was made of none effect by the traditions of men, and the righteousness of God was supplanted by man-made righteousness.

Paragraph 21.

(c) The treatise "Bet-za," or "egg," generally known as "Youm Tov," "good day," a general term given to any Jewish festival, is found in the second division of the Mishna, " Order of Festivals."   It has five chapters, and over forty sections.

(*d*) This decision of the " Bath-kol," which gave the verdict in favor of Hillel, is found in the tractate, entitled, " Erubin," in the same division as the above.

Paragraph 22.

(*e*) These two men lived about the middle of the first century before Christ.   They were the greatest teachers of that century.   For the privilege of listening to their words of wisdom, Hillel came near freezing to death one Sabbath evening.

(*f*) Hillel was considered one of the greatest men that ever lived among the Jews.   He was a great scholar, philosopher, and thinker.   He added much to the burden of tradition, and caused many burdensome laws to be enforced.   He is said to have been a man of a very mild disposition. He was the grandparent of that Gamaliel, at whose feet the Apostle Paul sat in his youth.   He died when the Savior was about ten years of age.

GARMENTS WITH BORDERS. ENLARGED. NARROW.

CHAPTER VI.

The Wearing of the Garment and the Phylacteries.

"Who also hath made us able ministers of the New Testament; not of the letter, but of the spirit: for the letter killeth, but the spirit giveth life." 2 Cor. 3 : 6.

PHARISAICAL WISDOM LEADS AWAY FROM GOD.

HAVING compared, in our last chapter, the teachings of the Savior and those of the Pharisees; and having found that the teachings of the Savior were the true application of the Scriptures, it may now be in place to consider further some of the teachings of the Pharisees, and their misapplication of the word of God. Claiming to be wise and learned men, they depended upon their own logic and philosophy to expound the Bible, which, *they* considered, explained the correct idea of righteousness, [1] and the true way to worship God. As a result, all their righteousness became self-righteousness; all their wisdom became folly,[2] which often led to sensuality;[3] all their impartings of Scripture knowledge became departings from the right ways of the Lord. Of the many instances in which this was manifest, we shall select the wearing of the garment, and the use of the phylacteries. On this subject, the Savior said the following:

"But all their works they do for to be seen of men: they make broad their phylacteries and enlarge the borders of their garments." [4]

STRANGE IDEAS OF VIRTUE.

2. It should be observed the Savior did not condemn them for wearing either of the objects, as though it were sinful; but

[1] Matt. 5: 20; Rom. 9: 31, 32.   [2] 1 Cor. 1: 20.   [3] James 3: 13-15.   [4] Matt. 23: 5

[79]

the condemnation pronounced upon them was for making the objects so prominent. Thus it must be clear that they considered there was something in these things which had a certain degree of virtue. That the people were thus taught, must be evident from certain scriptures, for we read :

"And, behold, a woman, which was diseased with an issue of blood twelve years, came behind Him, and touched the hem of His garment : For she said within herself, If I may but touch His garment, I shall be whole." [5]

"And besought Him, that they might only touch the hem of His garment : and as many as touched were made perfectly whole." [6]

3. Jesus, however, did not consider that there was any virtue in the garment itself. When the woman touched it, He turned to the disciples and said :

"Who touched *Me?* And Jesus said, Somebody hath touched Me : for I perceive that virtue is gone out of Me." [7]

THE GARMENT.

4. Upon these garments were borders of blue, and around them hung fringes. For the wearing of this the Pharisee claimed he had Scripture, and this is the proof :

"And the Lord said unto Moses, saying, Speak unto the children of Israel, and bid them that they make them *fringes* in the borders of their garments throughout their generations, and that they put upon the fringe of the border a *ribband* of blue : and it shall be unto you for a fringe, that ye may look upon it, and remember all the commandments of the Lord, and do them." [8]

5. After a time a degree of sacredness was thrown around the garment; finally it became part of the synagogue service. While the Lord commanded them to put upon it a border of blue, the rabbi permitted to have one of white instead, if they chose. There would come a time, possibly, when a person could not get the exact color, hence they could secure *something* in order to fulfil "an affirmative precept," as the rabbi would express it, rather than completely to violate the command.

[5] Matt. 9: 20.   [6] Matt. 14: 36.   [7] Luke 8: 45, 46.   [8] Num. 15 : 37-39.

6. The reason, no doubt, why God gave the color blue, was because this was the color of the heavens, as well as a representation of the royal covenant. This command to wear the garment, as well as many other of the commands of God, was designed to teach the people a deep spiritual truth, if their eyes were only opened to see it. There is a Pharisaical saying which declares that if a person should do this (wear the fringed garment with the border) it would be almost as much as if he saw the throne of glory, which is like unto blue.

THE NUMBER OF FRINGES.

7. While the fringes might be all around the garment there was a *special* number that must be used; this was just four, one to be placed at each of the four corners. It is said the reason for doing this is found in a scripture which reads as follows:

" Thou shalt make thee fringes upon the *four quarters* of thy vesture, wherewith thou coverest thyself." [9]

THE MATERIAL OF THE GARMENT.

8. This garment also must be of only one kind of material; there must be no mixture whatever in it. The following was used as a proof for this custom:

" Thou shalt not wear a garment of divers sorts, as of woolen and linen together." "Neither shall a garment mingled of linen and woolen come upon thee. " [10]

9. As these garments were brought into continual use it was found necessary to define their mission explicitly, for the rabbis said there must be some virtue in their use. Therefore a number of laws and ordinances were passed, which finally became part of the daily worship, and if strictly followed, imparted to the worshiper a great deal of righteousness.

MANNER OF USE.

10. As used by the Jews of to-day this scarf, garment, " Talith," is worn only at the morning service in the synagogue,

9 Deut. 22: 12.   10 Deut. 22: 11; Lev. 19: 19.

6

and that alone by the males, and not till they reach the age of thirteen.   It should be remembered that the Pharisees had very little respect for the female sex, outside of their performing the home duties.   In fact they taught that every male ought to thank God every day for his belonging to the masculine sex. Here is the prayer:

"Blessed art thou, O Lord our God, King of the universe, who hath not made me a woman."   And the woman is obliged to say: ".Blessed art thou, O Lord, King of the universe, who hath made me according to His will."—"*Daily Prayer-book.*" (a)

NUMBER REQUIRED FOR SERVICE.

Furthermore, a service cannot be held for the worship of God among the Jews unless there are ten males, over the age of thirteen.   That is to say, if there were in a synagogue one thousand or ten thousand persons, and only nine of these were males over thirteen years of age, it would be unlawful to have a service.   Can we not see some suggestive thought relating to this matter in the following words of the Savior:

"For where *two* or *three* are gathered together in My name, there am I in the midst of them." [11]

11. The writer well remembers many a time in early life; of attending morning service at the synagogue where the worship would be delayed on account of there not being a "minyan," as the number of ten persons is called.   Such is tradition, the righteousness of men.

WHEN THE GARMENT IS WORN.

12. This garment is worn *every* morning throughout the year, with the exception of one,—the ninth of Av, the fast of the fifth month, [12] generally occurring in July, which commemorates the destruction of the first and second temple.   Instead of wearing it this day at morning service it is worn before the sunset of the day; sometime during the afternoon. (*b*)   Before the garment is put on the worshiper, the fringes at the four

[11] Matt. 18: 20.   [12] Zech. 7: 3, 5; 8: 19.

corners are gathered, and the first two verses of Psalms 104 are repeated. A prayer is then offered in which is repeated the text containing the words, "That they make them fringes in the borders of their garments throughout their generations,"—with the request that, as the garment is wrapped around the body in this world, so the soul may be wrapped with the enjoyments of the world to come in the Garden of Eden. The garment is then thrown over the shoulders and the following prayer is offered:

"Blessed art thou, O Lord our God, King of the universe, who hath sanctified us in His commandments, and hath commanded us to be covered with fringes."—"*Daily Prayer-book.*"

When this is done, verses 7–10 of the thirty-sixth Psalm are repeated.

RIGHTEOUSNESS IN THE GARMENT.

13. It will be observed from these latter scriptures that the people regard the wearing of this garment as being associated with receiving righteousness. For did not the Lord say:

"I will greatly rejoice in the Lord, my soul shall be joyful in my God; for He hath clothed me with the garments of salvation, He hath *covered* me with the robe of righteousness." [13]

14. Consequently the pious Pharisee was very particular in having a large garment, sufficient to cover himself, with very wide borders; because the larger the garment, and the greater the border, the more the righteousness. Thus this very object that the Lord designed to use as a means to a great end, was perverted from its purpose, and substituted for the Creator Himself. It is not at all surprising, then, that the Savior should say:

"Except your righteousness shall exceed the righteousness of the scribes and Pharisees, ye shall in no case enter into the kingdom of heaven." [14]

15. They might have known, from the words of the proph-

[13] Isa. 61:10.   [14] Matt. 5:20.

ets, that true righteousness was not found in the wearing of those objects; but in Him, " Jehovah, our righteousness." [15] In several of the prophets it is recorded that the righteousness of the people of God was in the Lord; and that this righteousness would be imparted to them by believing God, and obeying His will. [16] (*c*)

THE PHYLACTERIES.

16. While certain scriptures might be adduced as reason for the wearing of fringes, the garment, and the border, this could hardly be said for the use of the phylacteries. Nevertheless there was no task too Herculean, for the scribe or the Pharisee to accomplish, if he thought that by so doing he could add some outward observance which would make him appear righteous overmuch, and a good logician in Scripture. The basis for the wearing of the phylacteries is found in four different scriptures recorded in Ex. 13:1–10, 11–16; Deut. 6:4–9, what is known as the " Shemang," a very precious service to the Jew. Deut. 11:13–20. The central thought in each of these texts being the words:

"And bind them for a sign upon your hand, that they may be as frontlets between your eyes." [17]

17. The " teachers of the law " concluded that these scriptures referred to something that was to be worn outwardly, which finally took form in the wearing of the phylacteries. It is claimed by some, however, that the phylacteries were originally designed as amulets or charms, which these rabbis used to practice magic. (*d*) However, upon this matter we shall not dwell at length.

DIVISIONS OF THE PHYLACTERIES.

18. These phylacteries are of two parts; one for the arm, the other for the head. The one for the arm consists of a receptacle, resembling a small box, in which is a piece of parchment

1. Jer. 23:5, 6; 33:14, 16.   16 Psa. 4:1; 35:28; Isa. 45:24; 54:17; Dan. 9:7; Hosea 2:19; Zeph. 2:3; Gen. 15:6; Deut. 6:25.   17 Deut. 11:18.

Worshipper Dressed in Phylacteries and Garment.

having written upon it the four texts previously mentioned, and having attached to it a long, narrow, black strap. The capsule is placed on the left arm, on the biceps, pointing towards the heart. Before this is placed in its position, however, a prayer is offered in which is contained the four scriptures already cited ; it mentions the location of these objects, and concludes that these may be as acceptable in the sight of God as though the individual had performed every command of God, even to the six hundred thirteen commands, upon which depend the wearing of these things. (*e*)   The following prayer is then said :

" Blessed art thou, O Lord our God, King of the universe, who hath sanctified us in His commandments, and hath commanded us in the wearing of the phylacteries."—"*Daily Prayer-book.*"

19. The strap is then wound around the arm seven times, during which seven Hebrew words are repeated. The following is a translation of these words :

" And cleave you unto the Lord your God all the days of your life."

The remainder of the strap is then placed three times around the hand. When this is finished the one for the head is placed in position. The receptacle is placed between the eyes, on the forehead, as the Scripture says, " between thine eyes." The straps are bound in a knot at the base of the brain ; then a long strap is allowed to fall on either shoulder. (See accompanying picture). When this is placed in position, the following prayer is offered :

" Blessed art thou, O Lord our God, King of the universe, who hath sanctified us in His commandments, and hath commanded us concerning the command of the phylactery." Then follow the words : " Blessed be His glorious name, His kingdom is forever."

20. The following scripture is said in conclusion :

" And I will betroth thee unto Me forever ; yea, I will betroth thee unto Me in righteousness, and in judgment, and in loving kindness, and in mercies.   And I will even betroth thee unto Me in faithfulness: and thou shalt know the Lord." [18]

[18] Hosea 2: 19, 20.

PHARISAICAL SELF-RIGHTEOUSNESS.

21. From the above prayers and scriptures it is evident that the Pharisee expected the wearing of these was bringing to him much of God's favor, and a large amount of righteousness. He was doing something for the Lord that not a Sadducee, or a Samaritan, or any other class who professed to believe in God was doing. Hence he thought he had a right to feel that the Lord ought to have more respect to him than to any other people. Of course the broader his phylactery the more imputation of righteousness. It is then not surprising that the Pharisee should want his phylactery broad, for this would indicate a greater amount of righteousness, as well as a nearness to the Shekinah.

MAN-WORSHIP.

22. Perhaps in nothing did the theocratical Pharisees put themselves in the place of God more than in the wearing of the phylacteries. Three blessings have been mentioned in connection with the wearing of the garment and of the phylacteries which say that the Lord, the King of the universe, commanded the wearing of these things, whereas the rabbis plainly teach that *they* made the ordinances. In one of the tractates of the Mishna, entitled "Sanhedrin," we find the following :

"It is more punishable to act against the words of the scribes than against the words of the Scripture. If a man were to say, There is no such thing as phylactery, in order to act contrary to the words of the Scripture, he is not to be treated as a rebel. But if he should say, there are five divisions in the tephillin [phylactery, the one worn on the forehead, instead of four as the rabbis teach], in order to add to the words of the scribes, he is guilty."

23. In the light of the above statements can we not read with new meaning the following words of the Savior :

" Why do ye also transgress the commandment of God by your tradition ? . . . But in vain they do worship Me, teaching for doctrines the commandments of men." "Making the word of God of none effect through your tradition, which ye have delivered: and many such like things ye do." [19]

CHRIST'S DESIRE TO FREE THEM.

24. How the Savior's heart must have felt toward those blind leaders, and blinded people, as He beheld them all going into the pit of destruction, as a result of such teachings! " O Jerusalem, Jerusalem, thou that killest the prophets, and stonest them that are sent unto thee, how often would I have gathered thy children together, even as a hen gathereth her chickens under her wings, and ye would not!" [20] Jesus longed for the people to see the truth; He longed to have them free from these errors and superstitions. " If the Son therefore shall make you free, ye shall be free indeed." [21]

25. When the Pharisee, clothed in his garment with the wide border, wore his phylacteries with the broad straps, and offered all the prayers connected with them, no one felt more secure of having received righteousness and God's smile than did he. [22] We can readily see why Paul felt as he did toward his brethren when he said:

" But Israel, which followed after the law of righteousness, hath not attained unto the law of righteousness. Wherefore? Because they sought it not by faith, but as it were by the works of the law. For they stumbled at that stumbling-stone." . . . " Brethren, my heart's desire and prayer to God for Israel is, that they might be saved. For I bear them record that they have a zeal of God, but not according to knowledge. For they being ignorant of God's righteousness, and going about to establish their own righteousness, have not submitted themselves to the righteousness of God." [23]

26. Righteousness comes not by the wearing of phylacteries, or garments, or in the observance of outward works of human devisings; but by faith in the righteousness of the Lord Jesus Christ, who in His own life worked out the great righteous character of God. [24]

[19] Matt. 15:3-9; Mark 7:13. [20] Matt. 23:37. [21] John 8:36. [22] Luke 18:9-11.
[23] Rom. 9:31, 32; 10:1-3. [24] Gen. 15:6; Rom. 3:21, 22, 25, 26; 4:3, 22-25; Gal. 3:6-9.

WHY THE GARMENT SHOULD NOT BE MIXED.

27. There is, however, one more thought in connection with the subject of the garment worthy of consideration. In several passages of scripture it is written that the Israelites should not mix the material in making the garment. In fact this was true of all their garments. Not under any circumstance were they to do this. While the Jews failed to see the lesson, there is no doubt a great truth which God wished to reveal to them in this. We read the following in the command of God :

"And the Lord commanded us to do all these statutes, to fear the Lord our God, for our good always, that He might preserve us alive, as it is at this day. And it shall be our righteousness, if we *observe to do all these commandments before the Lord our God*, as He hath commanded us." [25]

JESUS ONLY, THE RIGHTEOUSNESS OF GOD.

28. In two scriptures of the prophets, [26] the Lord declared that He would raise up a Branch unto David, who should bring safety and salvation; and His name was to be called, "Jehovah-Tsidkanu," "the Lord our righteousness." It is plain who was intended by "our righteousness," in the scripture above mentioned, only Jesus. See a similar comparison,—Rom. 10 : 6–8, with Deut. 30 : 11–14. In these commandments the Lord ever designed to have the people see Jesus, the Messiah, the Righteous One of God, who in Himself *was* the righteousness of God; [27] and not that righteousness was lodged in any mere abstractions. The reason, doubtless, why He forbade them to have mixture in their garments was to have them know that the righteousness of the Righteous One was *not to be mixed with anything outside of Himself.* Nothing of human invention must be woven into this loom. A few scriptures will make this plain :

" Who is this that cometh from Edom, with dyed garments from Bozrah ? this that is glorious in His apparel, traveling in the greatness of His strength ? I that speak in righteousness, mighty to save. Wherefore art

[25] Deut. 6 : 24, 25.   [26] Jer. 23 : 5, 6; 33 :14–16.   [27] 1 Cor. 1 : 30.

PHYLACTERIES, BROAD AND NARROW.

Thou red in Thine apparel, and Thy garments like him that treadeth in the winefat? I have trodden the winepress alone; and of the *people there was none with Me.* . . . And I looked, and there was *none* to help; and I wondered there was *none* to uphold: therefore Mine own arm brought salvation unto Me." [28]

CHRIST HIMSELF PAID THE PENALTY FOR SIN.

29. It needs no comment who is intended by these words of the prophet. When, however, was it that Jesus *especially* looked for some one to help Him, and could find none to uphold Him? Ah! in the Garden of Gethsemane, and at the cross of Calvary. Especially was this true in the garden, when He was drinking the bitter cup for a lost world. His sufferings were so intense that He sweat great drops of blood.[29] Of all the times in His experience in the flesh when He needed human sympathy to uphold and support Him, this was the time when it was the most desirable; but ah! He had none! none![30] "What, could ye not watch with Me one hour?"[31] were the repeated words of Him who longed to hear a few kind words from His disciples. But had they assisted Him with their human sympathy at this period, there might have been some human threads interwoven in the spotless garment of righteousness, which was to save the poor lost soul. But no! there was none. He did it, and did it all alone, bless His dear name. Not a thread of mixture in the loom. Thank God for the lesson in not mixing the garment. Oh that Israel had learnt it, what a wonderful revelation she would have had of Jesus, the Christ, the Anointed of God. But they stumbled at the stumbling-stone.[32]

30. Shall we not then see Him in all His word and works, and thrust aside all the commandments and traditions of men? "For all the promises of God in Him are yea, and in Him Amen, unto the glory of God by us."[33] He is the all in all.[34]

[28] Isa. 63:1-5.   [29] Luke 22:44.   [30] Heb. 5:7.
[31] Matt. 26:40.   [32] Rom. 9:31, 32; 1 Pet. 2:8.
[33] 2 Cor. 1:20.   [34] 1 Cor. 15:28.

EXPLANATORY NOTES.

Paragraph 10.

(*a*) There is much in the Mishna which clearly proves that women were, in a large measure, regarded as inferior to men. Here is a passage :

" Women are not qualified by the law to testify, because it is written, At the mouth of two witnesses.' The language is in the masculine and not in the feminine."

Here is another : " There are ten kinds of disqualifications. If in any person *any one* of these is found, this disqualifies his testimony. These are they : Women, slaves, children, idiots, deaf persons, the blind, the wicked, the outcast, relatives, those who have personal interest in the testimony,— these are the ten."—*Laws of Evidence.*

The above information, no doubt, explains why Simon the Pharisee felt as he did toward Jesus, when the woman, whom Simon regarded as a despised sinner, anointed the feet of the Savior, and He willingly allowed her to perform such a service. Luke 7 : 36–40.

Paragraph 12.

(*b*) The orthodox Jew still believes the biblical method of the computation of time,—from evening to evening,—from sunset to sunset. See Gen. 1 : 5, 8, 13, 19, 23, 31 ; Lev. 23 : 23 ; Deut. 16 : 6. This is God's method.

Paragraph 15.

(*c*) The orthordox Jew, in addition to the wearing of this garment in the synagogue service, wears a small garment, called " Arba-Kanfoth," literally, "four corners," on his person all the time. Various reasons are given for its use ; but the popular belief is that it might discriminate the Jew from the Gentile. In case the former might lose his way, or be taken ill and die suddenly, by his wearing this small garment, the Gentiles would know he was a Jew, and would have him buried in Jewish soil. For the Jews believe that they are to be raised from the dead at the last day ; but they either must be found in Palestinian soil, or soil purposely made sacred for the Jews' resting place.

Originally, all soil outside of Palestine was defiled, and not one particle was allowed to enter the Holy Land. Every bit of it must be shaken from the feet or from plants before entering the holy country. This leads us easily to understand what the Savior intended to convey to the Jews, when he told the disciples that they should shake off the dust of their feet against the Jews, if the people would not receive their testimony. Mark 6 : 11. They would then be considered as defiled, unclean, lost, just as the Gentile.

Since their persecutions and scattering, they have separate burial soil in which the dead are deposited, and they believe that the Lord will accept this as a substitute for the soil of Palestine.

Paragraph 17.

(*d*) In the tractate, "Sabbath," of the Mishna, the rabbis devoted a great deal of space to discussions of charms and amulets,—those that were approved, and those which were not approved. From all this it would seem evident that they did have something to do with the art and practice of magic. Might this not suggest a partial reason why the Savior told the Pharisees that they were the children of the devil, for they did the works of the devil. Astrology, sorcery, magic, were all the works of the devil,—which God strictly prohibited. Lev. 19:31; 20:6–27; Deut. 18:9–12.

Paragraph 18.

(*e*) The Pharisees claimed that all the law, the prophets, and all the commands, rested upon the wearing of these phylacteries. Too much stress and importance could not be placed upon the wearing of these things. Might we not see from this teaching a reason why the Savior should say that on the two great commands of love to God and to man, hung all the law and the prophets, instead of on the wearing of the phylacteries? Matt. 22:35–40.

CHAPTER VII.

Jesus Teaching the Law.

" Come unto Me, all ye that labor and are heavy laden, and I will give you rest.   Take My yoke upon you, and *learn* of Me; for I am meek and lowly in heart : and ye shall find rest unto your souls.   For My yoke is easy, and My burden is light."   Matt. 11 : 28–30.

THE Savior said: " Think not that I am come to destroy the law or the prophets : I am not come to destroy, but to fulfil. For verily I say unto you, Till heaven and earth pass, *one jot or one tittle* shall in no wise pass from the *law*, till all be fulfilled. Whosoever therefore shall break one of these least commandments, and shall teach men so, he shall be called the least in the kingdom of heaven : but whosoever shall do and teach them, the same shall be called great in the kingdom of heaven." [1]

PHARISEES MAKING A HEDGE FOR THE LAW.

2. These words of Christ are simply wonderful, as we view them in the light in which they were spoken.   In fact, what is true of these words is true of all the sermon on the mount. Every one of the beatitudes struck against some rabbinical view of the law; therefore the rabbis claimed that Jesus was seeking to break down, to subvert, and to change the law.   The one burden of these leaders was to teach the law. (*a*)   It was to make a hedge about it, to build a wall around it, to fence it in on every hand with so much explanation that it could not be subverted, nor could the people be led away from it.   The wise men said:

" Train up many disciples, and make a hedge for the law."—" *Ethics of the Fathers," chapter 1.*

[1] Matt. 5 : 17–19.

Blessed are the poor in spirit: for
theirs is the kingdom of heaven.
Blessed are they that mourn:
for they shall be comforted.
Blessed are the meek: for they
shall inherit the earth.
Matt. V 3 4 5.

SERMON ON THE MOUNT.

Hillel said:

"Love mankind, and allure them to the study of the law." "Who doth not increase his knowledge in the law, shall be cut off, and who doth not study the law, is deserving of death; and he who serves himself with the crown of the law, will be consumed."—*Ibid.*

"He who augmenteth his knowledge of the law, augmenteth life."

"Rabbi Eleazer said, 'Be expeditious to study the law, that thou mayest know how to controvert the Epicurean.'"—*Ibid.*

"Two who are sitting together, and have no discourse concerning the law, are accounted an assembly of scorners . . . but two who sit together, and discourse of the law, the divine presence may be said to rest upon them."—*Rabbi Chanena in "Ethics of the Fathers."*

"Rabbi Akeva said, 'Tradition is a fence to the law.'"

"Rabbi Myer said, 'Diminish your worldly affairs and engage in the study of the law: . . . if thou neglect the law, there are many hindrances to oppose thee; but if thou hast labored in the study of the law, there is much recompense to be given thee.—*Ibid, chapter 4.*

3. Much more might be cited as evidence that the burden of their toil was the fencing in of the law: yet everything that Jesus said seemed to contradict their views of the law, and to give it another meaning. The rabbis taught also the immutability of the law:

"A law of truth hath God given to His people, by the hand of our prophet, who was faithful in his house. *God will never change nor alter His law*; for evermore there is none but His."—*Daily Prayers.*

4. Thus we can see how the Savior was brought face to face with their teaching of the law.

THE BEATITUDES.

In his sermon on the mount, Christ said:

"Blessed are the poor in spirit: for theirs is the kingdom of heaven."[2]

5. We know from the New Testament that the Pharisees were a proud and haughty-spirited class,[3] and looked down on those who were poor spirited. They taught that a man who was poor in spirit was despised of God;[4] therefore they asserted

---

[2] Matt. 5:3.   [3] Luke 1:51; Luke 16:14.   [4] Luke 18:9-14.

that Christ's instruction was not in harmony with the law.

6. Jesus taught: "Blessed are the meek: for they shall inherit the earth."[5]

But true meekness was unknown among the rabbis. They were unforbearing, loved the uppermost rooms at feasts,[6] and delighted to be called by the title, "Rabbi, Rabbi." They considered that as God was high and lifted up, the more exalted their position, and the more influence that went with it by way of being above others, the nearer they came to God.

THE PHARISEES KNEW NO MERCY.

7. Jesus taught: "Blessed are the merciful: for they shall obtain mercy."[7]

But we know from what has already been quoted of their own sayings that they were strangers to this virtue. Jesus told them a little later; "Go ye and learn what that meaneth, I will have mercy and not sacrifice."[8] And at another time He said to them: "But if ye had known what this meaneth, I will have mercy and not sacrifice, ye would not have condemned the guiltless."[9]

8. This shows clearly they had not yet learned the meaning of this quality. Perhaps it may be in place to quote a few statements touching this point:

"A Gentile woman is not to be delivered on the Sabbath, not even for payment, neither is the enmity to be regarded. It is not to be done, even though no profanation of the Sabbath should be implied."—*Sabbath Laws.*

"Whosoever transgresses an affirmative commandment, for instance, he was commanded to make a tabernacle, and did not, he is to be beaten until his soul go out, without any consideration of his strength, and without dividing the flogging into three. And in like manner, whosoever transgresseth the words of the *wise men*, he is to be beaten without number, and without mercy. Why is this called "Ma-kath Mar-dooth," flogging of obstinacy? Because he has been obstinate to the words of the law, and to the words of the scribes."

[5] Matt. 5:5.   [6] Luke 14:7; Matt. 23:6, 7.   [7] Matt. 5:7.
[8] Matt. 9:13.   [9] Matt. 12:7.

"It is not permissible to give good advice to a heathen or to a slave.
—*Laws Governing Murder*.

CHRIST'S TEACHING STRANGE TO THE PEOPLE.

9. Thus every one of the beatitudes was a direct contradiction of what the rabbis taught upon the same subject. Not that it was opposed to the law which Moses gave, but to the exposition of that law as given by these theologians. The common people had not been accustomed to hear such a meaning given to the Scriptures : hence they were told by the scribes and rabbis that Jesus could not be a true rabbi or teacher, as He was opposing the words of the wise men, and the words of the law.

10. Here is what a notable writer has said on this point :

"As something strange and new, these words fell upon the ears of the wondering multitude. Such teaching is contrary to all they ever heard from priest or rabbi."

"As Jesus in His character and work represented to men, the holy, benevolent, and paternal attributes of God, and presented the worthlessness of merely ceremonial obedience, the Jewish leaders did not receive or understand His words. They thought He dwelt too lightly upon the requirements ; and when He set before them the very truths that were the soul of their divinely appointed service, they, looking only at the external, accused Him of seeking to overthrow it."

"The Pharisees noted the vast difference between their manner of instruction and that of Christ. They saw that the majesty and beauty and purity of truth, with its deep and gentle influence, was taking firm hold upon many minds, and they feared that if permitted, Jesus would draw the people away from them. Therefore they followed Him with determined hostility, hoping to find occasion for accusing Him before the Sanhedrin, and securing His condemnation and death."

"On the mount Jesus was closely watched by the spies, and as He unfolded the principles of righteousness, the Pharisees caused it to be whispered about that His teaching was in opposition to the precepts which God had given from Sinai. Many were saying in their hearts that Jesus had come to do away with the law; but in unmistakable language He revealed His attitude toward the divine statutes."—"*Thoughts from the Mount of Blessing*."

THE LAW IMMUTABLE.

11. Jesus, knowing the feelings and sentiments which the

Pharisees were endeavoring to instill into the minds of the masses, explained to the people his regard for the law. It was practically the same position that the scribes held. Here is a quotation, showing how strictly they believed in its immutability :

"These are they who have no part in the world to come, but are cut off, perish, and are condemned on account of the greatness of their wickedness and sin forever, even forever and ever,—*the deniers of the law.* . . . There are three classes of the deniers of the law. He who says that the law is not from God, yea, even *one verse or one word.* . . . He who says that the Creator has changed *one commandment for another*, and that the law has long since lost its authority."—*Laws of Repentance.*

12. Therefore the Savior said :

"*One jot or one tittle* shall in no wise pass from the law, till all be fulfilled. Whosoever therefore shall break one of these least commandments, and shall teach men so, he shall be called the least in the kingdom of heaven : but whosoever shall do and teach them, the same shall be called great in the kingdom of heaven." [10]

13. By this saying He not only claimed to believe the law as fully as they did, but to a still greater degree. They said that not one *verse nor one word* could be abrogated; the Savior declared not even *one jot or tittle*. It might be well to illustrate this jot and tittle.

HEBREW ALPHABET.

14. There are twenty-two letters in the Hebrew alphabet. Then there are five finals, and many double letters. Letters are doubled by inserting a dot in the center of them. Of these twenty-seven letters, the smallest is the tenth, the letter "Yoth," or "Jot." It is about as large as a comma in English punctuation. Some of the letters have what is known as crowns, small points on the top of them, twice the size of the dot of an "i." This letter "Jot," the smallest of all the letters, had this point or tittle attached to it. So the Savior, showing the people how he regarded the law, said in substance : Not only do I believe

[10] Matt. 5: 18, 19.

Hebrew Alphabet.

¹ JOT AND TITTLE.

in the law as given by Jehovah and by Moses; not only do I believe in its perpetuity; not only do I believe that not a verse or a·word can be changed; but I believe and strongly advocate that not the *smallest letter in the entire Hebrew alphabet*, or the *smallest point joined to the smallest letter of God's law*, can under any circumstance be set aside, or lightly esteemed. As long as the heavens and the earth shall remain, not a single point of the law shall be annulled. Yea, still more: Heaven and earth could more easily pass away than the smallest tittle of the law could fail. [11]

PHARISAICAL RIGHTEOUSNESS INSUFFICIENT.

15. The people by this time began to wonder then what would become of all those Pharisees who taught them their view of the law, and who placed their standard of its righteousness as the correct one? For the standard of righteousness as advocated by the Pharisees did not compare favorably with His exalted view of the law. Theirs, only concerned the exterior personage; His, dealt with the inward life. Knowing what was passing through their minds, the Savior continued:

"For I say unto you, that except your righteousness shall exceed the righteousness of the scribes and the Pharisees, ye shall in no case enter into the kingdom of heaven." [12]

16. This assuredly was an open challenge. The rabbis had given their definitions of the law, and Jesus said they were erroneous; there was no salvation in them. In order then that the people and the Pharisees might get His view of the righteousness of the law, the Savior took up certain principles of the decalogue and gave His exposition of them:

CHRIST TEACHING THE LAW.

"Ye have heard that it was said by [margin, to] them of old time, Thou shalt not kill; and whosoever shall kill shall be in danger of the judgment: but I say unto you, that whosoever is angry with his brother without a cause shall be in danger of the judgment: and whosoever shall

[11] Luke 16:17.   [12] Matt. 5:20.

say to his brother, Raca, shall be in danger of the council : but whosoever shall say, Thou fool, shall be in danger of hell fire." [13]

THE RABBIS UNNECESSARILY ANGRY.

17. What a cutting saying this must have been to these theologians as they heard the words, " Whosoever is angry with his brother without a cause." If this be so, they must have reasoned, then our greatest men must be condemned ; then there can be no hope for some of the great lights of Israel. This is the way many of them must have felt as they heard these truths, for it was not at all infrequent for a rabbi or scribe to get angry without any provocation. It was but natural then for the masses to imbibe the same spirit.

18. For instance : Shammi, the contemporary of Hillel the great, who lived about the time of the Savior, was approached by a Gentile, who asked to be made a proselyte. But the inquirer said you must teach me the whole law while I stand on one leg. This so angered the rabbi that he secured a stick, and in a violent manner drove him away. Certainly there was no cause to do this, but this disposition the rabbis claimed as their prerogative.

CHRIST'S DEFINITION OF MURDER.

19. This saying of Jesus also placed murder in an altogether different light from which it had been generally viewed. The Pharisees defined murder as an avenging of one person of his fellow, especially his Jewish brother. (*b*) But this must be done with some outward object or by physical force. According to the tractate, entitled, " Hilcoth Rotse-ach," the " Laws of Murder," there are scores, yes, hundreds of commands explaining rabbinical ideas of murder. Nevertheless, all of these must be committed by some outward force. Jesus, however, showed them that murder was not merely a result of certain outward forces brought to bear upon an Israelite, but he was a murderer who only harbored hateful thoughts against any person ; who said

[13] Matt. 5 : 21, 22.

harsh words to his fellow men; who cherished revengful feelings against his neighbor. And no doubt, at that very time, there were those in the audience who felt in their souls strong convictions of guilt.[14]

CHRIST DEFINING IMPURITY.

20. Having finished His exposition of this command, He passed on to the next:

"Ye have heard that it was said to them of old time, Thou shalt not commit adultery: but I say unto you, That whosoever looketh on a woman to lust after her hath committed adultery with her already in his heart." [15]

21. What depth of thought and truth this definition of the seventh commandment contained; such ideas of purity were unheard and undreamed of. The Pharisees had spent many hours in giving instruction on the subject of marriage; its lawful and unlawful functions. The wise men had made no less than six hundred laws upon the subject, divided into seventy-one chapters. Yes, one entire division of the Mishna is devoted to the consideration of woman, and all that pertains to her welfare. But never, absolutely never, are there statements made that could in any wise compare with this. There was not a person but what felt guilty of having violated this command. What a *strange* doctrine indeed such an exposition of the law of God must have seemed to them. It is not strange, therefore, that the people should say, after He finished His discourse on the mount, that they "were astonished at his doctrine: for He taught them as one having authority, and not as the scribes." [16]

22. To violate this command a person had but to think an impure thought; to have an evil eye; to look impurely upon a person. Such was the exalted view of the law, in the sight of God and of Christ. Certainly the people could not accuse Jesus of overthrowing the law after hearing such expositions, even if that was the Pharisees' claim. If they had only cor-

14 Luke 10 : 25-37.   15 Matt. 5: 27.   16 Matt. 7: 28, 29.

rectly understood the teachings of the prophets, how beautiful that scripture would have seemed to them as they listened to His precious and exalted principles of the law :

CHRIST MAGNIFYING THE LAW.

" The Lord is well pleased for His righteousness' sake; He will magnify the law, and make it honorable." [17]

23. Surely this the Savior did, as He caused these different principles to pass under the flashlight of His divine Spirit. How they shone with luster and brilliancy, as He portrayed them in their greatness and magnificence ! This text in Isaiah did not mean, as the rabbis claimed, that the Lord had given Israel special privileges and advantages over all others, therefore He increased the law to six hundred thirteen commands. It meant that the Messiah who was to come would exalt the law by magnifying its principles; by revealing its true significance; by exalting its every precept; by showing that the law reached to the very depths of the secret recesses of the soul. [18] This was exalting and magnifying the law. And why should not God be well pleased with this ? Would it not enable the people to see their exceeding sinfulness ? [19] Would it not bring a hungering to every soul who desired to be freed from sin, and who wished to properly perform God's will ? [20] Would it not make men hunger and thirst after righteousness ?—Of course it would ; then by the righteousness of the righteous Messiah, who would impart of the power of God, the people would be made better. Therefore God could be well pleased for His righteousness sake ; for Christ is His righteousness, [21] and He did magnify the law. Jesus did not come to change the law ; He did not abrogate it ; He did not allow even one tittle of it to fail. As long as heaven and earth shall stand, so long will the binding claims of God's law rest upon the human race. Neither a single jot nor tittle of it shall in any wise fail or pass away. It is by the life of Christ we see its exalted character.

[17] Isa. 42: 21.   [18] Mark 7: 21-23; Heb. 4: 12.   [19] Rom. 7: 7, 13; 8: 1-4.
[20] Rom. 7: 22-25.   [21] Rom. 3: 25, 26.

This definition of God's law will always remain the same; for Jesus Christ is the same yesterday, to-day, and forever. [22]

[22] Heb. 13 : 8.

EXPLANATORY NOTES.

Paragraph 2.

(a) The reader should bear in mind that the Jews had confused ideas of the law. Claiming that their teachings were equal to the commands of God, they made no difference between the law as spoken by Jehovah Himself, the laws which God gave to Moses, and the laws which they themselves made. Even the disciples failed in their early experience to see the real difference. In later years, however, when the Spirit of God was given to them as their teacher, they saw the broad distinction. Paul clearly teaches the difference between the law of God, the decalogue, and the law of Moses, which God gave him to teach the people. One was eternal, immutable; the other, temporal, changeable.

Paragraph 19.

(b) Here is a sample of their laws touching this question :

"An Israelite who unintentionally kills his slave, or a sojourning proselyte, is imprisoned. [That is, he is placed in one of the cities of refuge.] And also, a sojourning proselyte that kills a sojourning proselyte, or slave, unintentionally, is to be imprisoned. But a sojourning proselyte who *unintentionally* kills an Israelite, even though it be unintentionally, is to be put to death."

"An Israelite who kills a sojourning proselyte is not to be put to death by the Beth-din, the house of judgment, for it is said : ' But if a man come intentionally upon *his neighbor.*' " This, of course the rabbis taught, was only a Jew. The Scriptures, however, taught that this applied to the Gentile as well as to the Jew. Gen. 9 : 5, 6 ; Num. 35 : 15, 16.

CHAPTER VIII.

What the Jews Might Have Known.

"Oh that My people had hearkened unto Me, and Israel had walked in My ways! I should soon have subdued their enemies, and turned My hand against their adversaries." Ps. 81 : 13, 14.

"Oh that thou hadst hearkened to My commandments! then had thy peace been as a river, and thy righteousness as the waves of the sea." Isa. 48 : 18.

ACCEPTING THE TEACHINGS OF MEN.

FROM what has been written concerning the methods used by the rabbis in teaching the law and the word of God, the question, no doubt, must have arisen in the mind of the reader : " Could the people of the time have known any different, or could they have been taught other than they were ? " From the words of the Savior it is evident that they might have known. [1] In fact there was not a truth that Jesus taught concerning Himself and salvation, which the Christian church has believed for centuries, but what the Jews might have known and fully understood, if they had only believed the Bible, and read it in the light of the Holy Spirit.[2] When men, however, will accept the sayings of their fellows because of superior intellectual ability,[3] instead of believing the simple words of the Lord as they read, man-made traditions will surely be placed above the word of God, which in the end will lead men to become dark in their understanding,[4] and to lose the true knowledge of God and of Jesus Christ whom He has sent.[5]

JESUS AND NICODEMUS.

2. In the third chapter of John we find a very interesting

[1] Luke 19 : 41-44 ; Matt. 23 : 37 ; John 5 : 40. [2] John 6 : 45 ; compare Isa. 54 : 13.
[3] 1 Cor. 2 : 14. [4] Rom. 1 : 21. [5] John 17 : 3.

narrative which forcibly illustrates this truth. Nicodemus, a ruler of the Jews, came to Jesus by night. He had heard of Him in various ways, and had concluded he must have an interview with Him. Because of the position of this "ruler," he felt it best not to make it public that he had condescended to call upon Jesus, who was so poor in this world's goods; whose education was so limited, as compared with the extensive academical training the rabbis had, and whose early training was in such a low, outcast, and ostracized community. It is generally known that Nazareth and Galilee were so despised in the eyes of the rabbis that they scarcely could say a good word about them. Especially did the Pharisees mimic and mock the way the Galileans spoke. This is evidently why the little maid so easily recognized Peter as being one of Jesus' disciples; for, said she: "Surely thou also art one of them, for thy speech bewrayeth thee."[6] Their pronunciation of the Hebrew gutturals was very different from the Judean Jew, and the rabbis of Palestine used this against them in ridicule. As for the city of Nazareth, it was generally recognized among the "Tanaim," or teachers, that this place could produce nothing of service or honor to the Jews or to their religion. No doubt it was such teachings that led Nathaniel to reply as he did to Philip, when the former was invited to come and see the Messiah in Jesus of Nazareth. Said Nathaniel with astonishment: "Can there any good thing come out of Nazareth?"[7] It seemed to him so strange and absurd that the long-looked-for Messiah should emanate from that rude, unintellectual, obscure place, Nazareth. He changed his mind, however, when he personally investigated, for he saw in Him the Son of God, the King of Israel.[8]

NICODEMUS' OPINION OF JESUS.

3. On the other hand, Nicodemus was a man of great learning and skill, a member of the council of seventy-one, the Sanhedrin, (*a*) and no doubt a member of the executive committee

6 Matt. 26:73.   7 John 1:46.   8 John 1:49.

NICODEMUS INTERVIEWING CHRIST.   [105]

the three leading members of this august tribunal.   In other words, Nicodemus was one of the leading men of the Jewish nation at that time, a strict rabbi, one who closely followed the teachings and traditions of the Pharisees, a man of great wealth as well as of influence, holding the third position, probably, in all the government of Israel.   It must have been to him a very humiliating thing to go to the lonely house where Jesus was abiding, to seek an interview with this Galilean youth.

4. Nevertheless there was something in the man's heart that told him this youth was more than an ordinary man. He was performing great miracles;   had a great following of the common people; was giving clear, lucid and simple expositions of the law, and was a public benefactor. *His* miracles, in the eyes of Nicodemus, were considered greater than those traditional ones he had read about.   If those wonderful miracles which the rabbis claimed they and others performed gave them the title of " rabbi," surely, Nicodemus reasoned, this young man had a right to the title of rabbi, though the Pharisees would not sanction it.

5. Thus addressing the Savior, he continued: " We know that Thou art a teacher come from God: for no man can do these miracles that Thou doest, except God be with him." [9]

JESUS' REPLY A SURPRISE TO THE RULER.

6. Nicodemus considered this method of addressing Jesus as one of great honor and esteem.   Such a noble Israelite to thus speak to so uneducated a man, a Galilean at that, having no prestige among the rabbis, was certainly a remarkable thing, especially since Nicodemus was quite an old man, and the Savior was so young.   The Jewish teacher evidently expected to receive flattery and approval for this address, as such was the custom among the rabbinical class when addressing one another.   Instead of Jesus giving him what he expected, the man heard a most remarkable statement from the lips of the Nazarene :

9 John 3: 2.

" Verily, verily, I say unto thee, Except a man be born again, [margin, from above] he cannot see the kingdom of God." [10]

7. What could He mean? What could this young teacher imply by such a saying? Could it be possible that He does not consider me a fit subject for the kingdom of God? Me, a Jew, a rabbi, a member of the Sanhedrin, even a member of the *special committee* of the tribunal? Does He not know that any and every Jew, naturally, is a member of the kingdom of God? especially so when He has become a teacher of the people. Does He not know that the rabbis have taught that all the nations of the world would burn in the great day of judgment as a furnace, while all Israel, as a people, would be saved? Is He not aware that we have been instructed that Jehovah has set apart Israel for a people unto Himself? Could it be possible He was ignorant of that statement of the rabbis: 'All Israel have a part in the world to come?' And another statement: "God had sanctified the Jews for His people forever, and had placed them on a footing with all the angels of His presence, with all the angels of His praise, and with all the holy angels that stand before Him." These and many other thoughts must have passed through the mind of this " Master in Israel," as he contemplated this reply of Jesus. It seemed to him as though Jesus could hardly have intended to have said this to him, had He known who His guest was. No doubt the ruler was greatly perplexed; for he could not possibly see through the thought of Jesus. What did He mean? Was it that there must be a literal birth again, as of a child, in order to get into the kingdom of God? Hence the question:

" How can a man be born when he is old? Can he enter the second time into his mother's womb, and be born?" [11]

8. Then Jesus replied:

" Verily, verily, I say unto thee, Except a man be born of water and of the Spirit, he cannot enter into the kingdom of God. . . . *Marvel not* that I said unto thee, Ye must be born again." [12]

[10] John 3:3.   [11] John 3:4.   [12] John 3:5–7.

NICODEMUS STILL PERPLEXED.

9. This answer of the Savior seemed to perplex him still more. Such language he had never heard; such a qualification to become a member of the kingdom of God was unheard of by Nicodemus or his colleagues. But he evidently was at fault, for the Savior continued:

"Art thou a master of Israel, and knowest not these things?"[13]

10. This reply is not only intended to inform Nicodemus as to what he wanted to know, but it was also a stern rebuke for *not knowing* the word of God as he ought to have known it. Why should he not have known the birth of the water and of the Spirit? Had not the Scriptures told about it? Had not God declared it in His word? Had he never read the following from the word of God, and should he not have known how to apply it?

THE NEW BIRTH.

"Then I will sprinkle clean water upon you, and ye shall be clean: from all your filthiness, and from all your idols, will I cleanse you. A new heart also will I give you, and a new spirit will I put within you, and I will take away the stony heart out of your flesh, and I will give you an heart of flesh. And I will put My spirit within you, and cause you to walk in My statutes, and ye shall keep My judgments."[14]

"And I will cause the captivity of Judah and the captivity of Israel to return, and will build them, as at the first. And I will cleanse them from all their iniquity."[15]

"And I will give them one heart, and I will put a new spirit within you, and I will take the stony heart out of their flesh, and will give them an heart of flesh. . . ."[16]

"Create in me a clean heart, O God, and renew a right spirit within me. Cast me not away from Thy presence, and take not Thy Holy Spirit from me."[17]

EVERY TRUTH OF SALVATION MIGHT HAVE BEEN KNOWN.

11. There can be no doubt but that Nicodemus had read these scriptures more than once; but it must have been with a

[13] John 3:10.   [14] Eze. 36:25–27.   [15] Jer. 33:7, 8.   [16] Eze. 11:19.
[17] Ps. 51:10, 11.

clouded mind. His vision was blurred, because he had read them in the light of the teachings and traditions of the elders. It would seem from the statement of the Savior that all of the experiences relative to conversion, the new birth, the Holy Ghost, salvation, eternal life—all these were in the Scriptures. Nicodemus should have known them. Yes, as a master in Israel, he *ought* to have known them. The Savior expressed surprise that he did not know them. As a result of his not knowing them, the other rabbis also did not know them; the people, who depended for knowledge upon these leaders, were ignorant of them. Therefore, when the Savior came to earth, the whole Jewish nation was ignorant of Christ, His work, His salvation, eternal life.

JEWS MIGHT HAVE ENJOYED GREAT LIGHT.

12. The traditions of the rabbis had so hidden the purity of the truths of the gospel, that the people could not understand the spiritual truths which Christ sought to impart to them. Had they only read their Scriptures as the word expressed it; had they sought for the help of the Holy Spirit as it was their privilege, they might have had floods of light on all the great truths of salvation through the Messiah; then the Scriptures might have meant so much more to them.

MANY OF GOD'S SAINTS ENJOYED THE LIGHT.

13. It is often said that the Jewish people did not have the light of the gospel as people have it since the days of Christ's advent to earth; but if we examine the Scriptures, we shall see a vast fund of truth that the Lord intended the Israelites to know, and which they might have in a large measure enjoyed. Because they did not behold the light that was shining in their pathway, the Lord was not to blame. Some of the faithful servants of God saw it; all might have seen it. Those who saw the light of Christ, even before His advent to the world, rejoiced in it, and looked forward to the glad day when they should behold more.

14. We now turn to a few scriptures which will make clear what the Jews might have known concerning the real practical gospel of salvation, as revealed through the Holy Spirit, and what they lost as a result of not knowing these blessed messages. As we observe these truths, we shall the better see how much of the word of God is being lost to-day, because of a *lack of study of these very same truths.* It should ever be borne in mind that the Israelites were a typical people; [18] all their experiences, therefore, were but illustrations for the church after Christ came in the flesh. Their failures were to be as sign-boards and mile-posts for the church of Christ, by looking at which they were to take heed and beware, lest they fall into the same snares as the ancient people of God. [19]

THE GOSPEL.

15. The Apostle Paul tells us that the gospel of Christ is the power of God unto salvation to every one that believeth. [20] The salvation which the gospel brings, is a salvation from sin. [21] The sin-bearer, [22] or Savior, that brings this salvation, through the gospel, is Jesus Christ. [23] That there is no other gospel which has salvation from sin, [24] is evident by what the Apostle Peter says; [25] hence the means of salvation has always been the same. [26] This the Jews might have known; this they ought to have known. Abraham knew it, and was saved through it. For we read:

"And the scripture, foreseeing that God would justify the heathen through faith, preached before the *gospel* unto Abraham, saying, In thee shall all nations be blessed." [27]

16. It is thus clear that Abraham had the gospel. It was the gospel of Christ, too, that he had. For the Savior said:

"Your father Abraham rejoiced to see My day: and he saw it, and was glad . . . Jesus said unto them, Verily, verily, I say unto you, before Abraham was, *I am*." [28]

[18] 1 Cor. 10:11; Rom. 15:4.   [19] Heb. 2:1-3; 4:1, 11.   [20] Rom. 1:16, 17.
[21] Acts 13:38, 39; Matt. 1:21.   [22] 1 Pet. 2:24.   [23] Acts 3:26.   [24] Gal. 1:6-8.
[25] Acts 4:12.   [26] Isa. 43:11.   [27] Gal. 3:8.   [28] John 8:56-58.

ABRAHAM HAD THE GOSPEL.

17. We can see from this answer of the Savior to the Jews, that Abraham was saved through His merit, as the I Am here brought to view is none other than the Lord Himself, which is made clear in Exodus. [29] Paul also tells us that the Seed to whom and through whom the promises were made, was Christ. [30] Thus it is plain that Abraham, the father of the Jews, in whom the Jews trusted and believed, [31] had the gospel of Christ, which to him was the power of God unto salvation; and this blessed gospel gave to him righteousness through faith. " He believed in the Lord; and He counted it to him for righteousness." [32] " So then they which be of faith are blessed with faithful Abraham." [33] " If ye be Christ's, then are ye Abraham's seed, and heirs according to the promise." [34] Thus to Abraham was imparted the righteousness of God, through faith in the Lord Jesus. [35] This righteousness Paul tells us is the gospel of Christ, the power of God unto salvation to every one that believeth. [36] It was justification by faith [37] in the Lord Jesus alone, without good works outside of Christ. All this Abraham, the father of the Jews, had; Nicodemus might have had; the rabbis could have had; the people should have had.

THE GOSPEL GIVEN TO THE FATHERS IN THE WILDERNESS.

18. Not only did Abraham have the gospel, but the fathers in the wilderness also had it. They had all that Abraham had, and additional light beside. For says the apostle:

" For some, when they had heard, did provoke; howbeit not all that came out of Egypt by Moses. But with whom was He grieved forty years? Was it not with them that had sinned, whose carcasses fell in the wilderness? And to whom sware He that they should not enter into His rest, but to them that believed not? So we see that they could not enter in because of unbelief. Let us therefore fear, lest, a promise being left us of entering into His rest, any of you should seem to come short of it. For

29 Ex. 3:6. 13, 14.   30 Gal. 3:16.   31 Matt. 3:9; John 8:39.   32 Gen. 15:6.
33 Gal. 3:9.   34 Gal. 3:29.   35 Rom. 4:22.   36 Rom. 1:17.   37 Rom. 5:1.

unto us was the *gospel* preached, as well as unto *them :* but the word preached did not profit them, not being mixed with faith in them that heard it." [38]

19. It is here plainly stated that the gospel which the church had in the days of Paul, and which she has been enjoying ever since, was held by the Israelites first, and this in the wilderness during the forty years. The question, however, might arise whether this was the gospel of Christ that they had, and which had saving power in it for them, as it had for Abraham? This is answered again by the same apostle :

"Moreover, brethren, I would not that ye should be ignorant, how that all our fathers were under the cloud, and all passed through the sea; and were all baptized unto Moses in the cloud and in the sea; and did all eat the same spiritual meat; and did all drink the same spiritual drink : for they drank of that spiritual Rock that followed them : and that Rock was Christ." . . . " Neither let us tempt Christ, as some of them also tempted, and were destroyed of serpents." [39]

CHRIST WAS IN THE WILDERNESS.

20. It is clear from these scriptures that it was Christ who was with them in the wilderness; it was the gospel of Christ they had at that time; it was a lack of faith[40] in this Christ's gospel that caused them to lose the promised inheritance, and eternal life.[41] What was true of the Israelites at that time was true of their successors all through the ages. The men of God, who lived close to the Lord, knew of this saving power, and were saved. The majority living far from the Lord, did not believe in Christ, did not receive Him as their Savior, hence were lost. This is very beautifully as well as graphically described by the Prophet Isaiah :

"I will mention the loving-kindnesses of the Lord and the praises of the Lord, according to all that the Lord hath bestowed on us, and the great goodness toward the house of Israel, which He hath bestowed on them according to His mercies, and according to the multitude of His loving-kindnesses. For He said, Surely they are My people, children that will

[38] Heb. 3: 16–19; 4: 1, 2.   [39] 1 Cor. 10: 1–9.   [40] Deut. 32: 20; Matt. 17: 17.
[41] Num. 14: 30, 35.

not lie: so He was their Savior. In all their affliction He was afflicted, and the angel of His presence saved them : in His love and in His pity He redeemed them; and He bare them, and carried them all the days of old." [42]

THE PROPHETS KNEW CHRIST.

21. The prophets of God knew this saving power that was in Christ, and taught it to the people; but the latter did not see it because of their refusing to believe the word of the Lord.[43] They preferred to follow other teachers and leaders, who walked in the sparks of their own kindling.[44]

Says the Apostle Peter :

" Receiving the end of your faith, even the salvation of your souls. Of which salvation the prophets have enquired and searched diligently who prophesied of the grace that should come unto you: searching what, or what manner of time the Spirit of Christ which was in them did signify, when it testified beforehand the sufferings of Christ, and the glory that should follow." [45]

22. These men enjoyed the Spirit of Christ; and as many as are led by the Spirit of God, they are the sons of God.[46] If any man have not the Spirit of Christ, he is none of His.[47] It is thus clear and conclusive that from the days of Abraham, yes, from the days of Adam, [48] (*b*) the gospel of Christ was made known unto the sons of men, by the divine Spirit of God; and this blessed gospel through the Lord Jesus, brought salvation to every soul that believed in it. This was the Savior that Isaiah speaks of, for we read in the same book these words :

" I, even I, am the Lord; and beside Me there is no Savior." [49]

Peter tells us there is salvation in none other,[50] "for there is none other name under heaven given among men, whereby we must be saved," but the name of Jesus.

23. In view of these facts it is not surprising that the Savior should put the question to Nicodemus as He did :

"*Art thou a master of Israel, and knowest not these things?*" [51]

[42] Isa. 63: 7–9.   [43] Jer. 11: 10; 14: 13–15.   [44] Isa. 50: 11.   [45] 1 Pet. 1: 9–11.
[46] Rom. 8: 14.   [47] Rom. 8: 9.   [48] Gen. 3: 15.   [49] Isa. 43: 11.
[50] Acts 4: 12.   [51] John 3: 10.

8

We can see then added force in the Savior's words when He said :

"Thus have ye made the commandment of God of none effect by your tradition." [52]

Through their abundant traditions they lost the true knowledge of the gospel and its saving power, substituting therefor the sayings and doings of men.

CONVERSION AND THE HOLY SPIRIT.

24. It is often said that when Jesus came to earth a new era was brought about in the experience of mankind; and from this time forward men were to be regenerated through the Holy Spirit when the Holy Ghost would be poured upon them. Frequently the idea is conveyed that Pentecost marked the birth of the Holy Ghost; till this time very little, if anything, was known of the Spirit. The Jews had nothing but law; their legality, someway, brought them into certain favor with God.

NICODEMUS SHOULD HAVE KNOWN CONVERSION.

25. However, it must be readily seen from this answer of Christ to Nicodemus that this was not so; for the subject under consideration was the new birth, the regeneration of the soul by the Holy Spirit which convicts men of sin, and converts them to God. "Art thou a master of Israel, and knowest not these things?" [53] How surprised the Savior seemed, that Nicodemus did not know what it was to be born again, to give his heart to the Lord, to be converted. It was evident he should have known it, especially since he professed to be a student of the Word, as well as a leader of the people. His not knowing it, however, did not change the truth. It was *his* privilege as well as the privilege of every other man at that time to have known what conversion was; to have been born of the Spirit of God; to have received a new heart by the power of the Holy Spirit.

[52] Matt. 15:6.   [53] John 3:10.

DAVID'S EXPERIENCE IN CONVERSION.

26. Many instances of this truth might be cited, but one will suffice. This is the experience of David, and this experience is found in Psalms 51. It was his confession and repentance of the awful sin he had committed, as recorded in Second Samuel.[54] Hear his prayer:

"Purge me with hyssop, and I shall be clean : wash me, and I shall be whiter than snow. . . . Hide Thy face from my sins, and blot out all mine iniquities. Create in me a *clean heart*, O God ; and renew a right spirit within me. Cast me not away from Thy presence, and take not Thy Holy Spirit from me. *Restore* unto me the joy of Thy salvation, and uphold me with Thy free spirit. Then will I teach transgressors Thy ways, and *sinners* shall be *converted* unto Thee." [55]

27. From these scriptures we learn the following:

1. David had become a backslider, and had lost the Holy Spirit.

2. He had once known what salvation was; through sin he lost it, and was now asking the Lord to restore it to him.

3. He had once been a converted man with a soul which had been white ; this he longed for again.

4. He had been a missionary worker, as a result of his experience in salvation, and now longed for the power of the Holy Spirit that he might still see sinners reclaimed to God.

5. He had once thoroughly known the keeping power of God, and had enjoyed a free and full salvation.

ALL THE PEOPLE MIGHT HAVE ENJOYED THE SAME EXPERIENCE.

28. Now all this experience which David once had, and again longed for, came to him through Jesus, the Son of God, the Savior of men.[56] He knew the Lord,[57] and had received this saving power from Him. This, Jesus Himself proved, when conversing with the Pharisees. It is true that the people in general, even in David's day, did not know this, and he gives the reason:

[54] 2 Sam. 11 : 2-27.　　[55] Ps. 51 : 7-13.　　[56] Matt. 22 : 42-45.　　[57] Acts 2 : 29-31.

"I have more understanding than all my teachers : for Thy testimonies are my meditation. I understand more than the ancients [Hebrew elders], *because I keep Thy precepts.*" [58]

29. If the people, then, were as anxious to know the Lord as he was, and to understand God's word as he, and desired the truth of salvation in their inward parts as he desired, they, too, would have known this grand truth.[59]

HOLY SPIRIT GIVEN PRIOR TO JESUS' ADVENT.

30. That the Holy Ghost was given to the people before the Savior came, that David and others enjoyed it, is evident from the testimony of Jesus and the apostles. Many statements to this effect are also found in Moses and the prophets. We will first consider the testimony of the Savior.

THE TESTIMONY OF JESUS CONCERNING THE SPIRIT.

"And Jesus answered and said, while He taught in the temple, How say the scribes that Christ is the son of David? For David *himself said* by the Holy Ghost, The Lord said to my Lord, Sit Thou on My right hand, till I make Thine enemies Thy footstool." [60]

The Savior said that David had the Holy Ghost; and David lived more than a thousand years prior to the Pentecost of Acts 2. (*b*)

TESTIMONY OF PETER.

"And in those days Peter stood up in the midst of the disciples, and said, ... Men and brethren, this scripture·must needs have been fulfilled, which the Holy Ghost by the mouth of David spake before concerning Judas, which was guide to them that took Jesus." [61]

This was before the great outpouring of the Spirit.

DAVID'S OWN TESTIMONY.

"Now these be the last words of David. David, the son of Jesse, said, and the man who was raised up on high, the anointed of the God of Jacob, and the sweet psalmist of Israel, said, The Spirit of the Lord spake by me, and His word was in my tongue." [62]

"Then David gave to Solomon his son the pattern of the porch,

[58] Ps. 119 : 99, 100.   [59] 2 Chron. 19 : 7.   [60] Mark 12 : 35, 36.
[61] Acts 1 : 15, 16.   [62] 2 Sam. 23 : 1, 2.

"The Sweet Psalmist of Israel."

. . . and the pattern of all that he had by the Spirit." "All this, said David, the *Lord* made me understand in writing by His hand upon me, even all the works of this pattern." [63]

TESTIMONY OF OTHER PROPHETS CONCERNING THE SPIRIT.

"And Moses went out, and told the people the words of the Lord, and gathered the seventy men of the elders of the people, and set them round about the tabernacle. And the Lord came down in a cloud, and spake unto him, and took of the Spirit that was upon him, and gave it unto the seventy elders : and it came to pass, that when the Spirit rested upon them, they prophesied, and did not cease. But there remained two of the men in the camp, . . . and the Spirit rested upon them; and they were of them that were written, but went not out unto the tabernacle : and they prophesied in the camp. And there ran a young man, and told Moses, and said, Eldad and Medad do prophesy in the camp. And Joshua the son of Nun, the servant of Moses, one of his young men, answered and said, My lord Moses, forbid them. And Moses said unto him, Enviest thou for my sake? would God that all the Lord's people were prophets, and that the Lord would put His Spirit upon them !" [64]

WHY ALL THE PEOPLE COULD NOT RECEIVE THE SPIRIT.

31. What was this last statement of Moses, if not a longing desire that all the people might receive the Holy Ghost? God longed to give it to them; but they were not converted; they knew not the regenerating power of the Spirit in their life, consequently were not prepared to receive the Holy Spirit.

THE HOLY SPIRIT IN THE SCHOOL OF THE PROPHETS.

"And Saul sent messengers to take David : and when they saw the company of the prophets prophesying, and Samuel standing as appointed over them, the Spirit of God was upon the messengers of Saul, and they also prophesied. And when it was told Saul, he sent other messengers, and they prophesied likewise. . . . Then went he also to Ramah, . . . and he asked and said, Where are Samuel and David? And one said, Behold, they be at Naioth in Ramah. And he went thither, . . . and the Spirit of God was upon him also, and he went on and prophesied. . . ." [65]

THE HOLY SPIRIT IN THE WILDERNESS.

" I will mention the loving-kindnesses of the Lord, and the praises of

[63] 1 Chron. 28 : 11, 12, 19. [64] Num. 11 : 24-29. [65] 1 Sam. 19 : 20-23.

the Lord, according to all that the Lord hath bestowed on us, and the great goodness toward the house of Israel, which He hath bestowed on them according to His mercies, and according to the multitude of His loving-kindnesses. For He said, Surely they are My people, children that will not lie: so He was their Savior. In all their affliction He was afflicted, and the angel of His presence saved them: in His love and in His pity He redeemed them; and He bare them, and carried them all the days of old. But they rebelled, and vexed His *Holy Spirit:* therefore He was turned to be their enemy, and He fought against them." [66]

COULD NOT RECEIVE THE SPIRIT, BECAUSE OF LACK OF FAITH.

32. An abundance of evidence might be further produced from the Scriptures, clearly showing that the people in the days prior to the advent of Christ, enjoyed the experience of conversion, and the gift of the Holy Spirit, if they would only believe the Lord and receive this blessing. It was for every one, for God never has been any respecter of persons. The reason, however, why the majority of the people did not receive it, was because of their lack of faith in the salvation of God, [67] and in His servants who delivered to them the messages of salvation. [68] They preferred to have the *smooth* sayings [69] of the teachers and leaders, therefore they lost the precious gift of God.

THE SUBSTITUTE FOR THE SPIRIT.

33. As has been mentioned in a previous chapter, several centuries prior to the advent of the Savior, the rabbis instituted this spurious substitution for the Spirit of God, known as " Bath-kol," the daughter of a voice. This fraud, however, could not be discerned but by the rabbis; and the poor people were left in entire ignorance of this precious gift. This, no doubt, partially explains the reason why the disciples were so perplexed when Jesus told them of the coming of the Spirit to *them*, which they should receive, while the world and even the learned rabbis would reject [70] it. To think *they* could have the

---

[66] Isa. 63: 7–10. [67] Isa. 59: 1. [68] 2 Chron. 36: 15, 16. [69] Isa. 30: 10.
[70] John 14: 16, 17, 22.

real gift, which Jesus told them was so precious, and the rabbis and other learned men would not receive, was to them inexplicable. However, all *could* receive this blessed gift, if they would only open their hearts to it.

A GENERAL SUMMARY.

34. Thus salvation, conversion, the Holy Spirit, and all other gifts necessary for the salvation of the soul, were manifested in the word of God; and all these every one might have received through Jesus Christ, before His appearance in the flesh. Many of the people did avail themselves of its precious blessings, and were saved. This was true of Abel, of Enoch, of Noah, of Abraham, of other Patriarchs. Moses, many of the prophets, priests, and kings, as well as some of the more pious of the people of God, enjoyed this salvation.[71] Then the Old Testament Scriptures, rightly understood, clearly reveal that the Jews might have known many wonderful truths concerning the Lord Jesus; might have been prepared to receive Him when He came; might have been the heralds to the world of the grand and glorious gospel message of the Christ who had come; might have been freely and fully saved. Tradition, human theology, man-made teaching, and the philosophy[72] of so-called science[73] obstructed the channel of the soul; and those very people to whom He came, knew Him not.[74] What a sad thought! What a terrible fate![75]

THE CHURCH OF TO-DAY.

35. The church, however, should bear in mind the fact that all this which happened to the Jews has a very forcible lesson for the present time.[76] We are repeatedly admonished by the apostles and prophets that everything that happened aforetime was to illustrate to the church of Christ for to-day what the people might expect, should they follow now in a similar course.[77] If, however, the professed people of God will take

71 Heb. 11. 72 Col. 2:8. 73 1 Tim. 6:20. 74 John 1:11.
75 Matt. 23:34, 35; Luke 23:27-30. 76 Isa. 30:8, margin. 77 Rom. 11:17-23.

heed to the admonitions and rightly interpret that people and those times, a great deal may be received which they otherwise must lose. But we see at the present time so much of the experience of Israel being repeated, the teachings of philoso- phy, the teachings of science, the traditions of the elders and of the theological leaders, the higher criticism of the word of God, the destruction of much of the truth of the gospel, the neglect of the study of the blessed Bible. When we consider how little the Bible is studied at the present day, and how much less its grand truths are understood and practiced, we can dis- cern that the same path in which the ancient Jews travelled is being again beaten down. The masses are depending largely upon the few teachers to interpret the word for them, and many of these are constantly differing in opinion. Consequently spiritual death is resulting. Form is being substituted for de- votion ; outward demonstration takes the place of piety ; large edifices are an indication of spiritual growth.[78] Yet the form of godliness without the power of God is vain in His work and worship.[79] The teachings of men in the place of the word of God are lifeless and spiritless ; [80] and with God such worship is vain.[81]

WHAT THE JEWS OUGHT TO HAVE KNOWN, THE CHURCH SHOULD KNOW.

37. If men would but take heed and observe what trans- pired as a result of the Jews instituting so many customs, they might be saved from falling into the same snare, as well as from the same results. God's word is true ; His word is sure. What the Jews might have known they lost sight of ; what the church of to-day may know it is not earnestly seeking for, be- cause the teachings of Moses and the prophets are laid aside. Then while it is called to-day,[82] let the salvation of God be sought as revealed in His *own word ;* then life, power, and blessing will come to thousands of hearts,[83] which in turn will

[78] Hosea 8: 14.   [79] 2 Tim. 3: 1-5.   [80] 2 Cor. 3: 6.
[81] Matt. 15: 3, 6, 9 ; Mark 7: 3, 7, 9, 13.   [82] Heb. 3: 12-15.   [83] Joel 2: 23-27.

bless still others. The experience of the Jews will then be a valuable lesson. The Holy Ghost, faith, conversion, salvation, sanctification, obedience, as well as all the other gifts of the Spirit, will once more be manifested with power.

EXPLANATORY NOTES.

Paragraph 3.

(*a*) Just when the Sanhedrin came into existence is not definitely known. One thing is certain, it must have come into existence some time during the Grecian rule, as the word, *Sanhedrin*, though written in Hebrew characters, is a Greek word. It is true this council was called by a Hebrew title,— בֵּירַת דִין הַנָדוֹל — "the great house of judgment." But if this had been its original name, it never would have accepted the Greek title, for the Jews naturally abhorred the Grecians.

It is claimed, however, that it was in direct line of succession of the seventy elders appointed by Moses. The reason they had *seventy-one*, was to have the extra place filled, which Moses occupied in addition to the seventy. Ex. 18 : 19–26 ; Num. 11 : 16.

They had full power to judge the people and to execute the judgment. Their method of execution was originally strangulation; afterward they adopted crucifixion. This power of execution was removed about the middle of the second century before Christ.

Paragraph 22.

(*b*) The blessedness of the complete gospel of Christ is contained in this one verse, Gen. 3 : 15. It not only promises a Savior to die for the sins of the world; it also promises His second coming, the destruction of Satan, and the restoration of the earth to its Edenic beauty. All this was accomplished through Jesus only. He came and died for sins according to the Scriptures; He will come again according to the Scriptures; He will destroy Satan according to the Scriptures; He will restore all things to their Edenic beauty. Thus Christ was revealed to Adam, and the gospel, or good news of salvation, must have been known by him.

Paragraph 30.

(*c*) Matthew says, in chapter 1 : 17 of his Gospel, that twenty-eight generations elapsed from David to Christ. From the birth of the Savior to the outpouring of the Spirit on Pentecost was about thirty-one and a half years. According to chronology David was in his prime about 1050 B. C. Add to this the years from the Savior's birth to the experience of Acts 2, and we have nearly eleven hundred years.

CHAPTER IX.

"Art Thou the Christ, the Son of the Blessed?"

"Behold My Servant whom I uphold; Mine Elect, in whom My soul delighteth; I have put My Spirit upon Him; He shall bring forth judgment to the Gentiles." Isa. 42:1.

THE ISRAELITES HAD GREAT LIGHT.

THE saying of Jesus: "If therefore the light that is in thee be darkness, how great is that darkness!"[1] had a very practical and forcible application to the Jews at the time He said it. The belief is generally entertained that the Jewish people did not have much light; but by investigation of the word of God, as expressed by the Holy Spirit, we shall learn that they were a people who for decades and centuries had abundance of light. The trouble with them was that the light which the Lord gave them had become to them darkness, because of the mist which had been placed about the light. The light of God being covered up by their traditions and mysticisms, they could not see it. Christ came to remove the clouds of tradition, (a) and to make manifest the light which they had.

2. David said: "Thy word is a lamp unto my feet, and a light unto my path."[2] He also said: "The commandment of the Lord is pure, enlightening the eyes."[3] Solomon said: "For the commandment is a lamp; and the law is light."[4] They had the Scriptures;[5] they had the law;[6] they had the commandment; yet of these people the Savior said:

"And in them is fulfilled the prophecy of Esaias, which saith, By hearing ye shall hear, and shall not understand; and seeing ye shall see, and shall not perceive: for this people's heart is waxed gross, and their

[1] Matt. 6:23.   [2] Ps. 119:105.   [3] Ps. 19:8.   [4] Prov. 6:23.   [5] John 5:39.
[6] John 7:19; Rom. 9:4.

ears are dull of hearing, and their eyes they have closed; lest at any time they should see with their eyes, and hear with their ears, and should understand with their heart, and should be converted, and I should heal them." [7]

3. Again the Savior said:

" Do ye not therefore err, because ye know not the Scriptures, neither the power of God?" [8]

4. And the Apostle Paul says of them:

" But their minds were blinded: for until this day remaineth the same vail untaken away in the reading of the Old Testament; which vail is done away in Christ. But even unto this day, when Moses is read, the vail is upon their heart." [9]

ALL THINGS OFFERED TO THE JEWS.

5. Thus while they had great light in the Scriptures of the Old Testament and in the law which God gave them, they were blinded to the truth that they contained. But said the apostle:

" When it [the heart] shall turn to the Lord, the vail shall be taken away." [10]

6. It must be evident after perusing the contents of the last chapter, that the Jews had great opportunities of knowing all about Christ,—His mission to the world, His work among men. The very fact that salvation was offered them through Christ,—eternal life, the Holy Spirit, conversion, repentance, and every other gift which comes only through the Lord Jesus,—is in itself evidence that they might have known all about Him. Yes, Jesus told them that they did know it, but would not acknowledge it.

" Then cried Jesus in the temple as He taught, saying, Ye both know Me, and ye know whence I am: and I am not come of Myself, but He that sent Me is true, whom ye know not." [11] Nevertheless, " He came unto His own, and His own received Him not." [12]

NO MENTION OF MESSIAH IN MISHNA.

7. One thing is very strange concerning the traditions of

[7] Matt. 13: 14, 15. [8] Mark 12: 24. [9] 2 Cor. 3: 14, 15. [10] 2 Cor. 3: 16. [11] John 7: 28. [12] John 1: 11.

the Jews prior to the advent of Jesus, namely; not *once* in all the writings of the sages, and wise men, is the Messiah mentioned. The Bible abounds with that great Messianic truth; the rabbis knew it all the time; still they never mention a single instance in any part of their Mishnayos (or treatises) concerning the Messiah. There is a single notice of the near-coming Messiah in the tractate "Sotah;" but this statement is generally believed among writers to have been inserted after Christ had come.

ONE GREAT TRUTH IN ALL THE BIBLE.

8. If the Bible were properly understood, interpreted in the light of itself, there would be found one great, consecutive, central truth running through every one of the thirty-nine [13] books of the Old Testament; and that truth is the *Messiah*, the *Christ*, the *Son of the Blessed.* It will also be found that He always was with the Father; was co-creator with God; was the very essence of all light [14] and truth; [15] was the great Medium between God and the universe throughout all the ages of the past. [16] Every ray of light that has ever come to the world has come through Him; [17] every soul in the universe has been kept and preserved by Him; [18] and God the Father has trusted Him with the care and protection of this world, other worlds, the vast and great universe. [19] In Him the Father has placed all the riches of wisdom and knowledge and power and grace. [20] He is the one great Sun, around which everything in all God's vast domain revolves. This, the Scriptures declare; [21] this the Jews might have known; this they might have taught to the world; this knowledge lived, would have prepared them to have heralded to the world the birth of the Deliverer, instead of its being announced by the angelic hosts.

JESUS IS THE SON OF THE BLESSED.

9. That we might have a better appreciation of the text

[13] John 5:46, 47; Acts 3:24. [14] John 1:9. [15] John 14:6. [16] John 1:18; 1 Tim.2:5. [17] John 9:12. [18] Heb. 1:3. [19] John 1:10; Heb. 1:1, 2; Col. 1:19; 2:9,10. [20] Col. 2:2,3. [21] John 12:32; Col. 1:20.

heading of this chapter, we shall examine a number of scriptures, which will enable us to see more clearly that He *is* the Christ, the Son of the Blessed. And with this thought in view we may clearly perceive that *every* truth in all the Bible centers in Jesus, the Christ, the Son of the Blessed.

CHRIST'S PREEXISTENCE AS TAUGHT BY HIMSELF.

10. The Savior repeated again and again that He existed before He came to this world. He told the Jews that their own Scriptures taught it,[22] and His works proved it.[23] This they would know if they only laid aside their preconceived idea of the Messiah and the temporal kingdom they supposed He would set up,[24] and the expositions of the Bible as given by the Pharisees. If they had only devoted their thought and attention to the Scriptures themselves, and observed the work He was doing in fulfillment of the word of God, they would have seen that all that the Scriptures declared in Moses and all the prophets concerning the Messiah, were fulfilled in Him.

11. He said:

"No man hath ascended up to heaven, but He that came down from heaven, even the Son of man which is in heaven."[25]

"For *I came down from heaven*, not to do Mine own will, but the will of Him that sent Me."[26]

"What and if ye shall see the Son of man ascend up where He was before."[27]

"And He said unto them, Ye are from beneath; I am from above: ye are of this world; I am not of this world."[28]

"Your father Abraham rejoiced to see My day: and he saw it, and was glad. . . . Verily, verily, I say unto you, Before Abraham was, *I am*."[29]

"I and My Father are one."[30]

"And now, O Father, glorify Thou Me with Thine own self with the glory which I had with Thee before the world was."[31] "For I have given unto them the words which Thou gavest Me, and they have received them, and have known surely that I *came out from Thee*, and they have believed

22 John 5:39.   23 John 8:32; 14:10, 11.   24 Matt. 20:20, 21.   25 John 3:13.
26 John 6:38.   27 John 6:62.   28 John 8:23.   29 John 8:56–58.
30 John 10:30.   31 John 17:5.

that Thou didst send Me." [33]   "And now I am no more in the world, but these are in the world, and I come to Thee." [34]   "Father, I will that they also, whom Thou hast given Me, be with Me where I am, that they may behold My glory which Thou hast given Me : for Thou lovedst Me *before the foundation of the world.*" [35]

CHRIST'S EXALTED POSITION IN THE UNIVERSE.

12. Innumerable more testimonies from the lips of the Savior might be given, all of which show that He existed before he came in the flesh, and filled a position in the universe which none other could occupy.   All this the Old Testament Scriptures taught, and the Jews might have known, had they not so covered up the light of this blessed truth.   It might be well, perhaps, to cite a few :

" In the beginning God created the heaven and the earth. . . . And God said, Let there be light, and there was light." [36]

The Apostle John tells us that :

" In the beginning was the Word, and the Word was with God, and the *Word was God.*   The same was in the beginning with God.   All things were made by Him ; and without Him was not anything made that was made. . . . And the Word was made flesh, and dwelt among us, (and we beheld His glory, the glory as of the only begotten of the Father,) full of grace and truth." [37]

13. Hence when it says that in the beginning God created the heaven and the earth, we see that the Deity here referred to, included the Son with the Father.   In fact, the term *God*, in Genesis one, itself proves that.   The word *God* in the Hebrew, is *E-lo-him*, literally, *Gods.*   The word *E-lo-him* is the plural form of the word *El.*   *El*, the singular, is *God* ; *E-lo-him*, the plural, is *Gods.*   That is to say, if the word *God*, in Gen. 1:1, were properly translated, the plurality in the Godhead would be more clearly manifest.   This same thought is expressed in Gen. 1 : 26, where it says :

" And God said, Let us make man, in our image, after our likeness."

[33] John 17 : 8.   [34] John 17 : 11.   [35] John 17 : 24.   [36] Gen. 1 : 1-3.   [37] John 1 : 1-14.

Here the plural form of *El, God*, is used in expressing the creative work; but the word *God* is the same here as in verse one, namely, *E-lo-him*. (*b*)

DIFFICULTY OF JEWISH WRITERS TO EXPLAIN THE E-LO-HIM.

14. The Jewish writers recognize there is a plurality in this text (verse twenty-six) that seems difficult to harmonize with the idea of the rabbis that the Godhead is only one personage. Hence they have various ways of explaining it. One writer, in commenting on it (and this writer's idea largely prevails among the Jews even to this day), says it means that " God said to the *angels*, let us make man, in our image and in our likeness; that is, with reason and understanding such as we have." Perhaps it might be well to give the entire comment on this verse, as handed down by the great and learned commentator, Rashi. He says on Gen. 1 : 26, first part :

RASHI'S COMMENT.

" From this [that is, God said to the angels let us make man in our image and after our likeness, with understanding and reason such as we have], we learn concerning the plans of the Holy One, blessed be His name. Because man was made in the image of the angels, and for fear lest the angels should feel provoked concerning this matter, the Lord counselled with these angels, and received their approval in the matter. The Lord said : 'Between the angelic hosts and Myself there is a similarity in creation; that is to say, the heavenly hosts are created in My image and after My likeness. Now if the earthly creation should not be after My image and My likeness, there would be a jealousy and rivalry in all My created works, because the earthly would be jealous of the heavenly.' Therefore, He took counsel with the heavenly universe, that is, with the angels, and said, ' Let us make man.' Since, however, they did not assist Him in the creation of the earthly family, and here is an opportunity for the Epicurean [a synonym for the Christian, the follower of the Nazarene] to contemn the Holy One, blessed be His name, and to say that the angels *did* assist in the creation of man, for it is written, ' Let *us* make man,' that is to say in the plural form,—it is designed on the part of God to teach us great respect for others, and to inculcate the idea that the greater should counsel with and take advice of the younger. If it should have been written in the singular form, ' I will make man in My image and after My likeness,' we would not then have known that He was consulting with the heavenly hosts about the matter, but would have thought that He were speaking to Himself.

"And the alternative we have whereby to answer the Epicurean is written, beside this verse, in the next; that is, 'And God created man in His own image, in the image of God created He him; male and female created He them.' It does not say and they created him in their image after their own likeness."

THE FACT REMAINS THE SAME.

15. After all this elaborately drawn-out exposition of this commentator to hide the glorious truth of the co-creatorship of the Son, the fact still remains that the term *God* is used in the plural in *every verse* in the first chapter of Genesis. How sad it is to see men devote their time and thought to exegesis, rather than to the simplicity of the word of God. And amid this great labyrinth of explanation the light concerning the Son of God has been hid, or as the Apostle Paul states it:

"But if our gospel be hid, it is hid to them that are lost : in whom the god of this world hath blinded the minds of them that believe not, lest the light of the glorious gospel of Christ, who is the image of God, should shine unto them." [38]

MAKING THE SCRIPTURE VOID.

16. Another translator of the Old Testament from the Hebrew into English, finding the same difficulty to overcome, and not wishing to advance such strange ideas as Rashi advocates, says thus of Gen. 1 : 26 :

"This phrase is employed here, as in other places, to express the purpose of the Deity to affect His will. This construction is called, 'the plural of majesty.'"—*Leeser's Translation of the Old Testament, Introduction.*

17. It seems strange, however, that such phrases are very rare in the Bible, and nowhere in the Scripture do we find the nomenclature, "the plurality of majesty." How true it is that not to see Christ in the Old Testament is to have the vail of blindness and unbelief cover the soul.[39]

[38] 2 Cor. 4 : 3, 4.   [39] 2 Cor. 3 : 14, 15.

CHRIST THE TRUE LIGHT.

18. Concerning the third verse of Genesis one, previously mentioned, we find the Apostle Paul alluding to it in this manner:

" For God, who commanded the light to shine out of darkness, hath shined [margin, is He who hath shined] in our hearts, to give the light of the knowledge of the glory of God in the face of Jesus Christ." [40]

And the Savior repeatedly told His hearers that *He* was the light of the world; [41] that in Him was light; [42] and the light was the life of men. He is the light which lighteth every man that cometh into the world. [43] The true intent of all light, is Christ. [44]

WHAT SOLOMON SAID OF CHRIST.

" The Lord possessed Me in the beginning of His way, before His works of old. I was set up from everlasting, from the beginning, or ever the earth was. When there were no depths, I was brought forth; when there were no fountains abounding with water. Before the mountains were settled, before the hills was I brought forth : while as yet He had not made the earth, nor the fields, nor the highest part of the dust of the world. When He prepared the heavens, I was there, when He set a compass upon the face of the depth : when He established the clouds above : when He strengthened the fountains of the deep : when He gave to the sea His decree, that the waters should not pass His commandment : when He appointed the foundations of the earth, then I was by Him, as one brought up with Him : and I was daily His delight, rejoicing always before Him." [45]

19. Here Solomon, under the name of Wisdom, gives a brief yet accurate description of the position of Christ before the creation of this world. That Jesus is indeed the Wisdom here spoken of is plainly stated in the following scriptures :

" But we preach Christ crucified, unto the Jews a stumbling-block, and unto the Greeks foolishness ; but unto them which are called, both Jews and Greeks, Christ the power of God, and the *wisdom* of God. . . . But of Him are ye in Christ Jesus, who of God is made unto us *wisdom*, and righteousness, and sanctification, and redemption." [46]

[40] 2 Cor. 4:6.   [41] John 8:12; 9:5.   [42] John 1:4.   [43] John 1:9.
[44] 1 John 1:5.   [45] Prov. 8:22-30.   [46] 1 Cor. 1:23, 30.

MOSES' TESTIMONY CONCERNING CHRIST'S PREEXISTENCE.

" For this commandment which I command thee this day, it is not hidden from thee, neither is it far off. It is not in heaven, that thou shouldest say, Who shall go up for us to heaven, and bring it unto us, that we may hear it, and do it ? Neither is it beyond the sea, that thou shouldest say, who shall go over the sea for us, and bring it unto us, that we may hear it, and do it ? " [47]

20. Concerning the commandment here brought to view, and what is intended by it, Paul thus speaks :

" But the righteousness which is of faith speaketh on this wise, Say not in thine heart, who shall ascend into heaven ? (that is, to bring Christ down from above); or, Who shall descend into the deep ? (that is, to bring up Christ again from the dead)." [48]

Here we have a divine comment, given by the Holy Spirit to the Apostle Paul, (c) to tell us what is meant by that expression in Deuteronomy. It is Christ ; He is the great Command of God.

OTHER PROPHETS CONCERNING THE PREEXISTENCE.

21. In fact nearly all the prophets of the Old Testament have expressed themselves concerning Christ before His advent in the flesh, showing Him to be the Lord, the Word, the Jehovah, (d) the God of Moses and the prophets. This was true of David, Isaiah, Jeremiah, Daniel, and there is scarcely a prophet but what has spoken concerning Him and His glorious power which He manifested before He came into this world, clothed with the sinful flesh of humanity. Peter sums it up as follows :

" Of which salvation the prophets have inquired and searched diligently, who prophesied of the grace that should come unto you : searching what, or what manner of time the Spirit of Christ which was in them did signify, when it testified beforehand the sufferings of Christ, and the glory that should follow." [49]

THE SPIRIT OF CHRIST IN THE PROPHETS.

22. Since it was the Spirit of Christ which dwelt in the

[47] Deut. 30: 11-13.   [48] Rom. 10:6, 7.   [49] 1 Peter 1: 10,11.

prophets, there must have been the Christ to inspire these men with this blessed Spirit. How could they have had His Spirit to give utterance, if He were not there to impart to them the gifts? Yea, more: How could there have been any Spirit of Christ dwelling in these holy men of God, if there were no Christ present at the time? Even further: How could there have been any Spirit, if there were no one to give it? Yes, the blessed Christ was before the world was.[50] All the blessings that have come into the world since it existed, in whatever form they came, have come through Him who is the Christ, the Son of the Blessed.[51]

TESTIMONY OF JOHN.

23. Passing from the Old Testament writers, we come to the inspired men of God, who wrote the New Testament. The beloved John says of Christ:

"He was in the world, and the world was made by Him, and the world knew Him not." "All things were made by Him; and without Him was not anything made that was made." [52]

"No man hath seen God at any time; the only begotten Son which is in the bosom of the Father, He hath declared Him." [53]

"That which was from the beginning, which we have heard, which we have seen with our eyes, which we have looked upon, and our hands have handled, of the Word of life." [54] "I write unto you, fathers, because ye have known Him that is from the beginning." [55]

24. The apostle here tells us that Christ, the Word of God, is He who not only was in the beginning before the world was; but it was He who made *this world*; He, who came into the world, who came unto His own, and who was not received by them. Here then we have a plain statement that *Christ was* the Creator of this world. For without Him was not anything made that was made.[56]

TESTIMONY OF PAUL.

25. Of all the men of God, who were filled with the spirit of

[50] John 17: 5. [51] Matt. 16: 16; Mark 14: 61, 62. [52] John 1:10, 3.
[53] John 1: 18. [54] 1 John 1: 1. [55] 1 John 2: 13. [56] John 1: 3.

inspiration after the ascension of the Savior to the Father, no one received greater light and more glorious truth in visions and revelations that did Paul, the apostle. He himself says:

" It is not expedient for me doubtless to glory. I will come to visions and revelations of the Lord. . . . And lest I should be exalted above measure through the *abundance of the revelations*, ..." [57]

" But I certify you, brethren, that the gospel which was preached of me is not after man. For I neither received it of man, neither was I taught it, but by the revelation of Jesus Christ." [58]

And that the people might know the certainty of the truth of his claims, he says :

" The God and Father of our Lord Jesus Christ, which is blessed for evermore, knoweth that I lie not." [59]

He takes the solemn oath before God, which to every Jew is an end of all controversy.[60]   This is what He says concerning Christ's preexistence, and His position in the universe of God.

1. " God, who at sundry times and in divers manners, spake in time past unto the fathers by the prophets, hath in these last days spoken unto us by His Son, whom He hath appointed heir of all things, by whom also He made the worlds." [61]

Here we are plainly told, in addition to what John has said concerning Christ as Creator, that Christ not only created *this* world, but that all the worlds that have been created by the great Creator, were brought into being through His Son. Oh what a blessed Redeemer ! What a powerful and mighty Savior ! What a glorious and precious Deliverer ! The Creator of all the worlds in the vast domain of this endless universe is the Redeemer and Savior of the lost soul !

26. And that people should not receive a vague idea from *this* statement of the apostle, he specifies very minutely what is comprehended in this great workmanship:

2. " For by Him were all things created, that are in heaven, and that are in earth, visible and invisible, whether they be thrones, or dominions,

[57] 2 Cor. 12 : 1–7.   [58] Gal. 1 : 11, 12.   [59] 2 Cor. 11 : 31.   [60] Heb. 6 : 16.
[61] Heb. 1 : 1, 2.

or principalities, or powers : *all things* were created by Him, and for Him ; and He is before all things, and by Him all things consist." [62]

Then absolutely nothing that has ever had existence in the domains of God has ever been brought into being save as Jesus was the Maker of it, and that it was made for Him. The apostle, however, continues :

3. " But to us there is but one God, the Father, of whom are all things, and we in Him; and one Lord Jesus Christ, by whom are all things, and we by Him." [63]

4. " And to make all men see what is the fellowship of the mystery, which from the beginning of the world hath been hid in God, who created all things by Jesus Christ." [64]

5. " But unto the Son He saith, Thy throne, O God, is forever and ever : a scepter of righteousness is the scepter of Thy kingdom. Thou hast loved righteousness and hated iniquity; therefore God, even Thy God, hath anointed Thee with the oil of gladness above Thy fellows." [65]

JESUS' STATEMENTS TO THE JEWS AND TO PHILIP.

Here, then, we find the apostle giving to Christ the term *God* the same right, title, and prerogative that the Father Himself has. We can the better understand why Jesus said to the Jews :

" I and my Father are one." [66]

And to Philip :

" Jesus saith unto him, Have I been so long time with you, and yet hast thou not known Me, Philip ? he that hath seen Me hath seen the Father; and how sayest thou then, Show us the Father ? Believest thou not that I am in the Father, and the Father in Me ? " [67]

Paul throws a little light on this last expression of Jesus to Philip :

" Who being the brightness of His glory, and *the express image of His person*, and upholding all things by the word of His power, when He had by Himself purged our sins, sat down on the right hand of the Majesty on high." [68]

[62] Col. 1 : 16, 17.   [63] 1 Cor. 8 : 6.   [64] Eph. 3 : 9.   [65] Heb. 1 : 8, 9.   [66] John 10 : 30.
[67] John 14 : 9, 10.   [68] Heb. 1 : 3.

WHAT THE JEWS MIGHT HAVE SEEN IN JESUS.

27. What a wonderful privilege it must have been for the Jews to see God in the flesh [69] of humanity, and yet how much they lost by not beholding His glory. An opportunity to behold the Shekinah of Heaven, in the form of human flesh—divinity wrapped up in humanity—God manifest in the flesh—and yet their eyes were so blinded by the perversion of the truth of the word of God, as not to see or understand its import.

28. But the apostle gives still more evidence:

6. " And Thou, Lord, in the beginning hast laid the foundation of the earth; and the heavens are the works of Thine hands : they shall perish ; but Thou remainest; and they all shall wax old as doth a garment; and as a vesture shalt Thou fold them up, and they shall be changed; but Thou art the same, and Thy years shall not fail." [70]

WHY PAUL WAS RAISED UP.

29. As a result of the erroneous views of the Jewish leaders and people, the true position of Christ in the world and universe was misunderstood and misrepresented. God raised up this special servant of His, this learned and cultured Jew, removed the scales of human traditions and philosophy from his distorted and discolored vision ; opened his blind eyes [71] which had been tightly shut to every ray of light that came from Christ through the Apostles and disciples ; and gloriously, vividly, illustriously revealed to him the matchless splendor, the glorious beauty, the inexpressible and surpassing grandeur that was, is, and had been, wrapped up in Jesus.[72]

GOD'S WORK IN REVEALING CHRIST.

30. God designed to overthrow forever, through Paul and His other servants, the wrong estimate which had been placed upon His own dear Son, the Son of His love, the bosom companion of His fellowship. By instructing the church who Jesus Christ is, and had been, and the marvelous divine power that has been placed in Him since the days of eternity, God intended

[69] 1 Tim. 3:16. [70] Heb. 1:10-12. [71] Acts 9:15-17. [72] 2 Cor. 12:4, margin.

to encourage, to uplift, to ennoble, to refine, to glorify the sons of men through the redemption and salvation which exist in Jesus Christ. Because He has been given creative power is the reason, the strong reason, why He has redemptive power.[73] He who had power to create the world, is the same who has been given power to save the world. He who has the wisdom to uphold the world,—yea the universe in all its varied changes and experiences,—is He who has been given power, all power, both in heaven and in earth, to uphold, beneath the shadow of His wings, every man and woman, in all the varied changes of life, that will trust in Him.

31. No doubt this thought the Savior had in mind when He so beautifully responded to Peter's confession, " Thou art the Christ, the Son of the living God," [74] in saying to him : " Blessed art thou, Simon Bar-Jona; for flesh and blood hath not revealed it unto thee, but My Father which is in heaven."

LOSS TO THE JEWS IN NOT SEEING CHRIST.

32. It must be apparent to all that the Jewish people, because of their traditions and blindness, lost much in not seeing Jesus as the Christ, the Son of the Blessed. In their not properly understanding the Scriptures, He, the pearl of great price, was hidden from their view beneath the rubbish of human philosophy. The loss to them meant the breaking up of their nationality ; the destruction of their glorious temple ; [75] the abandoning of their beautiful city ; the loss of thousands, yes, millions of their lives ; the captivity of untold numbers of their posterity ; the hatred and animosity of mankind for decades, centuries, even millenniums; their being scattered abroad to the four winds of heaven, as a by-word, a reproach, a hissing, a perpetual opprobrium. O, what a sad picture ! " If thou hadst known, even thou, at least in this thy day, the things that belong unto thy peace !" said Jesus, " but now they are hid from thine eyes." [76]

73 Eph. 2: 10; 2 Cor. 5: 17.   74 Matt. 16: 16, 17.   75 Matt. 23: 37–39.
76 Luke 19: 42.

CHRIST, HUMANITY'S GREAT NEED TO-DAY.

33. To whom much is given, we read, from him much shall be required.[77] The great book of experience which records the deeds of the Jews can be easily read by the professed people of God at the present time. The one great theme which humanity needs to have presented now is Jesus Christ, the Savior of men, the Son of the Blessed; Christ as the Creator; Christ as the re-Creator. If any man be in Christ Jesus, he is a new creature, or creation. But in order to rightly know and to understand Jesus as He is, we must see Him in the word of God, the blessed Bible. We must read Him in Genesis, as well as in Revelation. We must see Him in Leviticus, as well as in Hebrews. We must know Him in Ruth, as well as in Matthew. In other words, we must search the Scriptures; for in them there is eternal life; and they all testify of Jesus.[78]

[77] Luke 12:48.   [78] John 5:39.

EXPLANATORY NOTES.

Paragraph 1.

(a) It is generally believed that when Christ died on the cross, He abolished a great many of the truths of the Bible that the Jewish people had believed during their national existence. But this is not so. Christ's life and death did not, neither could, abolish anything which in itself was from God; and therefore was truth. Because Christ, being "the truth" personified, could not thrust aside any truth that God had ever given. Certain things naturally ceased by limitation. Even these He did not abolish. The larger light that was manifested by His life and in His death, swallowed up the lesser light which shadowed His coming.

What Christ, however, *did abolish*, was the tradition and slavishness of men which had bound the people from exercising the freedom of their personal will and choice. He made men free. He destroyed sin. Not that He did away with any truth, or invalidated any of the teachings of the word of God. This the reader should bear in mind.

Paragraph 13.

(b) In every verse of Genesis one, wherever the term *God* is used, it is always in the plural form. No doubt there is a strong reason for this.

The singular is אֵל=*God*. For illustration, see Gen. 33 : 20. The plural, אֱלֹהִים=*Gods*. For example, see Ps. 82 : 6

Of the thirty times the word *God* is used in the first chapter of Genesis, in no case is the term used in the singular. We find the singular number used in other parts of Genesis, which shows clearly God could have used it here if he chose. But the very fact that the term is used in the plural form is proof positive that the Son was with the Father at this time in the creative work.

A statement from Paul, at this juncture, might be suggestive on this point. In writing to the Corinthians, he says:

" But if our gospel be hid, it is hid to them that are lost : in whom the god of this world hath blinded the minds of them which believe not, lest the light of the glorious gospel of Christ, *who is the image of God*, should shine unto them." 2 Cor. 4 : 3, 4.

Now in this connection, in verse six, he mentions the fact of the creation of light, as proof of the giving of light to the soul, in the face of Jesus Christ. It would seem then from this that Paul is carrying the minds of the people back to the first chapter of Genesis, where the record states that man was created in the image of God. But the text referred to in Gen. 1:26, plainly says that man was made in the image of אֱלֹהִים=*Gods;* and the *whole clause is in the plural* form. Here is the text in the original :

. . . וַיֹּאמֶר אֱלֹהִים נַעֲשֶׂה אָדָם בְּצַלְמֵנוּ כִּדְמוּתֵנוּ וְיִרְדּוּ. Literally translated: " And Gods said, let us make Adam in *our image*, according to *our likeness*, and they shall rule," etc. Thus we see that there was some other one associated with the Father when the first man was created ; and these personages had the *same image*, after which man was created. But the Apostle Paul says that Christ " is the image of God," and the " *express image* " of God. Heb. 1 : 3.

It is therefore conclusive that Christ was the person referred to here in Gen. 1 : 26; hence was with the Eternal in the creation of everything contained in the first chapter of Genesis. And this is the strong reason why Moses was inspired of God to use the term *E-lo-him*, in the first chapter, instead of the word *El*. Truly Moses did write of Him. John 5 46, 47.

Paragraph 20.

`(c) The Apostle Paul received his views and knowledge of Christ directly by revelation. The entire gospel was revealed to him by visions and revelations from the Lord. He, therefore, was thoroughly qualified to express the truth correctly. Gal. 1:11, 12; 2 Cor. 12:1–4.

Paragraph 21.

(*d*) It is generally supposed that the Jehovah of the Old Testament is applied directly, and only, to the Father. But this is not so. The Jehovah of the Old Testament is a term applied to the Son. For instance: In Gen. 12:1–4, Abraham was called of the Lord to leave his home, to go to a place where he should be told. The word *Lord* here is יְהֹוָה-*Jehovah.*

In Gen. 18:1, the *Lord* is also יְהֹוָה-*Jehovah.* But in Ex. 3:4, 6, 7, the term *Lord* in these texts is likewise יְהֹוָה-*Jehovah.* Thus the Jehovah in all of these texts is the one and the same person. The Savior, however, said to the Jews that "before Abraham was, I am." John 8:58. The word *I am*,-אֶהְיֶה is from the same word as Jehovah. Therefore the Jehovah of Abraham is the Christ of the New Testament. It was He that appeared to the Patriarch. The Jehovah of the Old Testament is God's title of His dear Son.

The objector, however, may say that in Ps. 110:1, the term יְהֹוָה-*Jehovah* is applied to the Father. For it is written: "Jehovah said unto my Lord, sit Thou at My right hand." נְאֻם יְהוָה לַאדֹנִי שֵׁב לִימִינִי Very true; but the Father has declared He has put His name in His Son, in the Angel of His presence. Ex. 23:20, 21. His name being Jehovah, this naturally would be the name of His Son.

Thus we again see that the Jehovah of Moses and the prophets is the title belonging to Christ. For in Isa. 43:11, it is written:

אָנֹכִי אָנֹכִי יְהוָה וְאֵין מִבַּלְעָדַי מוֹשִׁיעַ:

"I, even I, am Jehovah; and beside Me there is no Savior." By comparing this scripture with Acts 4:12, it is apparent it has reference to Jesus, the only Savior. It is certain that Jesus is the Jehovah.

Paragraph 26.

(*e*) The word *one* in this verse is the same as in the Hebrew אֶחָד-*echod.* There are two words in the Hebrew which mean one; though they have a similarity, yet they have a difference in meaning. These are אֶחָד-*echod*, יָחִיד-*yo-chid.* The word *e-chod*, translated *one*, expresses and contains the thought of unity. It frequently has the idea of at least *two*; but one in thought, action, expression. In Gen. 2:24, we read: "Therefore shall a man leave his father and his mother, and shall cleave unto his wife : .and they shall be *one* flesh." The last clause of this verse is as follows in the Hebrew : וְהָיוּ לְבָשָׂר אֶחָד; Literally translated,—" And they shall be to *one* flesh. In every respect they were to be one, two persons with *one* plan, one purpose.

The word יָחִיד-*yo-chid*, is used in the absolute sense of aloneness, singly, individually. Several such texts might be furnished; but the most pointed one in the Scripture is found in Abraham's experience, when commanded to offer Isaac. The Lord said : קַח נָא אֶת בִּנְךָ אֶת יְחִידְךָ;

" Take now, thy son, thine only, or only one son."

'This expression, however, is not used at any time when referring to God. The term is always אֶחָד-*e-chod*. For instance : " Hear, O Israel : the Lord our God is one Lord." אֶחָד;

Here again we have a strong proof of the presence of Christ with the Father, before the world was ; and as part of the Godhead.

CHAPTER X.

God's Purpose in Building the Sanctuary.

"For we know that if our earthly house of this tabernacle were dissolved, we have a building of God, an house not made with hands, eternal in the heavens." 2 Cor. 5 : 1.

THE LORD DESIROUS TO REVEAL HIS SALVATION.

SINCE the purpose of God with the Israelites was to make known to the world, as well as to them, His plans and wishes concerning His great salvation from sin through Jesus Christ, His only begotten Son, the Lord did all in His power[1] and wisdom to make this great truth so plain, simple, and clear that there could be no excuse [2] why every one could not know and understand His will. Therefore, soon after the exodus from Egypt, He commanded, through Moses, the building of the sanctuary upon a most elaborate and splendid scale,[3] which was designed to convey to their sight as well as to their intelligence some of the *visible* proofs of the glory of His Son, and to give them a clearer view of the salvation He was working out for a lost and sin-cursed world.

FIRST MENTION OF THE SANCTUARY.

2. After they crossed the Red Sea on dry land, Moses and the people sung the song of deliverance,[4] in which we find the following words :

"Thou shalt bring them in, and plant them in the mountain of Thine inheritance, in the place, O Lord, which Thou hast made for Thee to dwell in, in the sanctuary, O Lord, which *Thy hands* have established. Jehovah shall reign forever and ever." [5]

[1] Isa.5:4.　[2] Matt. 22:12; Rom. 1:20.　[3] Ex. 25–30.　[4] Ex. 15.　[5] Ex. 15:17, 18.

FURNITURE OF THE SANCTUARY.

THE PURPOSE OF THIS PROPHECY.

3. Here we have a great prophecy of a holy place which was prepared by the hands of God, into which these people were to be brought, in which God Himself was to dwell. There can be no question or doubt but what this prophecy had a double significance, and would have been completely fulfilled in these people who were delivered from Egypt, had they only been true and loyal to God.

4. In them the Lord designed to dwell in His fullness in this world; not only in a general way by dwelling in a tent; but by so completely taking possession of their lives, as to show them, and through them, the world, how the Messiah would be the dwelling-place of God, and how the Anointed One would dwell in the hearts of all humanity. If they had only been true to this desire of God, when the earthly sanctuary should have fulfilled its mission, God would have revealed to them the real sanctuary which He built with His own hands.[6] He would have placed it in this earth, and it would have been with them forever, and among them God would have personally reigned.[7] Both the type, the lesson, the antitype, would have all been fulfilled to them. This, no doubt, is all contained in this text.

A SPIRITUAL PEOPLE.

5. The Israelites were designed to be a spiritual people.[8] Everything that the Lord did for and through them was to be done by the Spirit. In other words, while they were in this world, they were not to be of it. Their minds,[9] their hearts, their deeds, were to be centered on heavenly things. They were to be led of the Spirit, to be taught by the Spirit, to eat in the Spirit, to drink of the Spirit, to walk in the Spirit, to be a truly and thoroughly spiritual people. For how could God reveal to the world the truth of the Messiah, only as He would be recognized as born of the Spirit?[10] The Deliverer must be

6 Heb. 8: 1, 2.   7 Deut. 26: 16–19.   8 Neh. 9: 20; 1 Cor. 10: 3, 4.
9 Isa. 26: 3.   10 John 3: 5, 6.

from heaven; His life must be a heavenly one. These people through whom He was to come must correctly represent Him. So the Lord intended to do for them everything by the power of the Spirit. This no doubt explains why the Lord gave them the manna and the water as He did. It is written:

MIRACULOUS PROVISION OF BREAD AND WATER.

"Then said the Lord unto Moses, Behold, I will rain bread *from heaven for you.*" [11]

"Though he had commanded the clouds from above, and opened the doors of heaven, and had rained down manna upon them to eat, and had given them of the *corn of heaven.* Man did eat angels' food: He sent them meat to the full." [12]

"And the Lord said unto Moses, Go on before the people, and take with thee of the elders of Israel; and thy rod, wherewith thou smotest the river, take in thine hand, and go. Behold, I will stand before thee there upon the rock in Horeb; and thou shalt smite the rock, and there shall come water out of it, that the people may drink." [13]

"Then Jesus said unto them, Verily, verily, I say unto you, Moses gave you not that bread from heaven; but My Father giveth you the true bread from heaven. . . . And Jesus said unto them, I am the bread of life: he that cometh to Me shall never hunger; and he that believeth on Me shall never thirst." [14]

"Moreover, brethren, I would not that ye should be ignorant, how that all our fathers were under the cloud, and all passed through the sea; and were all baptized unto Moses in the cloud and in the sea; and did all eat the same spiritual meat; and did all drink the same spiritual drink: for they drank of that spiritual Rock that followed [15] them: and that Rock was Christ." [16]

GOD STILL CARRYING OUT HIS PLAN.

6. However, the people soon murmured and rebelled,[17] and plainly manifested that they had not the Spirit in their hearts,[18] nor were they willing to be led in the ways of God. The Lord, nevertheless, continued to do all in His power to carry out His plan, to reveal to them His truth, to show unto them His grace and salvation: He still desired to have them reveal to the

[11] Ex. 16:4.   [12] Ps. 78:23-25.   [13] Ex. 17:5, 6.   [14] John 6:32-35.
[15] 1 Cor. 10:4; margin.   [16] 1 Cor. 10:1-4.   [17] Ex. 16:2,3; 18:23.
[18] Ps. 78:18.

world His purpose with them concerning the Messiah. To Moses then the Lord gave this commandment :

"Speak unto the children of Israel, that they bring Me an offering : of every man that giveth it willingly with his heart ye shall take My offering. . . . And let them make Me a sanctuary ; that I may dwell among them. According to all that I shew thee, after the pattern of the tabernacle, and the pattern of all the instruments thereof, even so shall ye make it." [19]

"And look that thou make them after their pattern, which was shewed thee in the mount." [20]

"And thou shalt rear up the tabernacle, according to the fashion thereof which was shewed thee in the mount." [21]

"Hollow with boards shalt thou make it : as it was shewed thee in the mount, so shall they make it." [22]

MOSES RECEIVING INSTRUCTION TO BUILD.

7. Moses had gone up to the mount to receive the decalogue,[23] the ten commandments, which God had personally spoken to the people in the hearing of them all.[24] Here he was with the Lord forty days and forty nights.[25] While in the presence of God, to him was revealed all these plans of God concerning the building of the sanctuary, and its appurtenances. One thing is very remarkable about these commands of the Lord to Moses in the construction of this sacred edifice ; that is, *everything* was to be made after a pattern.[26] It will be noticed in the scriptures quoted that God specifically points out to His servant that *everything* must be made according to this pattern.

GOD'S IDEAL SANCTUARY.

8. In other words, the Lord had an ideal ; this ideal He wanted worked out on the earth ; this ideal was to be of heavenly origin. Everything, therefore, connected therewith, must be made according to the purpose which God had in mind. All the vessels, all the instruments, all the garments, all the furniture,—everything must be carried out after God's own divine order.

[19] Ex. 25:2-9.   [20] Ex. 25:40.   [21] Ex. 26:30.   [22] Ex. 27:8.   [23] Ex. 24:12.
[24] Ex. 20:1-17.   [25] Ex. 24:18.   [26] Num. 8:4.

SOLOMON'S TEMPLE.

9. What was true of the sanctuary erected by the command of Moses, was equally true of the one that Solomon built. It will be remembered that David on one occasion had a strong desire to build a permanent residence for the ark of God, after it had been returned from the Philistines.[27] He finally expressed his wishes to Nathan the prophet, who encouraged him in his project. The Lord appeared, however, to the prophet the following night, and told him that this building should not be erected by David, but should be built by his son. David, however, desired very much to share in the blessing of this undertaking; therefore he collected a vast amount of wealth and material of every description, preparatory to Solomon's building the house.[28] The Lord saw that the longing of David to do this work was so intense, that He communicated to this faithful servant His plans of the building. And of these plans, David says:

"Then David gave to Solomon his son the pattern of the porch, and of the houses thereof, and of the upper chambers thereof, and of the inner parlors thereof, and of the place of the mercy-seat, and the pattern of all that he had by the Spirit, of the courts of the house of the Lord, . . . All this, said David, the Lord made me understand in writing by His hand upon me, even all the works of this pattern."[29]

AFTER GOD'S IDEAL.

10. We thus see that the Lord did the same way by David as He did by Moses—He revealed to David, though not while the latter was in the mount with Him in His presence, but by the Holy Spirit, all the details and working of this temple. Both, therefore, were of heavenly origin; both were planned by the Lord; both were after the divine order.

THE SANCTUARY A TYPE OR SHADOW.

11. It would seem from the expressions the Lord made to .Moses concerning the sanctuary, that not only did He show

[27] 2 Sam. 7: 1, 2.   [28] 1 Chron. 29: 1-5.   [29] 1 Chron. 28: 11-19.

him the mere patterns of the things He wanted built, but He must have had the *real things themselves* which Moses saw; and with those things as patterns from which Moses was to work, the objects on earth were to be made. That is to say, the Lord not only showed Moses merely patterns such as we would consider, but the very objects themselves from which he was to pattern the things for the sanctuary. In other words, the Lord showed Moses a real sanctuary in heaven, in the mount which God had there; and after which he was to build the one in the wilderness. This is evident from the text of Ex. 15:17, which was mentioned in the previous part of this chapter. Had the Israelites only been true, they would not only have had a typical sanctuary, but the real sanctuary which God Himself made would eventually have been revealed to them. For the sanctuary spoken of in the text just mentioned, was said to have been prepared by the hands of God Himself; whereas the one that was built by Moses was made by the hands of men.

12. That this earthly sanctuary was built after a real one, and was therefore but a shadow of one that God had actually Himself built, is clearly taught in the following scripture:

"Who serve unto the example and *shadow of heavenly things*, as Moses was admonished of God when he was about to make the tabernacle: for, See, saith He, that thou make all things according to the pattern shewed to thee in the mount." [30]

13. From this text we learn the following:

1. That the sanctuary and its services on earth were used as an example or illustration of the things that really are in heaven.

2. That the sanctuary and its services on earth were merely shadows of the things that are in heaven.

3. There could be no shadow, or illustration, or example of any object, if there were no object itself to cast the shadow. The very fact that the apostle says that the earthly sanctuary was a

[30] Heb. 8:5.

shadow, is in itself sufficient proof there must have been a substance. Since the apostle further says that this was a shadow
and an example of heavenly things, and since the matter under
consideration was the earthly sanctuary and its services, it very
naturally follows that the apostle is endeavoring to prove that
when the sanctuary was built by Moses, there must have been
a real sanctuary in heaven, which God showed to Moses and
after which Moses patterned.

THE HEAVENLY SANCTUARY.

14. That there really was a sanctuary in heaven is plainly
stated by the apostle in the first part of this chapter in Hebrews :

"Now of the things which we have spoken this is the sum : We have
such an high priest, who is set on the right hand of the throne of the
Majesty in the heavens ; a minister of the *sanctuary, and of the true tabernacle, which the Lord pitched and not man.*" [31]

15. And again :

"For Christ is not entered into *the holy places made with hands*, which
are *the figures of the true ;* but into heaven itself, now to appear in the
presence of God for us." [32]

"But Christ being come an high priest of good things to come, by a
greater and more perfect tabernacle, not made with hands, that is to say,
not of this building." [33]

16. Thus we see that both the shadow and the substance
was contained in that first promise mentioned in the fifteenth
chapter of Exodus, which the Lord would have fulfilled to them,
had they been obedient to his will. However, he sought to impress them with the truth by the objects contained in the
earthly tabernacle, built by the hands of men; and the way
they would appreciate this would be seen by their conduct
toward its services and worship.

THE PRACTICAL LESSON.

17. While we have seen that the sanctuary Moses was admonished to build was but a " figure," " example," " shadow,"

[31] Heb. 8:1, 2.   [32] Heb. 9:24.   [33] Heb. 9:11.

of the heavenly, and while we see that there was a real temple in heaven,[34] one that God Himself had built, both these were designed to teach the people of all times,—the Israelites at that time, and the people who should follow after,—a great, a wonderful, an extremely practical lesson. When God admonished Moses to build the sanctuary, He said it was to be a dwelling-place for Himself. But the Hebrew word, בְּתוֹכָם in Ex. 25 : 8, translated in the English, "amongst them," is a stronger expression than this. Literally translated the word, *Be-tho-com*, is "in their midst," or "*in them.*" Thus the tabernacle was to be a dwelling-house for God, a tabernacle for Himself, a place for Him to dwell in. But Solomom said at the dedication of the temple, that the mere building which he had builded, was not really the true dwelling-place of God. He says:

"But will God indeed dwell upon the earth? behold, the heaven and heaven of heavens cannot contain Thee; how much less this house that I have builded?"[35]

18. Then what was the practical lesson in it all that God was teaching the Israelites? What was the meaning of the temple? What was the real dwelling-place of God to be? The answer is given by many of the prophets; but Isaiah expresses it the most forcibly:

"For thus saith the high and lofty One that inhabiteth eternity, whose name is Holy; I dwell in the high and holy place, with *him* also that is of a contrite and humble spirit, to revive the spirit of the humble, and to revive the heart of the contrite ones."[36]

THE HEAVENLY TEMPLE.

19. Yes, it was the wish of God to make the human soul His dwelling-place, His temple, his sanctuary. But the sanctuary that was built on the earth was made after the heavenly pattern. Then the dwelling-place of God in the temple of the soul must, too, be made after the heavenly pattern. In other words, there must be a temple of heavenly origin, not made by the power of

[34] Rev. 11 : 19.   [35] 1 Kings 8 : 27.   [36] Isa. 57 : 15.

men, but made by the power of God, and after God's own ideal, which should be the pattern for all to follow.   Hence the Savior, when speaking to the Jews, after he had cast out the money-changers, who asked Him for a sign of His authority, from the temple, said :

" Destroy this temple, and in three days I will raise it up.   Then, said the Jews, Forty and six years was this temple [the one which Herod improved] in building, and wilt Thou rear it up in three days ? But He spake of the temple of his body." [37]

And the Apostle Paul, in speaking of the body of the Savior which He had when He came into the world, says :

" Wherefore when He [Christ] cometh into the world, He [Christ] saith, Sacrifice and offering Thou wouldest not, but a *body hast Thou* [the Father] *prepared Me* : . . By the which will we are sanctified through the offering of the *body* of Jesus Christ once for all." [38]

20. When the angel Gabriel came to Mary to tell her that she was to give birth to a child, in answer to her questions, he said :

" The Holy Ghost shall come upon thee, and the power of the Highest shall overshadow thee : therefore, also that holy thing which shall be born of thee shall be called the Son of God." [39]

Jesus Himself said :

" I *came down from heaven*, not to do Mine own will, but the will of Him that sent Me." [40]

And the Apostle Peter says :

" For even hereunto were ye called : because Christ also suffered for us, leaving us an *example*, that ye should follow His steps." [41]

21. Thus we have the lesson that God wanted to teach the Israelites, and through them all people, of the sanctuary. It was to represent to them that as God would dwell in that building by his own holy Shekinah, thus glorifying all their services, so He desired to dwell in their hearts, to glorify their lives.   But this earthly building was but an illustration of the one which

[37] John 2: 19–21.   [38] Heb. 10: 5–10.   [39] Luke 1: 35.   [40] John 6: 38.   [41] 1 Peter 2: 21

was built in the heavens; hence the glory of this earthly was but a reflection of the greater glory shed forth by the Shekinah in the heavenly. Yet both these temples were but to teach the lesson that Jehovah wished to dwell in the temple of the human soul, and fill it with the glory of His own divine Spirit. But there must be an Heavenly-human Temple, which should be a Pattern or example for all the temples that abide on the earth. So Jesus Christ, the Lord from Heaven, the second Adam, or Man, had " prepared " by the Father, a special body fitted for Him, which was filled without measure with the Holy Ghost, the Shekinah of God; [42] and this being of His was the real Temple for the indwelling of God's presence, after which every temple must be patterned. *He* is the ideal; *He* is the real Temple: *He* is the practical Lesson of the sanctuary, and of the dwelling-place of God.

THE EARTHLY TEMPLES.

22. What then was true of this heavenly Temple must be true of the earthly also. These earthly temples of men are, as it were, shadows of the heavenly; nevertheless they are to be real dwelling-places for the indwelling of the Holy Spirit, the glory of God, that God might fully dwell in the heart through Jesus Christ. So the Apostle Paul just takes this figure of the sanctuary and of the temple, and applies it to the people of God. He says:

" Know ye not that ye are the temple of God, and that the Spirit of God dwelleth in you? If any man defile the temple of God, him shall God destroy; for the temple of God is holy, *which temple ye are.*" [43]

" What ? Know ye not that your body is the temple of the Holy Ghost, which is in you, which ye have of God, and ye are not your own ? "

" And what agreement hath the temple of God with idols? *for ye are the temple of the living God;* as God hath said, *I will dwell in them and walk in them ;* and I will be their God, and they shall be My people." [44]

If the reader will notice some of the texts from which the

[42] John 3:34.   [43] 1 Cor. 3:16, 17.   [44] 1 Cor. 6:19; 2 Cor. 6:16.

apostle quotes, he will observe that the sanctuary of Israel is what is referred to. (*a*)

23. The Apostle Peter also speaks on this same point:

"Knowing that shortly I must put off *this my tabernacle*, even as our Lord Jesus Christ hath showed me." [45]

And when the Lord Jesus showed it to him it is recorded as follows:

"Verily, verily, I say unto *thee*, When *thou* wast young, *thou* girdedst thyself, and walkedst whither *thou* wouldest: but when *thou* shalt be old, *thou* shalt stretch forth *thy* hands, and another shall gird *thee*, and *carry thee* whither *thou* wouldest not. This spake He, signifying by what death he should glorify God." [46]

GOD'S PURPOSE IN THE SANCTUARY.

24. Thus the purpose of God in having the sanctuary built for the children of Israel was ever to keep before them Jesus Christ, the true Temple of God. Every time the pillar of cloud by day and the pillar of fire by night would lead and guide them, they were to see in this the leading of the Spirit of the Lord Jesus, their Messiah, their Deliverer. As He was to be the dwelling-place of the glory of God, as His life was to be the outshining of the face of God,[47] by their continually looking at Him through these objects, their own lives would be temples for the Shekinah, the Holy Ghost, to dwell in. They, too, would be led of God. Thus they would constantly be illustrating to the world the one grand truth of the Messiah, the Christ, the Deliverer, the Anointed of God; and they would become His personal representatives, by carrying out in their lives these grand truths and illustrations which God gave to them. Oh what exalted privileges the Lord gave the Israelites; what they might have enjoyed and known and heralded to the world, if they had only seen Him, the Deliverer from all their iniquities and bondage of sin! What pathos must have been mingled with

[45] 2 Peter 1: 14.   [46] John 21: 18, 19.   [47] 2 Cor. 3: 18; 4: 6; Heb. 1: 3.

THE TABERNACLE AND COURT.

these statements of the Lord, as He contemplated what Israel might have been :

" O that thou hadst hearkened to My commandments! then had thy peace been as a river, and thy righteousness as the waves of the sea! Thy seed also had been as the sand, . . ."[48]

" O that My people had hearkened unto Me, and Israel had walked in My ways! I should soon have subdued their enemies, and turned My hand against their adversaries. The haters of the Lord should have submitted themselves unto Him: but their time should have endured forever."[49]

THE WRONG CONCEPTION OF THE SANCTUARY.

25. Instead of the Jews seeing all this in the temple, in the object of its erection, in the presence of the Shekinah, in the pillar of cloud by day and the pillar of fire by night, they looked upon the material building, the outward grandeur and beauty, priding themselves that they were more favored than any other people, because *they* had a temple, and others did not. As the Prophet Jeremiah says of them :

" Trust ye not in lying words, saying, The temple of the Lord, the temple of the Lord, the temple of the Lord, are these."[50]

26. The temple had been defiled for centuries ; the symbol had lost its meaning to them ; the life had departed from the form ; the shadow had become to them the real substance. Or, as it was in the days of Christ, the gold was of greater value than the altar.[51] The outward stones were more highly prized than *the Lesson* who was with them ; and the size, and dimension of the building were of greater importance than the truth it taught. Thus in the Mishna, we find no less than four chapters in the tract, Middoth, on the dimensions of the temple. Many pages filled with masses of matter, simply discussing details of size, of space, of structure.

ALWAYS HAVING WITNESS.

27. Nevertheless God left not Himself without witness, as to the meaning of these things. Moses knew the true import

48 Isa. 48: 18.　　49 Ps. 81: 13–15.　　50 Jer. 7: 4.　　51 Matt. 23: 16.

of the sanctuary, Aaron and many of the people of God in that day, as well as a goodly number all through the ages. Isaiah, Jeremiah, and other men of God kept the truth alive, till the true Temple of God appeared direct from heaven, filled unutterably full of the Holy Ghost, the Shekinah of God. He was ever led by the pillar of cloud by day, and by the pillar of fire by night, the Holy Spirit; for Jesus said, that the Father would never leave Him alone; He was always with Him.[52] He would always and constantly guide Him. He would ever glorify His life.

GOD'S SPARING MERCY TILL HIS PLAN WAS FULFILLED.

28. The Lord bore with the Israelites for centuries, seeking to teach them the real meaning of the tabernacle, till at last there was no remedy.[53] Then they were sent into Babylonian captivity for seventy years;[54] their temple was reduced to ashes.[55] However, they returned after that period and rebuilt the temple;[56] but many of the objects which were in the first temple, and in the sanctuary in the wilderness, were not in this last temple, such as the Shekinah over the mercy-seat, the Urim and Thummim, the Spirit of Prophecy, (b) the Ark, and the Ten Commandments.

29. Nevertheless, the Lord said through the prophet that the glory of the latter house would be greater than the glory of the former house.[57] How could this be, when many who beheld the second wept because of its inferiority when compared with Solomon's?"[58] The *practical Lesson* that the sanctuary was to teach for nearly fifteen hundred years, the Temple of God, the Messiah, the Deliverer, would *personally appear* in the flesh;[59] and *then* they should see, in all its fullness worked out, what should have been observed all through these centuries. The Temple was glorified, God was glorified in His Temple. Jesus

---

[52] John 8:29.   [53] 2 Chron. 36:14-16.   [54] Jer. 29:10.   [55] 2 Chron. 36:17-20.
[56] Ezra 1:2; 6:7.   [57] Haggai 2:7-9.   [58] Ezra 3:12.
[59] Mal. 3:1-3.

learned and taught the lesson of the sanctuary. " As He is, so are we, in this world." [60]

[60] 1 John 4 : 17.

EXPLANATORY NOTES.

Paragraph 22.

(*a*). By reading Ex. 29 : 45, and Lev. 26 : 12, and comparing these with 2 Cor. 6 : 16, the reader will see that the apostle is alluding to the earthly sanctuary. In both the places the context states that God would dwell among the children of Israel in the tabernacle that had been established. But the words translated, " among," in both the verses referred to, are in the Hebrew בְּתוֹכְכֶם :בְּתוֹךְ=*Be-thoc, Be-thoc-cem*, literally, *in them.* That is, as the glory of the Shekinah dwelt *in* the sanctuary, so the glory and character of God would dwell in the people, and glorify their lives. This, evidently the people did not understand, even as they did not understand what Jesus meant when He spoke of raising the temple of His body. His own disciples did not understand this spiritual truth when He told the Jews ; and they did not comprehend it, until after His resurrection. See John 2 : 19–22.

Paul, however, understood clearly the meaning of all these things, and realized its application to the human heart.

Paragraph 28.

(*b*) The last of the Old Testament prophets was Malachi. He prophesied about B. C. 400. From that time onward the Jews say that the voice of the prophet was no more heard in their midst. And we have no record of any until we read the New Testament, where we find that Anna and Simeon both exercised the gift. But the Jews refused to believe that God was still speaking through prophets.

How frequently it is said at the present time that these gifts were in the early church, with Christ and the early Apostles ; but they long have ceased, and God does not talk thus to people at the present time. But if we read the word of the Lord, we find that God said these gifts were placed in the church of Christ, and must remain there until His church has been perfected, and till He comes. Would it not then be well for the church of to-day, to believe what God says, instead of accepting popular ideas of men, contrary to the word of the Lord ? See Acts 2 : 16–18 ; Acts 13 : 1 ; 1 Cor. 12 : 28 ; Eph. 4 : 8–13 ; Rev. 12 : 17 ; 19 : 10 ; 1 Cor. 1 : 1, 2, 6–8.

CHAPTER XI.

Why the Law was Given on Sinai.

"Thou camest down also upon Mount Sinai, and spakest with them from heaven, and gavest them right judgments, and true laws, good statutes and commandments." Neh. 9 :13.

BEFORE we continue the subject of the sanctuary, its sections, its ministrations, its feasts, its priesthood, it will be in place to ascertain some of the real causes that led to the building of it. This will necessitate a consideration of the giving of the decalogue on Sinai. The foundation truth of the temple service, we have already seen is Christ. This whole plan was to present the Messiah to the people, and always keep Him and His work before their eyes. This is no doubt the real thought that Paul had in view, when he made the following statement :

"For Christ is the end of the law for righteousness to every one that believeth." [1]

Everything in the law, in one form or another, was but a means in the hands of God toward a great end, and that *end* or *object* was Christ. He was to be seen through everything; He was the central object of all plans and purposes. "It pleased the Father that in Him should all fullness dwell." [2]

THE REAL NEED OF CHRIST.

2. The question, therefore, would naturally arise, What was the cause that should lead people to need a Christ, a Messiah, a Redeemer, a Deliverer? The answer very readily comes to hand,—Sin. Adam sinned; through him the whole world was involved in ruin.

[1] Rom. 10:4.   [2] Col. 1:19.

" Wherefore, as by one man sin entered into the world, and death by sin ; and so death passed upon all men, for that all have sinned." (Margin, in whom all have sinned.) [3]

" The wages of sin is death ; but the gift of God is eternal life through Jesus Christ our Lord." [4]

" For all have sinned, and come short of the glory of God." [5]

The whole world being involved in sin, the whole needed deliverance from sin and its terrible consequences. Hence we read :

" For God so loved the world, that He gave His only begotten Son, that whosoever believeth in Him should not perish but have everlasting life." [6]

GOD'S DEFINITION OF SIN.

3. It might be well, however, to inquire, What is sin ? What is the biblical definition of it? We find the answer in the following language :

" Whosoever committeth sin transgresseth also the law : for *sin is the transgression of the law.*" [7]

" Therefore, by the deeds of the law there shall no flesh be justified in His sight : for by the law is the knowledge of sin." [8]

" Because the law worketh wrath : for where *no law is, there is no transgression.*" [9]

"For until the law, sin was in the world : but *sin is not imputed where there is no law.*" [10]

" Nay, I had not known sin, but by the law."

It is evident, therefore, that God's definition of sin *is the transgression of the law*, and without transgressing the law there can be no sin.

THE LAW DEFINES SIN.

4. The thought which naturally comes to the mind next is, Which law is it that defines sin ? and which was it that man had transgressed? The Apostles Paul and James answer the question :

" What shall we say then ? Is the law sin ? God forbid. Nay, I had

[3] Rom. 5: 12.   [4] Rom. 6: 23.   [5] Rom. 3: 23.   [6] John 3: 16.   [7] 1 John 3: 4.
[8] Rom. 3: 20.   [9] Rom. 4: 15.   [10] Rom. 5: 13.

not known sin but by the law : for I had not known lust, except the *law had said, ' Thou shalt not covet.'* " [11]

" But if ye have respect to persons, ye commit sin, and are convinced of the law as transgressors. For whosoever shall keep the whole law, and yet offend in one point, he is guilty of all. For He [margin, that law] which said, Do not commit adultery, said also, Do not kill. Now if thou commit no adultery, yet if thou kill, *thou art become a transgressor of the law.*" [12]

" Now we know that what things soever the law saith, it saith to them who are under the law : that every mouth may be stopped, and all the world may become guilty before God." [13]

From these texts we learn that the law which points out sin, and the violation of which was the cause of the downfall of Adam, and through him the entire human race, is what is generally known as the decalogue, the ten commandments, the law of God, the moral law.

WHO FIRST KNEW THE MORAL LAW.

5. It may be said, however, that *Adam* did not know this law, neither had he ever received it. In specific detail we have no record of the fact; but it is evident from the scriptures already quoted that he must have been acquainted with it. In addition to the evidence given, we quote the following from the Prophet Isaiah :

" Thy *first father* hath sinned, and thy teachers have transgressed against Me." [14]

From the inspired definitions already cited, we must conclude that, though not all of the details of the commands which were given to Adam were recorded, he knew them nevertheless. (*a*) Even the Talmud specifies certain commands that Adam had received, which certainly shows that there was a general belief among the Israelites that Adam had a knowledge of God's law.

" Concerning six things the first Adam was commanded—against idolatry, against blasphemy, against murder, against adultery, against robbery, and concerning the administration of judgment. Although we have these things given to us *only* through Moses our Master orally, and reason

[11] Rom. 7 : 7.   [12] James 2 : 9–11.   [13] Rom. 3 : 19.   [14] Isa. 43 : 27.

naturally leans that way, yet from the direct words of the law, it doth not appear that they were commanded."—*Laws of Kings, chapter 9, section 1.*

NO LAW, NO SIN.

6. Since sin is the transgression of the law, and where there is no sin there is no transgression, and only by the law is the knowledge of sin, it is evident that before the Israelites could appreciate the work of salvation as revealed in the sanctuary and in its ministrations, they must know and understand the nature and consequences of sin. Therefore it was necessary upon the part of God to proclaim amid the awful thunders of Sinai His law, His great detector and informer of sin.

THE PEOPLE LOST THE KNOWLEDGE OF GOD.

7. During the sojourn of the Israelites in Egyptian bondage, they largely lost sight of the knowledge of God and of His law; in their constant mingling with heathenism and idolatry they lost almost all the knowledge of the true God and of his laws, which had been entrusted to them. In fact, God said that this was one of the reasons why He brought them forth from Egypt:

" He brought them forth also with silver and gold: and there was not one feeble person among their tribes. Egypt was glad when they departed: for the fear of them fell upon them. . . . And He brought forth His people with joy, and His chosen with gladness: . . . That they might *observe His statutes, and keep His laws.* Praise ye the Lord." [15]

EGYPT A TYPE OF SIN; THE EXODE, OF ITS DELIVERANCE.

8. The Israelites after their exode had a degree of appreciation of their deliverance from the physical servitude from which God had delivered them. But with God this mere physical deliverance was a minor matter; there was a deliverance which the people needed infinitely greater than the freedom from Egyptian servitude. This was the deliverance from sin, or from spiritual Egypt. The Lord plainly says there is a spiritual Egypt as well as a literal one.

[15] Ps. 105:37–45.

" And their dead bodies shall lie in the street of the great city, which spiritually is called Sodom and Egypt." [16]

Had the Israelites realized their need of a Savior from sin, there never would have been that continuous murmuring among them that always existed.[17]   For they would have appreciated the Lord and His salvation, because of His constant power manifested in their behalf.   But simply regarding their help from God as mere temporal benefits, when everything did not come just as they wished, and instantly at that, they were all ready to murmur.   Therefore the necessity on the part of God to give them His law in order that they might see the sinfulness of their sins, and thus learn to appreciate the Lord as their Deliverer from sin, as well as their Friend in time of physical necessities.

THEY MIGHT HAVE KNOWN THE LAWS BEFORE SINAI.

9. That they might have known God's law and commandments before they were given on Mount Sinai, is evident from what we read in the first part of the Pentateuch before the decalogue was given.   We will here enumerate some of them for the benefit of the reader; but before doing this, we wish to notice what the Lord said of Abraham :

" Because that Abraham obeyed my voice, and kept my charge, my commandments, my statutes, and my laws." [18]

It is therefore evident that God must have given Abraham laws, commandments, and statutes, which were well known to the Patriarch, and which he kept.

10. Concerning the commands of God which were known and in operation before the decalogue was given on Sinai we have the following record:

THE FIRST COMMANDMENT.

" Then Jacob said unto his household, and to all that were with him, Put away the *strange gods* that are among you, and be clean, and change

[16] Rev. 11 : 8.   [17] Ex. 15 : 23, 24 ; 16 : 2, 3 ; 17 : 2, 3 ; Ps. 78 : 17, 40, 56.
[18] Gen. 26 : 5 ; 18 : 19.

your garments:" "And they gave unto Jacob all the *strange gods* which were in their hand, and all their earrings which were in their ears; and Jacob hid them under the oak which was by Shechem."[19]

"And Joshua said unto all the people, Thus saith the Lord God of Israel, Your fathers dwelt on the other side of the flood in old time, even Terah, the father of Abraham, and the father of Nachor: and *they served other gods*."[20]

Now if this command on Mount Sinai was its first introduction, how then does it appear that they were apprised of it at the time of the flood, and in the days of Jacob? Moreover, how could it have been wrong for them to have other gods, if there were no law which forbade such things? And where there is no law, there is no transgression.[21] It is evident, however, that Jacob regarded it a sin to have strange gods in the dwellings of his family. This then being true, it naturally follows that he must have been informed of the fact and must have known the sinfulness of violating the first commandment of the decalogue, which was afterwards given to the children of Israel on Sinai.

THE SECOND COMMANDMENT.

"And Laban went to shear his sheep: and Rachel had stolen the *images* that were her father's. . . . Now Rachel had taken the *images*, and put them in the camel's furniture, and sat upon them."[22]

We see then that Laban was a violator of this second precept by having images; for if there had been no precept against them why should his daughter have them, that her father might not worship them. It is evident from the history of Laban that he was not a follower of the true God; hence he was an idolator. He violated God's law and served and worshiped images. We can see then that the second commandment was known at this time.

THE THIRD COMMANDMENT.

11. This commandment of the decalogue warns against profanity, the taking of the name of God in vain. We know from

[19] Gen. 35: 2-4.   [20] Josh. 24: 2.   [21] Rom. 4: 15.   [22] Gen. 31: 19-34.

the experience of the antediluvians that they were a very profane people, as through their conduct the earth was literally
teeming with violence.[23] But we have the record of at least
one person who violated this commandment, and who in the
Scripture is called a *profane person :*

"And Jacob said, Sell me this day thy birthright. And Esau said,
Behold, I am at the point to die : and what profit shall this birthright do
to me ? And Jacob said, Swear to me this day ; and he sware unto him ;
and he sold his birthright unto Jacob." [24]

And the Apostle Paul, in commenting on this experience of
Esau says :

" Lest there be any fornicator, or *profane person*, as Esau." [25]

As a result of his course of conduct, he failed to get the
blessing of God, though he sought it with many tears.[26] Surely
he must have known the terrible sin of violating the third commandment; for sin is not imputed where there is no law.   And
since he could find no favor, because of this wicked course of
his, it is evident the sin of that blasphemous conduct must have
been very great.

THE FOURTH COMMANDMENT.

12. This commandment, as all are aware, is concerning the
Sabbath day, the seventh day of the week.   It is often said that
this Sabbath day was given to the Jews, hence it is Jewish.   But
we will observe that, according to the teachings of Moses, this
institution was in existence before there was a Jew :

"And it came to pass, that on the sixth day they gathered twice as
much bread, two omers for one man : and all the rulers of the congregation came and told Moses.   And he said unto them, this is that *which the
Lord hath said*, To-morrow is the rest of the holy Sabbath unto the Lord.
. . And Moses said, Eat that to-day : for to-day is a Sabbath unto
the Lord : to-day ye shall not find it in the field.   Six days ye shall gather
it ; but on the *seventh day, which is the Sabbath*, in it there shall be none.
And it came to pass that there went out some of the people on the seventh
day for to gather, and they found none.   And the Lord said unto Moses,

[23] Gen. 6 : 5.   [24] Gen. 25 : 31–33.   [25] Heb. 12 : 16.   [26] Heb. 12 : 17.

The Ten Commandments.

The First.

I am the Lord thy God, which have brought thee out of the land of Egypt, out of the house of bondage. Thou shalt have no other gods before Me.

The Second.

Thou shalt not make unto thee any graven image, or any likeness of anything that is in the heaven above, or that is in the earth beneath, or that is in the water under the earth: thou shalt not bow down thyself to them, nor serve them: for I the Lord thy God am a jealous God, visiting the iniquity of the fathers upon the children unto the third and fourth generation of them that hate Me; and showing mercy unto thousands of them that love Me, and keep My commandments.

The Third.

Thou shalt not take the name of the Lord thy God in vain: for the Lord will not hold him guiltless that taketh His name in vain.

The Fourth.

Remember the Sabbath day, to keep it holy. Six days shalt thou labor, and do all thy work: but the seventh day is the Sabbath of the Lord thy God: in it thou shalt not do any work, thou, nor thy son, nor thy daughter, thy manservant, nor thy maidservant, nor thy cattle, nor thy stranger that is within thy gates: for in six days the Lord made heaven and earth, the sea, and all that in them is, and rested the seventh day: wherefore the Lord blessed the Sabbath day, and hallowed it.

The Fifth.

Honor thy father and thy mother: that thy days may be long upon the land which the Lord thy God giveth thee.

The Sixth.

Thou shalt not kill.

The Seventh.

Thou shalt not commit adultery.

The Eighth.

Thou shalt not steal.

The Ninth.

Thou shalt not bear false witness against thy neighbor.

The Tenth.

Thou shalt not covet thy neighbor's house, thou shalt not covet thy neighbor's wife, nor his manservant, nor his maidservant, nor his ox, nor his ass, nor anything that is thy neighbor's.

how long refuse ye to keep My commandments and My laws? See, for that the Lord hath given you the Sabbath, therefore He giveth you on the sixth day the bread of two days; abide ye every man in his place, let no man go out of his place on the seventh day." [27]

From these texts we learn that the Sabbath at this time was not a new institution; neither *could* it have been new three months after when given on Mount Sinai. The Lord here repeats the statement that the people *refuse to obey* His commandments and laws. So it is evident the people must have had these laws, and certainly must have known them. How could the Lord charge them with violating His law, if they had never heard anything about it? But God says that He had already told them, and they were apprised of it. Is there any command previously given to this effect? We find its record in the second chapter of the Bible, and several times in Exodus. (*b*) At creation God made the Sabbatic institution.[28] He gave it to Adam, the first man, the father of the race. From him it was to be handed down to all his posterity, to be guarded sacredly as a treasure from heaven. Jesus says this same thing to the people:

" The Sabbath was made for man." [29]

Certainly this must have included Adam, the first man. We thus see clearly that this command was known to the people before it was proclaimed amid the thunders of Sinai.

THE FIFTH COMMANDMENT.

13. This commandment, as every one knows, must have been in force before the giving of the law at Sinai; or how could the conduct of Jacob's sons in selling Joseph to the Midianites, be considered as sinful against their father?[30] They abused their brother; they falsified to their father;[31] they certainly failed to give honor to their parents. They knew it was wrong at the very time they were doing it; but because of their

---

[27] Ex. 16: 22-29.   [28] Gen. 2: 1-3.   [29] Mark 2: 27.
[30] Gen. 37: 27, 28.   [31] Gen. 37: 32, 33.

JOSEPH'S BROTHERS DECEIVE THEIR FATHER.

jealousy they sold him.[32]   If there were no law against disobedience to parents ; if there were no command that parents should
be respecɩed, then certainly these sons of Jacob had committed
no sin against their father, even though they had wronged their
brother.   For where no law is, there is no transgression. But
they knew it was wrong ; the Bible speaks of it as sinful ;[33] the
results show that their course was an evil one.

THE SIXTH COMMANDMENT.

14. Very little needs to be said touching the enforcement of
this commandment before the days of Mount Sinai.   The first
family violated this command in its literal language.   Cain slew
his brother, the book of Genesis tells us.[34]   John says he killed
his brother.[35]   Cain was a murderer.   The Lord accused him
of this deed,[36] and for it he was punished.   Cain himself said
that his punishment was greater than he could bear.[37]

15. If, however, there were no law against murder till the
time this precept was announced from the summit of the smok-
ing mountain, why was Cain accused of its violation, and punished for killing ?   Where there is no law, there is no transgression.   By the law is the knowledge of sin.   It is thus clear that
this commandment was known and violated.   The Israelites
might have known all this.   They knew the record ; it was
handed down from father to son ; the history of the world was
traced from one family to another.

THE SEVENTH COMMANDMENT.

16. We might give much proof of the knowledge of this command, and its violation as being sin.[38]   Just one case to the
point, and this must suffice.   When Joseph was again and again
tempted by his mistress to betray the sacred trust of his master,
he said.

" How then can I do this great wickedness, and *sin against God ?* "[39]

He evidently knew that the law against adultery was in

[32] Gen. 37 : 4, 8, 11.   [33] Gen. 50 : 16–20 ; Acts 7 : 9.   [34] Gen. 4 : 8.   [35] 1 John 3 : 12.
[36] Gen. 4 : 10, 11.   [37] Gen. 4 : 13.   [38] Gen. 34 : 1, 2, 31.   [39] Gen. 39 : 9.

force; and should he commit that terrible wickedness he was aware that it would be sinning against God. But sin is the transgression of the law; and the law which declares sin is generally known as the decalogue. Joseph therefore must have known this fact; the Israelites, who knew all about this experience of Joseph, might have known this, too, and have found deliverance from this sin, even as Joseph did.

THE EIGHTH, NINTH, AND TENTH COMMANDMENTS.

17. These three commands were all in force, as they were violated by Joseph's brothers; by Jacob, when he stole the blessing; by Abraham, when he twice falsified concerning his wife.

GOD AWAKENING THE PEOPLE.

18. Thus we have shown that every one of the ten commandments must have been *and was in force*, before God gave them to the Israelites. This knowledge, however, the people lost; hence, in order to awaken their consciences to what sin is, to reveal to them their sinful course of conduct, and to prepare them for the salvation there was to be revealed to them in the services and ministrations of the sanctuary, He declared to them the basis of His government,—His own wonderful law. When they once knew this and then violated it, they would be liable to its penalty,—death. Then realizing their lost and undone condition without any Deliverer from the consequences of their guilt, God could reveal to them the truths of the Messiah and of the great salvation which He should give to them, as portrayed in the work of the sanctuary. Every part of this service would teach them some phase of healing from sin; in everything they had presented to them, they would find deliverance from the bondage of evil. They must see the awfulness of sin, then they would have the remedy, when they realized they had committed trespass against the Lord.

WHAT THE LAW WAS.

19. However, the Israelites never saw what there was even

in the law. When God spake amid the awful thunders of Sinai His fiery law in the hearing of all the multitudes, the people begged that God would refrain from talking to them, but that He would let Moses talk with them, lest they should die.[40] The reason that this law made them feel so fearful and spoke only condemnation, was because of the sinful state of their own hearts.[41] This, however, was not so with Moses. He had no fears; he had no misgivings. He *wanted* God to speak, because it was to Him the voice of sweetness and mercy. Every precept he heard was filled with blessing; every statement that was made, meant life and salvation. What to the people was condemnation, to Moses was life and salvation. (*c*) The reason was, because Moses saw the Messiah, the Christ, even in the giving of the law, (*d*) as a merciful and loving Savior toward His people; the masses, with the consciousness of sins committed, felt the guilt and condemnation in everything that was said. This no doubt will assist in a better understanding of those verses in the third chapter of Second Corinthians. To the people it was merely the letter; therefore it meant death. And in reality would have killed them in a little while, for while they promised to heed the precepts the Lord gave,[42] in less than forty days they broke the law and should have died.[43] But Moses interposed, and most of them were saved.[44]

THE LAW WAS GLORY TO MOSES.

20. To Moses it was glory, it was the shining of his face as a result of that glory;[45] to the people it was darkness and condemnation so that they even could not look at Moses.[46] The trouble lay in the heart. It was dark; it was blinded.[47] They could not, therefore, see any light nor glory, but only condemnation and death. The law itself, however, was all right.[48]

21. When after a short period, they violated their promise and realized that they ought to die, the Lord then prepared

[40] Ex. 20: 19; Deut. 18: 16–18. [41] Neh. 9: 13–17. [42] Ex. 19: 4, 5, 8; 24: 3.
[43] Ex. 32: 9–14. [44] Ex. 32: 25–29. [45] Ex. 34: 29–35. [46] 2 Cor. 3: 7.
[47] 2 Cor. 3: 14–16. [48] Rom. 7: 10–14.

Moses to impart to them the instruction He gave him in the mount for the building of the sanctuary. Salvation was then in place for them. They then could have a better appreciation of it, as they realized what sin was, a result of transgressing the law of God.

THE LAW PROPERLY UNDERSTOOD.

22. Even in the law, if the people had only understood it, they could have seen the Christ, the Savior. It is a fact that there is not one attribute that the Bible gives to the law of God, but what is also inherent in Jesus Christ. He was simply the law of God in the flesh.[49] We shall now consider some of the attributes of God's law, and compare them with the character of Christ. Thus we shall see that if the law of God were only rightly understood by the people then, by their successors later, and even by the people of the present day, they would see some wonderful light and revelation in the life and character of Jesus Christ. David's words would then be appreciated : " How love I Thy law ! it is my meditation all the day."[50]

23. THE LAW OF GOD.   THE CHARACTER OF CHRIST.

1. Love.[51]	1. Love.[65]
2. Truth.[52]	2. Truth.[66]
3. Delight.[53]	3. Delight.[67]
4. Perfect.[54]	4. Perfect.[68]
5. Sure.[55]	5. Sure.[69]
6. Righteous.[56]	6. Righteous.[70]
7. Eternal.[57] (e)	7. Eternal.[71]
8. Spiritual.[58]	8. Spiritual.[72]
9. Peace.[59]	9. Peace.[73]
10. Holy.[60]	10. Holy.[74]

[49] Rom. 8: 3, 4.   [50] Ps. 119:97.   [51] Ps. 119:97.   [52] Ps. 119:142.
[53] Ps. 1:1, 2; Rom. 7:22:   Ps. 119:77, 92, 143.   [54] Ps. 19:7.   [55] Ps. 111:7.
[56] Ps. 19:9; 119:172.   [57] Ps. 119:89.   [58] Rom. 7:14; 8:2.   [59] Ps. 119:165.
[60] Rom. 7:12.   [65] Rom. 8:35, 39.   [66] John 14:6.   [67] Isa. 42:1.   [68] Heb. 2:10; 5:9.
[69] Heb. 7:22.   [70] 1 John 2:1.   [71] 1 John 5:11.   [72] 1 Cor. 15:45, 46.
[73] Eph. 2:14.   [74] Acts 4:27.

11. Unchangeable.[61]	11. Unchangeable.[75]
12. Liberty.[62]	12. Liberty.[76]
13. Good.[63]	13. Good.[77]
14. Just.[64]	14. Just.[78]

From this we see that the law of God is simply an expression of the character of Jesus Christ. Hence David prophesied of Him, through the Spirit:

"I delight to do Thy will, O My God: yea, *Thy law is within My heart.*" [79].

CHRIST'S SOLE OBJECT.

24. Since out of the heart are the issues of life,[80] the one great vital issue of the life of Christ when on earth, was simply to reveal to the Jews and to the world, the life principles of the law of God. He was the law of God in action. When the people saw only letter, they could and should have observed life. This was why the Lord built the Israelites the sanctuary that the principles of the law might be seen in the light of the life of Christ, in all the offerings they offered up, which were symbolizing the Christ, the Son of the living God.

ISRAEL DID NOT SEE THE GREAT TRUTH.

25. Israel did not see these grand truths in the giving of the law, nor in the law itself. Instead of learning the great lessons God wished to teach the world through them, they considered themselves as the most favored people on earth, because to them were entrusted these sacred oracles. Then they spent much of their time in after years elaborating upon the circumstances connected therewith. Thus many traditions have been written commenting upon the giving of the law, and of the peculiar advantages to them in receiving it.

DEFINITION OF THE END OF THE LAW.

26. Can we then not see the force of that grand truth, as expressed by Paul:

[61] Ps. 89:34.   [62] James 2: 10-12.   [63] Rom 7: 12.   [64] Rom. 7:12.   [75] Heb. 13: 8.   [76] 2 Cor. 3: 17.   [77] John 10:11, 14.   [78] Acts 3: 14.   [79] Ps. 40: 8; Heb. 10:7.   [80] Prov. 4: 23.

" Christ is the *end of the law* for righteousness to every one that believeth." [81]

Yes, *Christ is the End* in every sense of the word. Not that in Him the law is abolished or done away; but under the illumination of the blessed Spirit, in whichever form we find it, the law is a means to the great End or Purpose, which is Christ.

THE PRESENT LESSON.

27. Is there not then in all this a great lesson to be learned by the people living to-day? How great a need there is of seeing Christ in all the truths of the Bible. The law has not been nullified through Christ, as Antinomianism seeks to teach; the law of God to-day shows the beauty of Christ and of His character, the need of the complete fulfillment of the sanctuary service, the gospel of Christ, the remedy for sin. If there were no law to-day, there would surely be no need of a gospel. Christ died for sin; [82] to take away its transgression. He was manifested to take away sin, [83] and in Him there is no sin. [84]

THE WORLD'S GREAT NEED.

28. Since the greatest thing the world needs to-day is the elevating and refining power of the gospel of the grace of God, it is also proof that the world needs to know more of the beauty and glory of the principles of the law of God. The one is dependent on the other. The one is inseparable from the other.

THE LAW AND THE GOSPEL.

The law is the gospel infolded; the gospel is the law unfolded.

The law is the gospel inclosed; the gospel is the law disclosed.

The law is the gospel concealed; the gospel is the law revealed.

The law is the gospel-fullness delayed; the gospel is the law-fullness portrayed.

[81] Rom. 10:4. [82] 1 Cor. 15:3. [83] 1 John 3:5. [84] 1 Peter 2:22.

THE LAW AND THE GOSPEL.

The law is the gospel in minimum; the gospel is the law in maximum.

The law is the gospel contained; the gospel is the law maintained.

The law is the gospel sighted; the gospel is the law lighted.

The law is Christ designed; the gospel is Christ enshrined.

EXPLANATORY NOTES.

Paragraph 5.

(*a*) There was much given to prophets and apostles of which we have no direct word. We know, however, there were other things they said, though they do not state the fact; because other apostles say so. For instance: Jude tells us of a prophecy which Enoch bore to the people of his day; but we have no record of it in Genesis, or in any other account in the Bible, connected with Enoch's life. Jude 14, 15. Nevertheless it is true that he said it; and this information given by Jude is just as much the inspired word of God as though we found it in Genesis.

Again: Jude tells us that Michael came down and raised the body of Moses from the dead. We have no other record of his resurrection. That he must have been raised is evident from the fact that at the transfiguration of Jesus, Peter said he saw Moses, and the latter talked with the Savior. See Matt. 17:1–8; Mark 9:2–5; Luke 9:28–31. But we read in Deut. 34:5, 6, that Moses died, and God buried him. If, then, he ever came to life again, there was but one way that it could be accomplished, viz., by a resurrection. Job 14:14; 17:13; 14:15; John 5:28, 29.

Even though we have no other statement of the fact than this of Jude it is as truly inspired as though we found it in an earlier part of the Scripture.

Paul tells us that Jesus said *one* thing of which we have no record in any other place: "It is more blessed to give than to receive." Acts 20:35. This is just as important and necessary as though we found it in any of the Gospels. In fact John tells us that it would need a great many books to record all the sayings and doings of Jesus. John 21:25.

So it is with the laws as given to Adam. Though it is not so stated in as many words, we find sufficient in the writings of later apostles and prophets to show conclusively that Adam and his posterity did know the law of God.

Paragraph 9.

(*b*) In the fifth verse of Exodus 5, there is a strong statement which would plainly show that Moses revived the Sabbath among the Israelites. They accepted it, and began to observe it. Pharaoh's attention was called to this fact, and as a result he laid upon the people heavier burdens than before. That this is so is clear from the following: Moses and Aaron were accused by Pharaoh of hindering the people in their work. Verse four. He also said to these leaders: "Behold, the people of the land now are many, and ye make them rest from their burdens." The word *rest* in this text is in the Hebrew, וְהִשְׁבַּתֶּם, literally, and *ye make them sabbatize*. The root word of this expression is the word שָׁבַת *rest—Sabbath*. This is the very same word which in Ex. 20 : 8–11, is translated *Sabbath*, and in Gen. 2:3, rendered *rest*. In fact, the word *Sabbath* means *rest*. Hence Moses, before he was to deliver the people from their bondage, was to have them see the importance of keeping the Sabbath of the Lord. Thus it is clear that at this period Moses introduced the Sabbath to the people, and they actually began to observe it. Then Pharaoh, refusing to permit them to observe the Sabbath of the Lord, became indignant against Moses and Aaron. When they were not allowed to keep it in Egypt, God brought them out, where they could keep it, if they chose to. Ps. 105:36, 37, 45. It was no doubt because of this fact that Moses told the people they ought to keep the Sabbath as an additional reason to what the Lord had given in Ex. 20:8–11. See Deut. 5: 13–16.

Paragraph 19.

(*c*) That this is evidently so is clear from the experience of the children of Israel just forty days after the law was given. They made a golden calf, for which God said they all should die. The people wanted to get away from God as far as they could, because of their dreadful sin ; whereas Moses asked of God gifts and favors such as none other man ever requested in this world. See Ex. 33 : 12–23. And God granted him the request. He allowed him to stand in the Rock (verse twenty-one), and this Rock was Christ. 1 Cor. 10 : 1–4. So in all this experience on the mount, in the giving of the law, Moses beheld the Christ ; hence he felt safe.

(*d*) There is much in the Scripture to show that Christ was with the Father in the giving of the law on Sinai. Stephen says that the Prophet which Moses speaks of in Deut. 18 : 15, 18, is Christ. See Acts 7. He also says that this Prophet, or Christ, was the Angel who gave the law on Sinai, who spoke to Moses in the mount, and who gave the oracles to the people. Hence it is clear from Stephen's testimony that Christ was with the Father in the giving of the law.

Again: James tells us there is one *law-giver*, who is *able to save and to destroy.* James 4:12. But we read in Heb. 7:25, that it is Jesus that is *able to save.* Thus we see again that the Bible tells us that Christ was at Sinai at the giving of the law.

Paragraph 23.

(*e*) The expression "for ever," in verse eighty-nine, is in the Hebrew, לְעוֹלָם —*L-O-lom*, the identical word used in Isa. 60:15, rendered *eternal.*

Thus God's law is an eternal law. Jesus could truthfully say, not a jot or tittle of the law *could* pass away.

CHAPTER XII.

The Articles of Furniture in the Sanctuary.

"And when Aaron and his sons have made an end of covering the sanctuary, and all the vessels of the sanctuary, as the camp is to set forward; after that, the sons of Kohath shall come to bear it : but they shall not touch any holy thing, lest they die." Num. 4 :15. " Depart ye, depart ye, go out from thence, touch no unclean thing ; go ye out of the midst of her ; be ye clean, that bear the vessels of the Lord." Isa 52 : 11.

AFTER the Lord had given to Moses the command to build the sanctuary, as noticed in Chapter X, He gave him specific directions for the building of all its parts, its furniture within, its decorations without. Every part had a special function, and in every way it must be made according to the pattern.[1] Nothing was left for conjecture or supposition ; not even the smallest minutia was passed by unheeded. The means of carrying on the services by the priesthood with the Levites as assistants,[2] after the building was completed,[3] were all directed by the Lord ; and the offerings with all the needed appurtenances received equal attention. Everything in this economy had its place ; and nothing must be misplaced.

THE ARK.

2. The first article of furniture which was commanded to be made was the ark.[4] It was a box-like object, about three and a half feet long, two and a fourth feet wide, and about the same dimensions in height. (*a*) It was made of shittim-wood, the acacia of the East. The chest was overlaid within and without with pure gold. A very beautiful crown adorned its top, all around, and at its four corners were rings of pure gold, in which

[1] Heb. 8: 5.   [2] Ex. 28:40-43.   [3] Num. 3:5-9.   [4] Ex. 25: 10-16.

THE ARK.

were placed the staves made of the same wood, covered with gold and used to carry the ark.[5] In the ark was to be placed "the testimony" (*b*) which God would give Moses.[6] What the testimony was, might be of interest to trace, for there is much importance attached to this fact.

THE TESTIMONY.

3. After Moses had received his instruction from the Lord, we read:

"And He gave unto Moses, when He had made an end of communing with him upon Mount Sinai, two tables of *testimony*, tables of stone, written with the finger of God."[7]

Here we observe that the *two tables of stone are tables of testimony;* and Moses was commanded to put into the ark the "testimony" which he was to receive.

"And Moses turned, and went down from the mount, and the *two tables of the testimony* were in his hand: the tables were written on both their sides; on the one side and on the other were they written. And the tables were the work of God, and the writing was the writing of God, graven upon the tables."[8]

"And it came to pass, when Moses came down from Mount Sinai with the *two tables of testimony* in Moses' hand, when he came down from the mount, that Moses wist not that the skin of his face shone while He talked with him."[9]

"And he was there with the Lord forty days and forty nights; he did neither eat bread, nor drink water. And He *wrote upon the tables the words of the covenant, the ten commandments.*"[10]

"And He declared unto you His covenant, which He commanded you to perform, *even ten commandments;* and *He wrote them on two tables of stone.*"[11]

"These words the Lord spake unto all your assembly in the mount out of the midst of the fire, . . . with a great voice: and He added no more. And He wrote them in *two tables of stone,* and delivered them unto me."[12]

4. Thus we find that "the testimony" referred to, which was placed in the ark, was the *ten commandments.* As we have

[5] Ex. 25: 14.   [6] Ex. 25: 16.   [7] Ex. 31: 18.   [8] Ex. 32: 15, 16.   [9] Ex. 34: 29.
[10] Ex. 34: 28.   [11] Deut. 4: 13.   [12] Deut. 5: 22.

seen, it is sometimes called "the testimony," at other times "the tables of testimony." Sometimes the term *testament* was used as a synonym.[13] The word *testimony* is from the Hebrew word עֵדוּת, *a-dus*, meaning *evidence, proof, witness*. Thus the ark came to be called the "ark of the testimony,"[14] or the "ark of the testament."[15] Therefore the decalogue, the ten commandments, the law of God, was ever to be to the people, God's great "evidence," "proof," or "witness." It was to testify who the true God is; it was to be proof of His mighty power; it was to be an evidence of His authority as the only, and the true, God.

OTHER OBJECTS PLACED IN ARK.

5. In addition to the law of God, there was placed in the ark the rod of Aaron which budded,[16] and a pot of manna;[17] *but nothing more*. Both these latter had evidently been removed from the ark for some cause in the days of Solomon; for we read that at that time there was nothing in the ark save the two tables of stone, the ten commandments, which Moses placed in there at Horeb.[18] However, there was none other law or laws deposited in that sacred chest *at any time*, save these ten commandments, written with the finger of God, spoken by the voice of Jehovah.

THE MEANING OF THE ARK.

6. What lesson was to be taught by the ark, with its contents? It is well known that an ark had been used at different periods in the history of this world prior to this time. When the Lord was to bring a deluge upon the world, He commanded Noah to build him an ark for the saving of himself and his house.[19] When Moses was born, and it was expected he would be drowned according to the command of Pharaoh, his mother secured an ark, and hid him therein.[20] In this ark he

13 Rev. 15:5; 11:19.   14 Ex. 30:6.   15 Rev. 11:19.   16 Num. 17:7-10; Heb. 9:4.
17 Heb. 9:4; Ex. 16:32-34.   18 1 Kings 8:9; 2 Chron. 5:10.
19 Gen. 6:13, 14; Heb. 11:7; 1 Peter 3:20.   20 Ex. 2:3.

was afterward discovered by the Egyptian princess, and his life was saved.[21] Thus we learn that the ark was a symbol of protection, safety, care, preservation. But in the ark which God commanded made, was deposited the law of God, the ten commandments. What can we therefore learn from both the ark and the law?

7. We read in Psalms 40, the following prophecy:

"Sacrifice and offering Thou didst not desire; Mine ears hast Thou opened: burnt offering and sin offering hast Thou not required. Then said I, Lo, I come; in the volume of the book it is written of Me. I delight to do Thy will, O My God: yea, Thy law is *within My heart*."[22]

8. And to whom this prophecy refers is explained by the Apostle Paul:

"Wherefore when He cometh into the world, He [Christ] saith, Sacrifice and offering Thou wouldest not, but a body hast Thou prepared Me: in burnt offerings and sacrifices for sin Thou hast had no pleasure. Then said I, Lo, I come (in the volume of the book it is written of Me) to do Thy will, O God."[23]

9. We thus see that the fulfillment of this prediction is none other than Jesus Christ. Then the place in which the law of God was deposited in His life, was His heart. In the fleshly tables of His divine-human soul were inscribed by the finger of God's own Spirit the divine and eternal precepts of Jehovah's unalterable law. Then it must be apparent that the ark, the place of safety, was a symbol of the life of Christ in which was placed the law of Jehovah.

WHAT CHRIST'S LIFE WAS.

10. Was not His heart a safe and secure place for the law of God to abide? Did He not prove to the world who the true God was? "This is life eternal, that they might know Thee, the only true God, and Jesus Christ, whom Thou hast sent."[24]

Was not His life a "proof" of the mighty power and wonderful care of God toward all whose hearts are right toward

[21] Ex. 2: 5–8; Acts 7: 20, 21. [22] Ps. 40: 6–8. [23] Heb. 10: 5–7.
[24] John 17: 3.

Him? Was not His life a living "witness" as to who the true and living God was, and what was His character? Oh, precious Ark of Safety! In Him is a sure and blessed Ark of Rest and Security![25] God could place His law in that heart, for He knew it was safe. It would never be betrayed; it would never be forsaken; it would never be misrepresented! It would always be preserved. What Jesus did with God's law, is what He will do in every soul who will trust in Him.[26] This was what He longed to do for the Jews. His heart sighed and cried for them. His heart burned within Him that He might shelter them in the bosom of His love.

"And when He was come near, He beheld the city, and wept over it, saying, If thou hadst known, even thou, at least in this thy day, the things which belong unto thy peace! but now they are hid from thine eyes."[27]

"O Jerusalem, Jerusalem, thou that killest the prophets, and stonest them which are sent unto thee, how often would I have gathered thy children together, even as a hen gathereth her chickens under her wings, and ye would not!"[28]

How He longed to free them from all their burdens of traditionalism, form, and servitude; but no! they would not receive Him.

"If the Son, therefore, shall make you free, ye shall be free indeed."[29]

How blessed, then, to know we can trust in Him, and to realize, personally, this beautiful lesson on the ark.

"How oft in the conflict, when pressed by the foe,
   I have fled to my Refuge and breathed out my woe;
How often, when trials like sea-billows roll,
   Have I hidden in Thee, O thou Ark of my soul."

But the promise of the new covenant is that God would do this in every heart; He would put His law in every soul.

THE HEAVENLY ARK.

11. It was shown in a previous chapter that the tabernacle

[25] Ps. 144:2. [26] Prov. 18:24; Heb. 13:5. [27] Luke 19:41, 42. [28] Matt. 23:37. [29] John 8:36.

12

on the earth was but a shadow of the real sanctuary which the Lord had in heaven.[30]　All the objects in the earthly were made after the pattern of the heavenly.　This, then, being true, we would naturally expect that there would be the same objects in the heavenly temple as there were in the earthly.　Perhaps it may seem strange to the reader to think there is a real temple in heaven, and real objects there as here.　But " thus saith the Lord."

12. That there is a temple in heaven, with an ark in it, and the law deposited in this ark, is evident from the following scriptures :

" And the temple was filled with smoke from the glory of God, and from His power; and no man was able to enter into the temple, till the seven plagues of the seven angels were fulfilled." [31]

" And the temple of God was opened *in heaven*, and there was seen in His temple the ark of His testament." [32]

" And after that I looked, and behold, *the temple of the tabernacle of the testimony* in heaven was opened." [33]

' GOD'S LAW IN THE HEAVENLY ARK.

13. Thus we see clearly stated that there is a temple *in heaven;* and in that temple is the ark; in that ark is the " testimony," exactly the same as we found existed in the earthly sanctuary.　But we discovered that the reason the ark in the earthly sanctuary was called the " testimony " was because of its contents, the ten commandments, which God called His " testimony." [34]　This being true, we must conclude that in heaven, in the temple of God, in the ark above, is deposited the *original transcript of the ten commandments*, the decalogue, the law of God.　Yes ; beneath the very throne of God, in His own abiding-place, is to be found the original copy of God's law. And as long as He shall dwell and rule, so long shall that " testimony " remain there. [35]　Therefore we see the absolute impossibility of the prevailing idea entertained that the law of

---

[30] Heb. 8 : 1, 2, 5.　　[31] Rev. 15 : 8.　　[32] Rev. 11 : 19.　　[33] Rev. 15 : 5.
　　　　　[34] Ex. 40 : 20.　　　　　　[35] Luke 16 : 17.

Jehovah is unimportant; is of little account; is of no special service; and even, as some assert, is abolished.[36] Heaven and earth shall pass away; but not one jot or tittle of the law can ever fail.[37] This cannot be otherwise; for justice and judgment are the habitation of His throne.[38]

THE MERCY-SEAT AND THE CHERUBIM.

14. The next article made after the ark was the mercy-seat.[39] This was to be of pure gold, and its position was above upon the ark. At each end of this mercy-seat Moses was commanded to make cherubim,[40] one at one end, and one at the other. These also were to be made of pure gold, beaten, of the same material as the mercy-seat. The position of the cherubim was to be erect, with their faces both looking at the mercy-seat. There were to be two wings upon each, so arranged that one of each would touch the other.

15. When this was completed, God would make the place on the mercy-seat between these cherubim, a sacred one, and would sanctify it with His own personal presence.

"And there I will meet with thee, and I will commune with thee from above the mercy-seat, from between the two cherubim which are upon the ark of the testimony, of all things which I will give thee in commandment unto the children of Israel." [41]

"And when Moses was gone into the tabernacle of the congregation to speak with Him, then he heard the voice of One speaking unto him from off the mercy-seat that was upon the ark of the testimony, from between the two cherubim: and He spake unto him." [42]

This position on the mercy-seat would represent the throne of God to the people. Whenever God wished to meet the people to give them commandments, or for any other reason He desired to speak with them, the glory of the Lord, the Holy Shekinah, would be manifest at this place between these two cherubim.

Ps. 119:172; Isa. 51:6.　[37] Matt. 5:17, 18.　[38] Ps. 89:14.　[39] Ex. 25:17. [40] Ex. 25:18-20.　[41] Ex. 25:22.　[42] Num. 7:89.

CHERUBIM ON EITHER SIDE OF MERCY-SEAT.

THE HEAVENLY CHERUBIM AND MERCY-SEAT.

16. As with the ark and the law, so with the cherubim and the mercy-seat. The real cherubim and mercy-seat, the antitypes of the earthly, were in the temple of God in heaven; for there is where the real throne of God is established. There God abides. There He has the seat and center of His government. We read concerning these truths the following scriptures:

"The Lord is in His holy temple, the Lord's throne is in heaven." [43]

"In the year that King Uzziah died I saw also the Lord sitting upon a throne, high and lifted up, and His train filled the temple." [44]

"The Lord hath prepared His throne in the heavens; and His kingdom ruleth over all." [45]

"Give ear, O Shepherd of Israel. . . . Thou that dwellest between the cherubim, shine forth." [46]

"The Lord reigneth; let the people tremble: He sitteth between the cherubim; let the earth be moved." [47]

"And Hezekiah prayed unto the Lord, saying, O Lord of hosts, God of Israel, that dwellest between the cherubim, Thou art the God, even Thou alone, of all the kingdoms of the earth: Thou hast made heaven and earth." [48]

"Let us therefore come boldly unto the throne of grace, that we may obtain *mercy*, and find grace to help in time of need." [49]

17. Yes, there is a throne of mercy to which every soul can come in time of need. There is a God whose glory fills that throne, who has cordially invited us to come and receive the sweet draughts of mercy. [50] Though He be high and lifted up, though He dwell between the cherubim in the temple of His dwelling, though the house be filled with that brilliant glory,— to the soul that cometh to this throne there is always a welcome hand extended. [51] What a blessed comforting thought to know the reality there is in the truth of salvation through the Lord Jesus Christ.

THE FALLEN CHERUB.

18. When God told Moses to make the cherubim, He spe-

[43] Ps. 11:4.   [44] Isa. 6:1.   [45] Ps. 103:19.   [46] Ps. 80:1.   [47] Ps. 99:1.
[48] Isa. 37:15, 16.   [49] Heb. 4:16.   [50] Micah 7:18-20.   [51] John 6:37.

SATAN, THE FALLEN CHERUB.

cified also the number; He said there should be two, one on each side of the mercy-seat. [52] From this we learn that on either side of the throne of God in heaven there is one cherub, in the same position as those which were made after the pattern. The earthly were made of gold; the heavenly, however, are living. The Scripture tells us that God *dwelleth* between the cherubim. These cherubim are the most exalted beings of ·the heavenly hosts, occupying the nearest position to the very throne of God. What an exalted place! What a high honor!

19. Yet strange as it may seem, the originator of sin, [53] the father of lies, [54] the perpetrator of all evil, who to-day is known as Satan, adversary, enemy, [55] once had the honor and privilege of holding that exalted, that high and glorious position. He it was who once was esteemed as one of the most favored and exalted beings in the universe of God. For thus saith the Scripture, concerning the position and fall of Satan, under the name of the " Prince of Tyrus :"

" Moreover the word of the Lord came unto me, saying, Son of man, take up a lamentation upon the king of Tyrus, and say unto him, Thus saith the Lord God: Thou sealest up the sum, full of wisdom, and perfect in beauty. Thou hast been in Eden the garden of God; every precious stone was thy covering. . .. . Thou art the *anointed cherub* that covereth; and I have set thee so: thou wast upon the holy mountain of God; thou hast walked up and down in the midst of the stones of fire. Thou wast perfect in thy ways from the day that thou wast created, till iniquity *was found in thee.* By the multitude of thy merchandise they have filled the midst of thee with violence, and *thou hast sinned:* therefore I will cast thee as profane out of the mountain of God; and I will destroy thee, O covering cherub, from the midst of the stones of fire." [56]

" Because thine heart is lifted up, and thou hast said, I am a God, I sit in the seat of God, . . . yet thou art a man, and not God, though thou set thine heart as the heart of God; behold, thou art wiser than Daniel; there is no secret that they can hide from thee." [57]

20. Here the Lord gives us a vivid picture of the origin of sin. Its originator was once the most exalted, beautiful, perfect,

[52] Ex. 25:18, 19.   [53] 1 John 3:8.   [54] John 8:44.   [55] Rev. 12:9; 1 Peter 5:8.
[56] Eze. 28:11–16.   [57] Eze. 28:2, 3.

wise being in all of God's creation, except His only begotten Son. (*d*) Not content with his position which God gave him to occupy, he sought to become as God himself.[58]   Though he were enshrouded with the very light of God's own personal glory which came directly from the throne, he coveted the very place and honor due to God alone.   This is the cause of all the sin and misery that has ever appeared in this great universe of God.   Selfishness, self-esteem, self-exaltation, is certainly the root of all wickedness and sorrow.

WHAT JESUS SAID OF SATAN.

21. Jesus Himself said that Satan was once in heaven, and that he fell from his dwelling-place.[59]   His home was there; but as a result of his desire for self-glorification he was exiled from heaven, with many of his evil sympathizers,[60] after a terrible and bitter conflict had been waged in the heavenly courts.[61]   Sin must be expelled from heaven; it cannot find any place there.   No doubt a very precious lesson was designed to be taught the people in this connection, as they realized that the cherubim and their glory were in the holy place of the temple.

THE PRACTICAL LESSON OF THE MERCY-SEAT.

22. There is, however, a very beautiful *practical* lesson connected with the mercy-seat.   The Jewish teachers spent a great deal of time in writing concerning the beautiful Shekinah, the cherubim, the mercy-seat, the ark; but of the real sweetness of the practical, helpful lesson they knew nothing.   The apostle, in Romans, speaking of Christ, says:

" Being justified freely by His grace through the redemption that is in Christ Jesus : whom God hath set forth to be a *propitiation* through faith in His blood, to declare His righteousness for the remission of sins that are past, through the forbearance of God."[62]

23. The word which in this text is translated " propitiation, "

[58] Isa. 14: 12-14.   [59] Luke 10: 18.   [60] 2 Peter 2: 4.
[61] Rev. 12: 3, 4, 9.   [62] Rom. 3: 24, 25.

really means "mercy-seat." In fact this is the same word which *is translated mercy-seat* in Heb. 9:5. Some of the translations so render it. The German gives it, *"gnaden-stuhl,"* gracious or mercy-seat. So we see that Jesus Christ is God's mercy-seat. The Jews, in fact the world, never understood God; He has always been misrepresented and misunderstood. His very essence is grace and mercy.[63] Thus He represented Himself to Micah;[64] also the same to other prophets. He delights in mercy. Jesus came to reveal God to the world. "He that hath seen Me hath seen the Father."[65] "Neither knoweth any man the Father save the Son, and He to whomsoever the Son will reveal Him."[66]

THE MEANING OF MERCY.

24. In order then that the world and the Jews might understand this wonderful trait of the character of God, Christ came to reveal this sweet mercy to men. The Jews did not know what it meant. Twice they were instructed to go and learn it; twice they were asked to ascertain its meaning; but they refused.[67] In their precisions and exactions; in their desire to rigorously carry out the letter of the law, they lost that sweet and beautiful trait of God's character. Christ, however, revealed it. They felt it incumbent to be just, and to perform true judgment; but mercy was a quality with which they were unacquainted. With the Lord Jesus, however, mercy and truth embraced each other in the loving arms of peace and righteousness.[68]

25. Is there not then a great significance in the words of Jesus when He said: "Him that cometh to me, I will in no wise cast out"?[69] In His soul God dispensed mercy; He was passing it along as rapidly as He received it. Let us then learn what that meaneth, "I will have mercy, and not sacrifice."

[63] Ex. 34:5, 6; Ps. 103:8, 17; Ps. 136.   [64] Micah 7:18.   [65] John 14:9.
[66] Matt. 11:27; Luke 10:21, 22.   [67] Matt. 9:13; 12:7.
[68] Ps. 85:10.   [69] John 6:37.

THE TABLE, THE SHEWBREAD, THE DISHES.

26. The next article of furniture we have a record of is the table for the shewbread.[70] This table was made of the same kind of wood as was the ark, and was similarly covered. A border around it was also made, and a crown of pure gold. At each of the four corners of the table a ring was made of pure gold for the golden covered staves, by which it was to be borne from place to place.

The various dishes required to furnish this table, with the spoons, the bowls, and the covers, were all made of pure gold. No alloy, no admixture of any kind. We can see there must have been something very significant about all these objects because of the precision which was demanded by the Lord in their making.

THE BREAD OF THE PRESENCE.

27. Upon the table was to be placed the shewbread. The words in the Hebrew, לחם הפנים *Le-hem Ha-ponim*, means *bread of the presence*, instead of *shewbread*, as we have it translated. The directions for the making of this bread were given by the Lord, even the exact amount necessary for every several baking. Just so many loaves were to be baked each time; no more, no less.[71] The twelve loaves were to be renewed every week;[72] they were to be placed upon the table in two rows, six in a row.[73] On Sabbath day the bread was to be brought in fresh, and to be eaten only by Aaron and his sons, as everything connected therewith was holy unto the Lord, and was designed as a memorial.[74] It must also be eaten in the holy place; it must not be eaten outside of the sanctuary. The table never was to be empty; it must always be supplied with the twelve loaves.

THE PRACTICAL APPLICATION OF THE BREAD.

28. How many beautiful lessons are here taught in the light

[70] Ex. 25: 23–30.　[71] Lev. 24: 5.　[72] Lev. 24: 8.　[73] Lev. 24: 6.
[74] Lev. 24: 7.

THE TABLE AND BREAD OF THE PRESENCE.

of the Holy Spirit,[75] intended as great blessings and spiritual help to the people as they were performing this work for God. How much of the life and work of the Lord Jesus was here given for the people to know which might be practical and helpful in their experience.

29. The bread here represents Christ who is the Bread of Life with which He feeds the people. This we find recorded in many instances. [76]   The reason it is called the " bread of the presence " is because it is He who always is in the presence of God ; and who from God is delegated to feed mankind with His own life and with His own power. (*e*)

" For the bread of God is He which cometh down from heaven, and giveth life unto the world   . . .   I am the Bread of Life." [77]

" I am the living Bread which came down from heaven : if any man eat of this bread, he shall live forever." [78]

" No man hath seen God at any time; the only begotten Son, which is in the bosom of the Father, He hath declared Him." [79]

He came down from heaven, from the very bosom and presence of the Father, to feed the people that He had been feeding all the time, though they were not aware of the fact. [80] It was He who had for centuries been caring for the Israelites, both temporally and spiritually ; [81] yet they did not know it. Well did the Lord say of this people through His prophet :" [82]

" My people are destroyed for lack of knowledge." [82]

No doubt the Apostle Paul must have had in mind this method of the Jews in speaking, in reading, in writing, that of which they knew not the meaning.   He says :

" What is it then ?   I will pray with the Spirit, and I will pray with the *understanding* also : I will sing with the Spirit, and I will sing with the *understanding* also." [83]

THE LESSON OF THE TWELVE LOAVES.

30. Beautiful thoughts too are suggested in the manner the

75 1 Cor. 2: 13.   76 John 6: 32, 33.   77 John 6: 33, 35.   78 John 6: 51.   79 John 1: 18.
80 Isa. 40: 10, 11.   81 Isa. 63: 7-9.   82 Hosea 4: 6.   83 1 Cor. 14: 15.

loaves were placed on the table; the purity of the dishes to be used in the serving of the bread. There must nothing come in contact with the food served on the table which had any adulteration or defilement. Everything must be without mixture.

31. The fact that there were but twelve loaves suggests the twelve tribes which the Lord separated for Himself, for whom He labored, whom He came to save. [84] Not only the twelve tribes in the flesh who were instantly serving God are intended, but the twelve complete tribes of Israel are included also. [85] The true Israel are those who are born of the Holy Spirit, [86] who are redeemed by the blood; who are saved through His precious salvation. For them He gave His life, upon which they might feed. [87] Every true child of God He carries upon His soul; and with Him these twelve spiritual tribes shall ever rejoice when they go no more out forever from the Father's presence; [88] they shall hunger no more; [89] they shall ever be priests of God and of Christ, [90] and shall reign forever and ever. [91]

THE GOLDEN CANDLESTICK.

32. One other beautiful article of furniture was the seven-branched golden candlestick, [92] a most beautiful as well as remarkable piece of workmanship made by human hands, but devised by divine wisdom. For a full and complete description of the same read the thirty-first and thirty-seventh chapters of Exodus. Made of one piece of pure gold, with its knops, its bowls, its branches, its glittering shaft, all very delicately and cunningly inwrought with figures and flowers, what a beautiful appearance it must have presented when lighted by the high priest. Its position was directly opposite [93] the table of " the bread of the presence." When completed it weighed nearly two hundred pounds, being almost five feet high and nearly three and a half wide. The gold alone in the candle-

[84] Acts. 26:7.   [85] Deut. 32:8, 9; Gal. 6:16.   [86] Rom. 9:6-8.
[87] John 6:54, 55, 63.   [88] Rev. 7:4; 14:1-5.   [89] Rev. 7:16. 17.   [90] Rev. 20:4.
[91] Rev. 22:5.   [92] Ex. 25:31-39.   [93] Ex. 40:24.

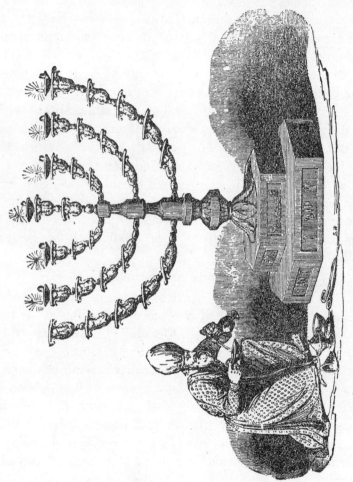

THE GOLDEN CANDLESTICK.

stick has been estimated to be worth almost twenty-five thousand dollars. Special oil was necessary for its use, [94] and it must be lighted every evening by the priest at the time of the burning of the incense, [95] and the wicks must be trimmed by him in the morning, when he burned the incense. [96] The object of the candlestick was to give light. It must be lighted every day ; it must be constantly supplied with oil ; it must have its wicks trimmed each morning ; great care must always be taken of it, that it might never become useless.

CHRIST THE LIGHT BEARER.

33. How naturally this suggests to us the Christ, the Light-bearer to the world. [97] He came to give to men light. His life was itself light. [98] The oil of divine grace was constantly replenished in His soul, and He was ever careful to have the light of His life free from everything impure and defiling. [99] Every time the priest trimmed the lamps how he should have felt the power of the Messiah to remove all the obstructions of his own life ! How he should have felt the blessing of having the Christ clear away all the impurity from his life, which might obstruct the light flowing through His soul ! Yes, the Messiah as the light-giver, was very vividly and forcibly taught by this seven-branched golden candlestick.

THE HEAVENLY GOLDEN CANDLESTICK.

34. A very forcible lesson from this candlestick is taught by the apostle, when he had revealed to him the antitypical candlestick in heaven, of which the one on earth was but a shadow.

"And I turned to see the voice that spake with me. And being turned, I saw seven golden candlesticks ; and in the midst of the seven candlesticks one like unto the Son of man, clothed with a garment down to the foot, and girt about the paps with a golden girdle." [100]

"The mystery of the seven stars which thou sawest in My right hand, and the *seven golden candlesticks*. The seven stars are the angels of the

[94] Ex. 27: 20; Lev. 24: 2.　[95] Ex. 30: 8.　[96] Ex. 30: 7.　[97] John 8: 12; 9: 5; 12: 46.　[98] John 1: 4, 5, 9.　[99] John 8: 46.　[100] Rev. 1: 12, 13.

seven churches : and the *seven candlesticks* which thou sawest are the seven churches." [101]

Thus John saw the seven golden candlesticks in heaven ; and the Savior said they were illustrative of the seven churches. But what is the mission of the church? When Christ was in the world He said He was the light of the world; when He was to leave, He told the church that *it* was the light of the world. [102] Therefore " let your light so shine before men, that they may see your good works, and glorify your Father which is in heaven." [103]   " As He is, so are we in this world." [104]

THE LESSONS FROM THE CANDLESTICK.

35. When we think of the wonderful amount of light that the Jews might have seen in the Lord Jesus, it is remarkably strange how they were blinded to all these glorious truths. Yet they which live in houses of glass should not be casting stones. It being true that the Jews in their day had great light, how much more does the professed church of Christ have at the present time. Do we always see Christ as the Light of the world in all things now? or is the philosophy and science of the present day the illuminator of mankind? The rabbis wrote many treatises on the objects of the sanctuary, and upon this candlestick; but as to its practical application to their own life they said very little.

CHRIST THE ONLY TRUE LIGHT.

36. At the present day we hear much said of light and advancement in the various branches of learning and education, yet it must be confessed that human philosophy and human intelligence are in a measure substituted for the Light of the soul, even Jesus Christ. He only is the Light of every man which cometh into the world. Neither learning, nor education, nor culture, nor philosophy, nor refinement, nor science can give the true light, which only can bring salvation to mankind

[101] Rev. 1: 20.   [102] Matt. 5: 14; Phil. 2: 15.   [103] Matt. 5: 16.   [104] 1 John 4: 17.

in the perils of these latter days. The blessed Bible, the word of God, is the means, and the only means, which can impart the light of truth to every person; and Jesus Christ only, is its source. The light must come from the oil that is furnished the candlestick. The candlestick is the bearer, the oil is the feeder, the snuffers the trimmer. This was God's plan.

37. So Jesus Christ is the Light-bearer to the world, to every individual soul; His oil of grace, the divine Spirit, is needed to feed the light; His blessed and precious Word *only*, will do the trimming. [105] This thought is forcibly brought out in the parable of the ten virgins. [106]

THE GOLDEN ALTAR.

38. Still another interesting article of furniture in the sanctuary was the altar of incense. [107] This, too, was made of shittim-wood, the top and sides being covered with pure gold.[108] It also had a crown of gold, and rings were made at its corners for transportation. It was about three feet high, two and a fourth feet long, and about the same measurement in width. The object of the altar was to burn the sweet incense thereon every morning and every evening. [109] A special compound was prepared which was burned each time, morning and evening, giving out a very sweet and fragrant perfume. [110] A special fire was needed for the offering of this perfume; and should this law be transgressed, death was likely to follow. [111] This was literally fulfilled to the two sons of Aaron. [112]

THE HEAVENLY ALTAR OF INCENSE.

39. In the vision that John had as given in the Revelation, he tells us of a very beautiful golden altar he saw in heaven, and describes it as follows:

"And I saw the seven angels which stood before God; and to them were given seven trumpets. And another angel came and stood at the *altar*, having a golden censer; and there was given unto him much

---

[105] Heb. 4 : 12. [106] Matt. 25: 1-10. [107] Ex. 30: 1. [108] Ex. 30: 3.
[109] Ex. 30: 7; Luke 1: 9. [110] Ex. 30: 34, 35. [111] Ex. 30: 9. [112] Lev. 10: 1, 2.

13

GOLDEN ALTAR OF INCENSE.

incense, that he should offer it with the prayers of all saints *upon the golden altar which was before the throne.* And the smoke of the incense, which came with the prayers of the saints, ascended up before God out of the angel's hand." [113]

"And the sixth angel sounded, and I heard a voice from the four horns of the golden altar which is before God." [114]

40. In heaven, right by the throne of God, stands a golden altar, the true altar of which the earthly was a type. We are also informed that on this altar was offered incense, even as on the altar in the earthly. [115] This incense, however, was added to the prayers of the saints of God, as they were offered up by the angel. We are told, however, in the word of God, that personally we know not how to pray; [116] hence our own prayers cannot reach the throne of God. But the Spirit maketh intercession for us with groanings which cannot be uttered; and then our petitions before God are made acceptable by their presentation through the Spirit.

HOW GOD ACCEPTS PRAYER.

41. What a beautiful truth then this altar of incense was designed to teach! The preciousness of the gift of the Spirit, by Jesus Christ, would be ministered by the angels,[117] in order that the prayers of the children of God might be made acceptable. As the sweet incense, amid the volumes of smoke, ascended heavenward, giving off its rich perfume and delightful fragrance, the Lord would have his children learn, by the altar of incense, that the precious merit of Jesus Christ, deposited in that most blessed Spirit of God, would also ascend to God amid the impediments and stammering of imperfect human language from the lips of man. These requests and earnest petitions of the soul would approach the very throne of God as the sweet and fragrant incense. Oh Thou blessed and kind and loving Christ! in so many, many ways revealing Thine own blessed life and truth! doing all in Thy power to make Thyself mani-

[113] Rev. 8: 2-4. [114] Rev. 9: 13. [115] Ex. 30: 7. [116] Rom. 8: 26.
[117] Heb. 1: 14.

fest to the children of men! opening so many avenues, and revealing such wonderful plans whereby Thou mightest be known to the children of men, to bring Thyself to them, and to raise them toward the throne!

THE RESULT OF OFFERING STRANGE FIRE.

42. What a blessed and precious hour it must have been, morning and evening, when the priest offered up the sweet incense before the Lord, and all the people were without offering their prayers to God.[118] How different this way of praying from the set and stereotyped manner of the rabbis. Every prayer was prescribed; every form was planned. The long-drawn-out, vain repetitions [119] expressed the self-satisfied egotistical personal merit of the self-praised and self-righteous sinner.[120] It was a strange fire offered upon the altar, which God forbade, and commanded not.[121] The Lord said that if one offered such fire he should die. It is not surprising then that the Jews died that spiritual death, when they refused to offer before God upon the altar of the soul, the righteous incense which He had prepared.

43. Did the church of the present day know how God is longing to kindle the fire of His love, as it burned on the altar of Jesus Christ's soul,[122] what fervency of spirit, what continuity of thought would pervade the minds of the children of God, that there should not be any strange fire offered; but that there should be the fire of the divine Spirit, offering to the throne of the eternal One the precious merit and fragrance of Christ's life, in order that the offering might be acceptable unto God.[123] Ah! how many then there would be, even at the present day who, though without the temple, would be offering up their prayers unto God.

THE LOCATION OF THE FURNISHINGS.

44. The furniture of the sanctuary thus far mentioned, con-

---

[118] Luke 1:10.   [119] Mark 12:40.   [120] Luke 18:9.   [121] Lev. 10:1.
[122] Isa. 6:5-7; Zech. 4:11-14.   [123] Rom. 8:26, 27.

stituted the principal part of the interior of the building. Each piece, however, had a specific location, which bore a given relation to the other. The tabernacle which contained these articles, was divided into two apartments, known as the holy and the most holy place. [124] The division was made as follows :

TRUE WORSHIP A PROTECTION AGAINST SUN-WORSHIP.

45. The ark, the testimony, the mercy-seat, the cherubim, were placed in the rear part of the building. Its position was toward the west; so that when the people worshiped toward the holiest place, their backs would always be toward the east. There was a strong reason for this, as will be seen from the following experience. While the children of Israel were in Egypt they were continuously surrounded with heathenish worship devoted to the sun-god. Sun-worship was the form of idolatry which was most abhorrent to the Lord. When they worshiped the sun they always did so facing the east. In order that they might show their abhorrence of this idolatrous worship, the Hebrews were commanded to turn their *backs* toward the sun, toward the east. Their thought and devotion then would be toward the true and living God. It is a singular fact that whenever the people turned their backs upon the true God and His worship, they always went to worshiping the sun; hence they worshiped with their faces toward the east. One illustration from the Scripture will make this very clear:

"Then said He unto me, Hast thou seen this, O son of man? turn thee yet again, and thou shalt see greater abominations than these. And He brought me into the inner court of the Lord's house, and behold, at the door of the temple of the Lord, between the porch and the altar, were about five and twenty men, *with their backs toward the temple of the Lord*, and their *faces toward the east; and they worshiped the sun toward the east.*" [125]

46. To avoid as far as possible anything that would incline them toward this awful and abominable worship, the Lord made

[124] Ex. 26: 33; Heb. 9: 2, 3.　　　[125] Eze. 8: 15, 16.

every possible provision whereby they might worship Him in spirit and in truth. [126]

47. In the synagogue service, even to the present day, the Jews intend, as far as possible, to have the ark, as they term the place where the scrolls of the law are preserved, located toward the west. As the people now worship with their faces toward the ark, they are still reminded of the abominable wickedness of sun-worship, and the necessity of worshiping with their faces toward the west.

THE VAIL OF SEPARATION.

48. Just in front of this ark the Lord commanded Moses to hang a very beautiful curtain, made of blue, purple, scarlet, and fine-twined linen, to be designed with embroidered figures of cherubim. [127] This was to form a partition for two places, called respectively the holy, and the most holy place. [128] Where the ark, and other articles directly connected with it, were placed, was called the most holy place. Into the most holy place no soul was permitted to enter at any time on pain of death, except the high priest, and he only on the Day of Atonement. [129] Even then he must be clothed with special garments, and must pass through a process of purification." [130]

HEAVENLY VAIL; OPEN AND SHUT DOOR.

49. As we think of these two places in the sanctuary, and the vail or door which was made to separate them, we can the better appreciate the statement which the Revealer gave to John:

"And to the angel of the church in Philadelphia write; These things saith He that is holy, He that is true, He that hath the key of David, He that openeth and no man shutteth; and shutteth, and no man openeth; I know thy works: behold, I have set before thee an open door, and no man can shut it." [131]

Having already seen that all the articles of the earthly

[126] John 4:24.　　[127] Ex. 26:31, 32.　　[128] Ex. 26:33.　　[129] Lev. 16:2; Heb. 9:7.
[130] Lev. 16:3 4.　　　　　　[131] Rev. 3:7, 8

THE HOLY PLACE WITH VAIL.

sanctuary were but shadows of the heavenly, the vail or door which separated the two apartments must be but a shadow or type of the same thing in the heavenly. That there were two apartments in the heavenly sanctuary is apparent from the types themselves;[132] but further evidence will be given in a future chapter.

A HELPFUL LESSON FROM THE VAIL.

50. One very precious practical lesson from the vail we can indeed appreciate, when we remember that the way which gives us an entrance unto God, the Father, is by the Vail, which is to say, His flesh.[133] Yes, He, Christ, is the Door;[134] He is the Vail; and through this blessed and precious Vail, we can come before the mercy-seat into the presence of God.[135]

POSITION OF FURNITURE IN HOLY PLACE.

51. Right in front of this beautiful vail was placed the golden altar of incense, about the center of the room.[136] To the south side of the sanctuary was placed the candlestick;[137] directly opposite the candlestick, on the north side, was placed the table of the bread of the presence.[138] The apartment in which these three articles were located was called the holy place.[139] The holy and the most holy places constituted the principal part of the tabernacle; and in these apartments the service and ministry were conducted by the priests only.

THE LAVER AND ITS USE.

52. Without the holy place was to be placed the laver, which God had commanded Moses to make. The purpose of the laver, and its description are as follows:

"Thou shalt also make a laver of brass, . . to wash withal: and thou shalt put it between the tabernacle of the congregation and the altar, and thou shalt put water therein. For Aaron and his sons shall wash their hands and their feet thereat: when they go into the tabernacle of the congregation, they shall wash with water, that they die not;

132 Heb. 9: 8, 24.   133 Heb. 10: 19, 20.   134 John 10: 9.   135 Heb. 4: 15, 16.
136 Ex. 40: 26.   137 Ex. 40: 24.   138 Ex. 40: 22.   139 Heb. 9 · 2.

or when they come near to the altar to minister, to burn offering made by fire unto the Lord : so they shall wash their hands and their feet, that they die not : and it shall be a statute forever to them, even to him and to his seed throughout their generations." [140]

"And he made the laver of brass, and the foot of it of brass, of the looking-glasses of the women assembling which assembled at the door of the congregation." [141]

THE LAVER.

The object of the laver was for the priests to wash their hands and feet before they entered the holy place to minister, or before they offered any burnt offering unto the Lord. Not to wash meant death. For refusing to do this they would certainly die. [142] Hence we can see that the Lord had a great lesson He designed to teach the people thereby. The laver

[140] Ex. 30: 17.　　　[141] Ex. 38: 8.　　　[142] Ex. 30: 21.

must always be provided with water, so that the priest should have a supply on hand whenever it was needed.

53. David, referring no doubt to this service, says the following:

"I will wash mine hands in innocency: so will I compass thine altar, O Lord." [143]

It will be remembered that the priest must wash before he can serve at the altar. David appreciated its meaning, and saw at least *one* lesson it taught.

MEANING OF THE WATER.

54. Water in the Bible is a symbol of various truths, of the Spirit; [144] of the Word; [145] of baptism; [146] of cleansing. [147] Here, however, we see that David refers to the washing as an illustration of innocency. This being so, how much of divinity is stamped upon this great truth. How then the priests should have seen, and taught the people, every time they washed, the Innocent One, [148] in whose mouth was found no guile; [149] His life had nothing that was not true, and pure, and innocent. What He said outwardly illustrated what He was inwardly. He did not act one thing outwardly, and contradict this by His inward life. Pilate washed his hands, when the Jews clamored for the blood of Christ. We read that he took water, and washed in the presence of all the people, saying, "I am innocent of the blood of this just person." [150] But oh, the guilt of the Man's blood which defiled his soul.

55. So with the Jews. They would not go into the judgment-hall to accuse Christ of blasphemy, [151] for fear of being defiled; but they had no scruples whatever to murder Him, and to take a robber as a substitute. [152] But *He* was innocent; there was nothing in Him that was defiling, and insincere.

143 Ps. 26: 6.   144 John 7: 37–39.   145 John 13: 10; 15: 3; Eph. 5: 26.
146 John 3: 5.   147 Titus 3: 5.   148 Matt. 27: 4.   149 Isa. 53: 9; 1 Peter 2: 22.
150 Matt. 27: 24.   151 John 18: 28.
152 Acts 3: 14, 15.

RABBINICAL IDEAS OF THE LAVER.

56. Some very interesting descriptions have been given by the rabbis concerning this laver, and also by Josephus. Its support, its supposed position, general construction, and weight, are all explained and elaborated upon. Various opinions prevailed among the rabbis concerning its general scope; but of the real lesson it was designed to teach they had no idea. It is one thing to say, Lord, Lord; but another altogether to do the will of the Father which is in heaven. [153]

THE BRAZEN ALTAR.

57. In addition to the altar of incense that was in the *holy place of the sanctuary*, another altar was made, which was placed outside of the first apartment of the tabernacle near the entrance. This was the brazen altar, generally known as the "altar of burnt offering." A full description of it is found in Exodus 27. [154] The particular purpose of this altar was the offering up of all the animals brought to the priest as offerings. It was about four and a half feet high, seven and a half feet long, and the same in width. It was made of the same wood as the rest of the furniture, and covered with brass. That is why it received the name, altar of brass.

58. A complete set of dishes were made to go with it, necessary to carry on the work of offering up the animals to the Lord. Several kinds of offerings were burned upon this altar; some entire, others only in part. However, the chief thought in connection with this was the offering up of the animals.[155] Hence the Psalmist, seeing the meaning of the offering of the animals on the altar, says:

"God is the Lord, which hath shewed us light: bind the sacrifice with cords, even *unto the horns of the altar*." [156]

THE GREAT OFFERING.

59. Every offering which was sacrificed upon this altar

[153] Matt. 7: 21.   [154] Ex. 27: 1–8.   [155] Lev. Chaps. 1 to 3.   [156] Ps. 118: 27.

THE ALTAR OF BURNT OFFERING.

symbolized the great and only Offering which could be offered in behalf of sinful man.[157] The only means which God had whereby the atonement for mankind could be affected,—was the Lamb of God, which beareth away the sins of the world.[158] It was He who was typified by the offerings sacrificed upon the altar, and the altar itself was a great lesson of Him ; for, says the apostle :

"We have an altar, whereof they have no right to eat which serve the tabernacle."[159]

60. The sanctuary and its service in Paul's day had completed its mission ; everything connected with it had been fulfilled in Christ. The priest and the Jewish people still followed the sacrifices and the offering.[160] As long as they did that, they could not see Christ. They could not partake with the followers of Christ. If they still clung to these offerings, they had no right to have a part with the followers of Christ.

61. When the vail of the temple was rent in twain at the time of the crucifixion,[161] sin offerings, and offerings of every kind which had been formerly offered upon the altar, forever ceased. Everything was fulfilled in Him. He offered Himself to God without spot and blemish, a whole burnt offering. Because of this, how we should regard the precious lessons we find in the brazen altar, and the offering up of its sacrifices.

62. It is no doubt but that Paul, when thinking of this altar and its offerings, wrote the following to the Romans :

"I beseech you, therefore, brethren, by the mercies of God, that ye present *your bodies* a living sacrifice, holy, acceptable unto God, which is your reasonable service."[162]

THE MAKING OF THE COURT.

63. All the vessels in the holy places, as well as those not therein, were inclosed by a court. Moses was commanded to have

[157] Heb. 9 : 14.   [158] John 1 : 29, margin.   [159] Heb. 13 : 10.   [160] Acts. 21 : 26.
[161] Matt. 27 : 51.   [162] Rom. 12 : 1.

a court made,[163] to surround all these objects of the service of God. The court was about one hundred fifty feet long and about seventy-five feet wide in all its parts.[164] It was made of very delicate material, and was to present to the people a very beautiful and impressive sight. The material was to be of fine-twined linen, with the exception of the gate, or the entrance, which was composed of blue, purple, scarlet, and fine-twined linen.[165] Everything about it was harmonious, and nicely blended; the colors as well as the material. The hangings on the north and south sides were to have each about one hundred fifty yards of the beautiful fine-twined linen, and the east and west sides, each about seventy-five yards of the same material. The blue, purple, scarlet, fine-twined linen for the gate was to be beautifully wrought with cunning needlework.

64. These curtains were supported by sixty pillars, equidistant, each pillar resting in a socket of brass. Very beautiful silver hooks and fillets joined the curtains to the pillars. Under the curtains which formed the rib work of the court were forty-eight boards, all of the same height and width, joined together with tenons, and resting in silver sockets. The boards were all covered with pure gold.[166]

65. There were also several coverings made for the tent, to cover it everywhere.[167] The first covering was made of blue, purple, scarlet, and fine-twined linen, cunningly wrought with beautiful cherubim. Above this was a covering of goats' hair; then one of rams' skins, dyed red, and lastly, the one which appeared to the eyes of all the people. It was a rough, coarse-looking badger skin. It certainly was not at all attractive, and to the casual observer would not be considered very beautiful and harmonious, as compared with the workmanship or material which was found within.

CHRIST THE OBJECT OF ALL THE SANCTUARY.

66. There was nothing in all this grand and elaborate work

163 Ex. 27:9.   164 Ex. 27:18.   165 Ex. 27:9-17.   166 Ex. 26:15-30.   167 Ex. 26:1-14
168 Rom. 10:4.

but what contained very beautiful, significant, spiritual truth ; and the vital force of it all was Jesus Christ, the Messiah. Yes indeed ;

"Christ is the end of the law for righteousness to every one that believeth." [168]

67. How different His life and teachings to that of the Pharisees. Everything about them was *beautiful without*, like the polished and garnished tombs ; while everything within was similar to the deposits under those tombstones. [169] The outward skin which covered the sanctuary was *apparently* unpleasant and undesirable to the eye, while the objects within were all beautiful and glorious. How forcibly we are reminded of what the prophet Isaiah said of Him :

" He hath no form nor comeliness ; and when we shall see Him, there is no beauty that we should desire Him. He is despised and rejected of men ; a Man of sorrows, and acquainted with grief : and we hid as it were our faces from Him ; He was despised, and we esteemed Him not." [170]

68. All this the Lord taught the people in the sanctuary ; all this the Lord was using to reveal Christ to them. God was teaching the people ; [171] but they were dull of hearing. While they admired the gold, the stones, the precious materials, and the rabbis enjoyed discussing about them, they did not see the application of the truth.

WHAT THE CHURCH WILL GAIN BY SEEING CHRIST.

69. O Church of God to-day ! keep thine eye fastened upon Him, the fulfillment of all the truths in the word of God ! See that in Him is all beauty, grandeur and glory ; and by beholding Him we shall become changed. [172]

[169] Matt. 23 : 27, 28. [170] Isa. 53 : 2, 3. [171] Isa. 54 : 13 ; John 6 : 45. [172] 2 Cor. 3 : 18.

EXPLANATORY NOTES.

Paragraph 2.

(*a*) A variety of opinions exist as to the exact measurement of a cubit. The Hebrew word for cubit is אַמָּה=*ammah*. The plural is

אַמָּתִים=, *two ammahs*. But the Jews consider that two ammahs equal an

anglo-saxon yard. That would make the ammah, or cubit, equal a half yard, or eighteen inches. While this perhaps is not the exact literal measurement that may have been in use in Bible times, this is as near to it as can be ascertained. Hence the cubit has been counted as eighteen inches.

Paragraph 3.

(*b*) From the reading of this verse alone, one might be led to think that it was Moses that wrote the ten commandments upon the tables of stone. But by reading the other scriptures cited in this same paragraph, it will be observed that it was God who did the writing, and not Moses. The pronoun *He*, therefore, refers to God and not to His servant.

A similar illustration of the use of this pronoun *he* is found in the experience of David numbering the people. In the record as given in 2 Sam. 24 : 1, it would seem that the pronoun *he*, in this text, referred to God; and, therefore, it was God who tempted David to number the people. But we know that God does not tempt any man to do wrong: for says the Apostle James: " Let no man say when he is tempted, I am tempted of God: for God *cannot be tempted* with evil, *neither tempteth He any man:* but every man is tempted, when he is drawn away of his own lust, and enticed." James 1: 13, 14.

By the reading, however, of the account of the numbering of the people as found in 1 Chron. 24 : 1, it plainly says that " *Satan* stood up against Israel, and provoked David to number Israel." The pronoun *he*, therefore, in 2 Sam. 24 : 1, is meant for Satan, and not for the Lord.

So then if the word of the Lord were studied itself, it would be seen that God explains Himself very clearly, and gives very lucid expositions of His own blessed Word. We should then see how beautifully the word of God explains itself, and how easy it is to be understood. Truly, the wayfaring man, though a fool, need not err therein.

Paragraph 15.

(*c*) The word *cherubims* is not the proper word to use. This word is not a *translated* word, but a *transferred* one. The Hebrew singular is כְּרוּב=*ke-roov*. The plural is כְּרוּבִים=*ke-roo-vim*. So the English reads

cherub for the singular ; hence for the plural, it should read either *cherubim*, or *cherubs*. The Hebrew plural is formed by the letter ם=*mem*. Hence the proper word in the English should be *cherubim*. But since the plural in the English is formed by adding *s*, or *es*, to the singular, the word *cherubs* would be proper. Either cherubs, or cherubim, should be used for the plural. In this work, the term *cherubim* is used.

Paragraph 20.

(*d*) There is a growing tendency at the present time to disbelieve in the personality of Satan. But the Scripture teaches very forcibly that there is such a being, who is a real personage, and who has wonderful and mighty powers. Jesus says that He saw Satan fall from heaven; and there are an abundance of scriptures which clearly teach that he and his associates are the leaders in this great rebellion of evil. Luke 10:18; Rev. 12:7-9. They are yet to work miracles, and do mighty works ere the Lord shall come; but the Savior warns and admonishes us that we may not be enslaved by them. God, however, has pledged that the devil and sin shall forever be destroyed. Rev. 13:13, 14; Rev. 16:14; 2 Thess. 2:1-12; Matt. 24:24; Isa. 14:15; Ezek. 28:19; Nahum 1:9; Matt. 25:4.

Paragraph 29.

(*e*) The very fact that the Savior compares Himself to the true manna lends additional force to the Hebrew definition of the shewbread, the bread of the presence. Soon after the manna began to fall in the wilderness the Lord commanded Moses to tell Aaron to "take a pot, and put an omer full of manna therein, and lay it up before the Lord, to be kept for your generations." Ex. 16:33. The words, *before the Lord*, are literally, לִפְנֵי יְהוָה, *before the face of the Lord*. That is to say, this manna, which was to be preserved throughout their generations, was to ever be kept in the presence of God, as a reminder to the people how God had fed their forefathers in the wilderness. Ex. 16:32.

As this bread was to ever keep before them the fact that God had fed their ancestors with bread from heaven, from his presence, even so He would feed them with the spiritual bread, the Messiah, the *le-hem ha-ponim*, the Real Bread of the Presence, who always was in the presence of God.

This the Jews ought to have known; for the priests and rulers acknowledged that the Messiah was to come from Bethlehem. Micah 5:2; Matt. 2:4-6. But the words בֵּית לֶחֶם-*Bethlehem*, mean *house of bread*.

Therefore the prophet predicted He was to come from a place known as the house of bread, because He was to be as a Shepherd, who should feed the people. See Matt. 2:6, margin.

Paragraph 45.

(*f*) Although the Israelites had received so much light, and so many helps to keep them from apostatizing from God, the larger part of

14

their national history deals with their experiences as worshipers of the sun-god. Their first experience was the making of the golden calf; and from this time till they were carried to Assyria and to Babylon, they were constantly worshiping Baal, the sun, Ashera, and Ashteroth. Judges 2:13; 2 Kings 23:5; 2 Kings 17:6–23.

Paragraph 60.

(*g*) While Paul had so decidedly taught the fulfillment of all the ceremonial law in Christ, and therefore, all offerings in the earthly temple were useless, in order to yield to the wishes of some of his brethren, he took upon himself to obey certain of the laws which had become obsolete, by the doing of which he practically brought himself under bondage. In order to keep the peace with the brethren, when he was aware they were catering to popular opinion, he involved himself and others in persecution; became separated from all those who were dear to him at Jerusalem; and the cause of Christ lost valuable help it might otherwise have had. An able writer, in speaking of this experience of Paul, says: "When we consider Paul's great desire to be in harmony with his brethren, his tenderness of spirit toward the weak in faith, his reverence for the apostles who had been with Christ, and for James, the brother of the Lord, and his purpose to become all things to all men as far as he could do this and not sacrifice principle,—when we consider all this, it is less surprising that he was constrained to deviate from his firm, decided course of action. But instead of accomplishing the desired object, these efforts for conciliation only precipitated the crisis, hastened the predicted sufferings of Paul, separated him from his brethren in his labors, deprived the church of one of its strongest pillars, and brought sorrow to Christian hearts in every land." —"*Sketches from the Life of Paul.*"

All this plainly teaches that it pays ever to stand firm and true to principle, and leave the results with the Lord. The Lord, however, knew the purposes of His faithful servant, and overruled it all to His own glory, and for Paul's good. Nevertheless, there was a loss to God's cause which might have been saved.

CHAPTER XIII.

The Priesthood and the Offerings.

"For such an high priest became us, who is holy, harmless, unde-filed, separate from sinners, and made higher than the heavens: who needeth not daily, as those high priests, to offer up sacrifice, first for His own sins, and then for the people's: for this He did once, when He offered up Himself." Heb. 7:26, 27.

THE PRIESTS TO REPRESENT CHRIST.

OF all the offices connected with the Jews that of the priesthood was the most solemn and sacred. The climax of truth and beauty concerning the work and ministration of the Lord Jesus Christ and the most graphic representation of the Messiah as He was to be, were met in the high priest, and those associated with him. Consequently, special laws and ordinances were given for the priesthood, which could not under any circum-stances be applied to any other class of people. The Lord sought to keep them pure, holy, spotless, living examples to all of the purity and spotlessness of their great Antitype, the Lord Jesus. They were to be the models of the people; and to them the people were to look for instruction, for blessing, [1] for truth, for light, for judgment.

THE PRIESTHOOD BECOMES CORRUPT.

2. Though the Lord had done all in his power to preserve them pure, it was but a short time after the priesthood was instituted before some of them became corrupt. [2] Corruption continued to increase among them, till the days just prior to the Babylonian exile; then all became so wicked and vile [3] that the Lord was obliged to send them into captivity for seventy years. After the return from Babylon, Ezra, Nehemiah, and a few

[1] Num. 6:22-26.   [2] Lev. 10:1, 2; 1 Sam. 2:12, 17, 27-29.   [3] 2 Chron. 36:14.

others sought to reform the priesthood, and for a while met with good success;[4] but soon after the men of God passed away, corruption again was rife among them,[5] and so wickedly at that, that when the Lord came to earth every bit of sacredness and solemnity connected with that office was entirely lost; and the priests in general were among the worst of the people.[6] This was especially true of the high priest. His position being the greatest, his influence the most extensive, using it for personal advantage only, naturally made him the most wicked and corrupt.[7] To see the force of this statement, we need to con sider such men as Annas and Caiaphas, from the accounts given of them in the New Testament.[8] And the Talmud tells us that a learned person, though he be an illegitimate child, is to be preferred before a high priest who is an ignorant man. Thus we can see how this most holy office had become vile, especially among the rabbis and priests themselves.

ORIGIN OF THE PRIESTS.

3. Much might be said concerning the priests and their work, but space will forbid an extended dissertation. In the patriarchal days the head of the family was also its local priest, who did the ministering for the family, before the Lord. The father of the family was supposed to represent the great High Priest before his household. In the days of the Israelites, after they had become a people, and the types of the gospel and of salvation through the Messiah, the priesthood was confined to a special tribe. The tribe chosen was that of Levi;[9] the gift was placed upon Aaron and his posterity.[10] All the male children of Aaron[11] were to be priests. This priesthood was to be confined only to the family of Aaron, and was not to be transmitted to any other portion of this tribe.[12]

4. The priesthood was divided into two sections, the high

4 Ezra 10:18, 19.　5 Mal. 1:6-8; 2:1, 2, 7, 8.　6 Matt. 21:15; 26:3, 4; Luke 10:31.
7 Matt. 26:65-67; Acts 23:2.　8 John 18:13-24; Acts 4:5-7.
9 Num. 3:11, 12, 41, 44, 45.　10 Ex. 28:1.　11 Num. 3:10.　12 Num. 3:10.

priest [13] and the regular priests.[14] The high priest was especially to be God's personal representative on the earth, a special type of Christ, to communicate His messages to the people. This is forcibly illustrated when Moses and Aaron were commanded to appear before Pharaoh. The Lord said thus to Moses:

"Is not Aaron the Levite thy brother? I know that he can speak well. . . . And thou shalt speak unto him and put words in his mouth: . . . And he shall be thy spokesman unto the people: and he shall be, even he shall be to thee instead of a mouth, and thou shalt be to him instead of God." [15]

THE ANOINTING OF THE PRIESTS.

5. When Aaron and his sons were called to the priesthood, they were to have special garments made,[16] and were also to be anointed with special oil of consecration.[17] The high priest was to be anointed differently from his sons, the other priests. The anointing oil was to be poured upon his head, was to flow down upon his beard, till it dropped upon the borders of his garments.[18] The other priests, however, were only anointed on certain parts of their body, and on their garments.[19]

SUCCESSION IN HIGH PRIESTHOOD.

6. The oldest son was to succeed his father in the high priesthood, when the latter deceased. If, however, the oldest son had died, the next in age was to be the successor. This was illustrated in the case of Eleazer, the third son of Aaron.[20] The two older ones were slain by the Lord, because of offering strange fire,[21] while under the influence of strong drink.[22] He was the successor in age.

THE MINISTRY OF THE PRIESTS.

7. The work of the priests was to minister before the Lord.

---

13 Lev. 21: 10: 2 Chron. 24: 11.   14 Num. 3: 2, 3; Luke 1: 8.
15 Ex. 4: 14-16.   16 Ex. 28: 2, 3; 31: 10.   17 Ex. 29: 5-10; 28: 41.
18 Ex. 29: 7; Lev. 8: 12; 21: 10; Ps. 133: 2.   19 Ex. 28: 41.
20 Num. 20: 25-28.   21 Lev. 10: 1, 2.   22 Lev. 10: 8-10.

They were to act as mediators between God and men. They were to bring the blood, which was shed by the people in the offerings they brought to the Lord for the forgiveness of their sins, and sprinkle it in the holy place, just before the vail. [23] Or when they did not do this, they were to eat of the flesh of the slain animals in the holy place, [24] thus bearing the people's sins into the sanctuary in this manner. By the sprinkled blood that was shed, and by the bearing of the sins in the flesh, the priests were to make known God's method of the atonement.

THE PRIEST'S GARMENTS.

8. The priest's garments were made from special material, worked in a particular manner. Speaking of them as a whole, they were to have two sets of holy garments, the linen garments, and the robes of beauty and of glory. Then there was to be the breastplate, the ephod, the broidered coat, the mitre, the girdle, to be worn by the high priest alone. All these garments were to be specially anointed and consecrated, even as the priest himself was. They were made of the most costly material, adorned, embellished, and decorated in a most beautiful manner. If the reader will study Exodus, chapters twenty-eight and thirty-nine, he will find a most sublime description of these beautiful articles. They deserve thought and study, for their truths shine with luster. While each one is deserving of much comment and consideration, we wish to notice especially a few thoughts concerning the ephod, and the breastplate.

THE EPHOD.

9. The ephod was made of gold, of blue, of purple, of scarlet, of fine-twined linen, very artistically embroidered. [25] It was in two parts, one for the front, one for the back. These pieces were joined together at the shoulder by their two edges. Then on each of the shoulder-pieces was to be placed an onyx stone, set in a beautiful golden case. On these two stones were

[23] Lev. 4:15-17, 20.　　[24] Lev. 7:6.　　[25] Ex. 28:6-14.

THE HIGH PRIEST IN LINEN ROBES.

to be inscribed the names of the twelve tribes of the children of Israel.[26]   On the one stone the names of six tribes, on the other stone the names of the other six.   It is then stated that the high priest was to regard these stones as a memorial unto the children of Israel, and he shall bear their names before the Lord upon his two shoulders.

10. What a beautiful and precious prophecy this is of Christ's work, and how was it possible that those Jews, who had read the Scriptures so much, and who knew what they said concerning this that the Messiah should do, could not understand ! Yet, when He accomplished that very thing while here on earth, the people were so full of their own distorted views of the Bible that they could not see it.   This was the fulfillment :

"For unto us a Child is born, unto us a Son is given : and the government shall be upon His shoulders [Hebrew שִׁכְמוֹ *Shech-mo*, plural, *shoulders*], and His name shall be called Wonderful, Counsellor, The Mighty God, The Everlasting Father, the Prince of Peace." [27]

How Christ did bear the people upon His shoulders ![28]   How by day He taught them,[29] He sought them,[30] He fed them,[31] He cared for them ! [32] How by night He prayed and pleaded for them ![33]   How the one burden of His life was to pity and care for the multitude ![34]   Gladly did He do all in His power for the sake of bearing the burdens of the people.[35]

THE PHARISEES MADE BURDENS.

11. While the rabbis were binding upon the people burdens grievous to be borne,[36] which they could not endure, the Savior was saying to them :

"Come unto Me, all ye that labor and are heavy-laden, and I will give

[26] Ex. 28 : 9, 10.   [27] Isa. 9 : 6.   [28] Isa. 63 : 8, 9 ; 53 : 4 ; 40 : 11.   [29] Matt. 5 : 2 ; 13 : 54 ; 26 : 55. [30] Luke 19 : 10.   [31] Mark 8 : 1–9.   [32] 1 Pet. 5 : 7. [33] Mark 6 : 46–48 ; Heb. 5 : 7 ; Luke 22 : 31, 32.   [34] Matt. 9 : 36.   [35] 1 Pet. 2 : 24. [36] Luke 11 : 46 ; Acts 15 : 10.

'you rest. Take My yoke upon you, and learn of Me; for I am meek and lowly in heart: and ye shall find rest unto your souls." [37]

What burdens they heaped upon the people! Hundreds, yes thousands, of traditions of every class and description, and all these the people must observe with severe punctiliousness.

12. Since He has departed to heaven, He has still been bearing his people [38] upon His shoulders, and He will bear the twelve tribes till He places them at the great white throne,[39] and they see their names engraved upon the gates of the beautiful city of God.[40]

THE BREASTPLATE AND ITS LESSON.

13. The breastplate was made of the same precious metal as the ephod, and inserted, double and bag-shaped, in the ephod. It was a perfect square, about a span each way. It was attached to the ephod above the girdle. Beautiful gold chains were attached to it above and below, giving it a rich and gilded appearance. What made it appear most beautiful was the four rows of precious stones which were inserted in it. Each row contained three stones, making in all twelve stones. [41] These stones were of the same material that is found in the walls of the beautiful city of God, the New Jerusalem.[42] On each stone was a name of one of the tribes of Israel, thus making in all twelve tribes. The breastplate was so worn that it covered the heart, so that he literally bore the twelve tribes upon his heart, when he went into the sanctuary to minister before the Lord. In addition to this there were two other stones in the breastplate, called Urim and Thummim.[43] These were the oracles by which the priest inquired of God, and through which the Lord answered him.[44] (a)

14. How this does illustrate to us the work of the great High Priest, even Jesus, the Son of God, who upon His own divine human soul, bears the names of all His children in the

[37] Matt. 11:28, 29.   [38] Heb. 4:14-16.   [39] Rev. 14:1, 3.   [40] Rev. 21:12.
[41] Ex. 28:15-29.   [42] Rev. 21:19, 20.   [43] Ex. 28:30.   [44] Num. 27:21; 1 Sam. 28:

THE HIGH PRIEST IN ROBES OF GLORY AND BEAUTY.

heavenly sanctuary before God. How glad He is to present the names of these twelve tribes of the true Israel of God to-day before His Father, and plead for them His precious merits through the shed blood.[45]

15. When we ask of Him what we need, and He grants it to us even as we ask, what light and joy comes into the soul, and what blessed peace follows. If, however, he sees that to answer according to His will, is the best way, though it may bring a cloud over our life's experiences, we should nevertheless remember that all things work together for good to them that love God ; and, therefore, in whatsoever state we are, therewith we should be content.[46]

URIM AND THUMMIM ABSENT IN SECOND TEMPLE.

16. Among the things the rabbis taught were missing in the second temple, was the breastplate. As a result, they record in the prayers which are read in the synagogue, even at the present day, the sadness and sorrow they endure because they have no breastplate, nor Urim and Thummim, that they might inquire of the Lord and find Him as aforetime. But they can find Him, if they will go where He is.[47] He said to the Jews, "Ye shall seek Me, and shall not find Me." [48] The reason is, they are not seeking for Him in the proper place.[49]

17. What was true of the Jews is true also of many who profess to love Him at the present time. He is in the heavenly sanctuary, in the most holy place, [50] bearing upon His soul, *now*, the names of all who desire His grace and salvation, pleading before the Father His own virtue and merit. The earthly priests are no more ; [51] (b) the Heavenly Priest abideth forever.[52]

THE SACRIFICIAL OFFERINGS.

18. After the priesthood had been instituted for the work of ministry, the Lord gave commands concerning the offerings. Everything connected with the offerings was to represent some

---

45 Rev. 1:5.   46 Rom. 8: 28; Phil. 4: 1.   47 John 6: 37.   48 John 7: 34.
49 Rev. 1: 12, 13.   50 Rev. 3: 8.   51 Heb. 7: 12,22-24.   52 Heb. 9: 26.

form of the great Offering, who was the true Sin-bearer; these offerings being but types and shadows. That there was no virtue in the blood of these animals is evident from what the apostle says:

"For it is not possible that the blood of bulls and of goats should take away sins." [53]

They were to see in these sacrifices the great Sacrifice, who would bear away the sins of the world. [54]

19. The offerings were divided into two great classes; the sweet savor offerings, and the sin offerings, or non-sweet savor. In the first division were the whole-burnt offering, the meat offering, the peace offering. [55]　In the second the sin offering, and the trespass offering. [56]　The sin and trespass offering were offered up before the others; because a person could not appreciate the meaning of the sweet-savor offerings until he had experienced the blessings of the sin offerings, and had received expiation. [57]

EVERY OFFERING HAD ITS SIGNIFICANCE.

20. Every one of these offerings taught some great truth concerning the Messiah, the Savior of the world. They were to teach the priests and people the forgiveness of sin, the atonement through the blood; the pardon of a trespass after a man had been forgiven his sin and committed error; the giving of his whole life to God after his sins were forgiven, as illustrated in the whole-burnt offering; the meat offering, the feeding of his whole life upon the salvation of God; the peace offering, the sweet peace which comes to the soul through the Lord Jesus.

THE SIN OFFERING.

21. While we could with much profit devote considerable space to each of these offerings individually, we *must consider* still further the sin offerings, as there is so much wrapped up

[53] Heb. 10:4.　　[54] John 1: 29, margin.　　[55] Lev. 1; 2; 3.　　[56] Lev. 4: 5; 6: 1-7.
[57] Lev. 4: 35; 6: 6, 7.

in them. The laws of these offerings found in Leviticus, chapters four and five, are as follows:

22. If a *priest* committed a sin he was to bring a sin offering,[58] and appear with it at the door of the tabernacle. Then he was to place his hand upon this offering, and confess his sins thereon. After this was done, he was to take of the blood of this slain animal, and carry it into the holy place of the sanctuary, and sprinkle it seven times before the vail, before the Lord.[59] Then some of the blood was also to be sprinkled upon the horns of the golden altar of incense,

MAN CONFESSING HIS SINS.

the rest of the blood to be poured at the base of the altar of burnt offering.[60] Then the animal was to be dissected; part to be burned on the altar of burnt offering;[61] the rest of the body including his inward parts, was to be taken away from the sanctuary, unto a clean place, at a distance from the

[58] Heb. 7:27.   [59] Lev. 4:5, 6.   [60] Lev. 4:7.   [61] Lev. 4:8–10.

camp, where a fire was built, and the parts burned. [62] This was carrying away the animal without the camp. The animal was slain; the blood sprinkled in the sanctuary before the Lord, before the vail; the fat burned; the rest of the animal carried without the camp.

SIN OFFERING FOR THE DIFFERENT CLASSES.

23. This was in general the way the animals were offered up as sin offerings. Beside the offering up of the sin offering for the priest, there were the sin offerings of the people as a whole, [63] the offering for the rulers, [64] the offering of the common people individually. [65] After the blood was sprinkled, the fat offered up, the animal taken "without the camp" and burned, the individual, or the people collectively, received the forgiveness of sins; [66] an atonement was made for the soul. He was reconciled to God; his sins were forgiven. [67]

CHRIST, THE GREAT SIN OFFERING.

24. Who cannot see in this offering a beautiful type of the offering up of the Son of God, the Savior, the Sin Offering? After the sins of the people had been confessed upon him, [68] He voluntarily bore them in the Garden of Gethsemane. [69] The people then took Him and shed His blood, clamoring for His crucifixion. " His blood be upon us and upon our children." [70]

25. He bore our sins in His own body on the tree. When He gave His life for us, He took upon Himself our own sins ; [71] He became sin for us, who knew no sin. [72] The fat, representing the sin, was offered up unto God. By offering His life to God for us, He offered up the sins also, [73] which He had purchased with His own precious blood, [74] and thus they became as the fat offered upon the altar.

26. Paul says that as the animals were taken, after they

[62] Lev. 4: 11, 12.   [63] Lev. 4: 13.   [64] Lev. 4: 22.   [65] Lev. 4·27.   [66] Lev. 4: 31.
[67] Lev. 4: 35.   [68] Isa. 53: 4, 6.   [69] Matt. 26: 36–45; Luke 22: 39–44.
[70] Matt. 27: 25.   [71] 1 Cor. 15: 3; 1 John 3: 5.   [72] 2 Cor. 5: 21.   [73] Gal. 1: 4.
[74] 1 Pet. 1: 18, 19; Heb. 9: 12–14.

CHRIST IN GETHSEMANE.

were slaughtered, and carried without the camp, even so was it done with Jesus.[75]   He bore reproach,[76] the curse, by hanging on the tree.[77]   He was carried without the camp, because He was *the* Sin Offering.

27. He afterward went to heaven, into the presence of God,[78] into the heavenly sanctuary, into the holy place,[79] before the vail of the ark of God, where is deposited the sacred and blessed law ; and there before that throne He presents to His Father the blood which had been shed for the sins of men. The Apostles could then well preach and teach :

" If we walk in the light, as He is in the light, we have fellowship one with another, and the blood of Jesus Christ His Son cleanseth us from all sin." [80]

Yes, the blood was sprinkled.[81]   As a result there was forgiveness.   The offering had been sacrificed ; the atonement was made.   Oh what a blessed Lamb, who bore away the sins of a doomed world !

THE PRIESTS LOST THE SIGNIFICANCE OF THE OFFERINGS.

28. When Christ came to earth the Jewish people had wholly lost sight of the meaning of the priesthood, and of the sacrifices.   The priests, who were to offer the offerings, had lost sight of the meaning of this service, for they had neither mercy nor compassion upon people.   This is forcibly illustrated in the parable of the " Good Samaritan," when the priest passed by, and walked on the other side.[82]   The animals were bought and sold in the temple, and were made a means of merchandise.[83]   These very blessings had become a curse to them.[84]

29. There was much said about the offerings, the different kinds, their different purposes ; volumes were written in one form or another.   Nevertheless the meaning of these offerings they never understood.   Perhaps the reader will form some

75 Heb. 13: 11, 12.   76 Rom. 15: 3.   77 Deut. 21: 23.   78 Heb. 9: 24.
79 Heb. 8: 1, 2; 9: 24.   80 1 John 1: 7.   81 Heb. 12:24; 1 Pet. 1:2.
82 Luke 10:31.   83 John 2: 14, 16.   84 Mal. 2:1, 2.

better idea of their view of the offerings at the time of Christ and since, by the following taken from the Jewish prayer-book :

"Which are the places of the offerings ? the holy of holies, their sacrifice was towards the north ; the bullock and the goat, on the Day of Atonement, their sacrifice was in the north ; the reception of their blood in the vessel of service in the north. Their blood required sprinkling over and between the staves, the vail, and the golden altar; one gift neglected interrupted the service. The rest of the blood was poured on the west side at the bottom of the outer altar; if not given it did not interrupt the service.

The bullocks and the goats which were burnt, their sacrifices at the north side. The reception of their blood in the vessel of service at the north. Their blood required sprinkling on the vail, and on the golden altar. One gift omitted interrupted the service. The rest of their blood was poured at the bottom, on the west side of the outer altar; if it was not given, it would not interrupt the service ; both were burnt in the house of ashes.

The sin offering of the whole congregation, and of particular persons, these are they : The sin offering of the whole congregation, the goats which were brought at the beginning of the months, and at the festivals, their slaughter was at the north ; and the reception of their blood was in vessels of service in the north ; and their blood required four gifts on the four corners. . . ."

30. We thus see how their tradition was mixed with the truth, and a jumbling confusion resulted. What the apostle wrote to Timothy, touching this very point, is not surprising :

"Now the end [or object] of the commandment is charity out of a pure heart, and of a good conscience, and of faith unfeigned : from which some having swerved have turned aside unto *vain jangling:* desiring to be teachers of the law; *understanding neither what they say, nor whereof they affirm."* [85]

PAUL SHOWED CHRIST FROM THESE LAWS.

31. Much more, similar to the above, might be cited, to illustrate the sayings of these teachers of the law. Paul reasoned with them out of the Scriptures ; [86] and from these very laws of Moses, [87] in the offerings and sacrifices, he proved to them that

[85] 1 Tim. 1 : 5–7.   [86] Acts 17 : 2.   [87] Acts 4 : 14.

Jesus was the very Christ. [88] He said he taught none other things than that which Moses and the prophets did say should come, [89]—that Christ should be the Savior of and Sacrifice for the world. [90] A most beautiful as well as a philosophical study of the priesthood and the offerings is contained in that wonderful book to the Hebrews, written by the Apostle Paul.

ADVANTAGE TO THE CHURCH TO STUDY THE LEVITICAL LAWS.

32. If the Jews could only have the vail of unbelief removed from their eyes, [91] and see the meaning of all the sacrificial system,—how perfectly and completely it was fulfilled in Jesus Christ and in His ministry,—what a wonderful power and marvelous light, by the illumination of the Spirit, might be given to the world. Then should not the church of Christ to-day study these grand truths; see what is written in Moses and in the law; find out what the book of Leviticus teaches? Eternal life through Jesus Christ will then be more and more appreciated. Repeatedly Jesus said that Moses had written of Him; [92] His whole life and work was contained in the law of Moses, as well as in the prophets. There is no offering, no sacrifice, no service, no phase of the priesthood but what all find in Him great significance, and much importance. " Blessed are your eyes, for they see : and your ears, for they hear." [93]

[88] Acts 17:3.   [89] Acts 26:22.   [90] Heb. 9:26.   [91] 2 Cor. 3:15, 16; Rom. 11:23.
[92] Luke 24:27, 44; John 5:46, 47.   [93] Matt. 13:16.

EXPLANATORY NOTES.

Paragraph 13.

(*a*) The words *Urim* and *Thummim* are Hebrew words, which have never been translated. The Hebrew word הָאוּרִים=*ha-oo-rim*, is the plural form of אוֹר=*or* *light*. The Hebrew word הַתֻּמִּים=*ha-too-mim*, is perfection, from the word תָּמִּים=*tam-mim*. When the Lord responded favorably to the individual, who came to the priest for counsel from God, a halo of light encircled the Urim. That was practically saying

15

to the man that God was pleased with his request, and there was light in it for him. But when the petitioner was to be denied his desire, a cloudy appearance was noticed at the Thummim. This was practically saying that God would take care of that matter; and everything should remain as it was.

Paragraph 17.

(*b*) Ever since the destruction of the temple in A.D. 70, by Titus, the Roman general, the sacrificial system has been done away by the Jews. There have been times when a few would attempt to revive the offering of animals; but the people know that this cannot be done, except there be an altar and a temple. Moreover, the lineage of the tribes has not been preserved since that time; therefore, a person cannot determine whether he really belongs to the tribe of Levi, or to any other tribe. But for many centuries there has been maintained a traditional genealogy among those who are supposed to have descended from the tribe of Levi, both the priests and the Levites. And this is the manner that it has been done:

The word *priest* in the Hebrew is כֹּהֵן=*Co-hen*. All these, therefore, that we find at the present day by the name *Cohen*, claim to be traditionally descended from this tribe. The way the word became Anglo-Saxonized is as follows:

It has been the custom among the Jews for many centuries, to give the child *one* name. This was generally done, and is followed by the orthodox Jews at the present day, at the time of the circumcision of the child,—when the child is eight days old. See Luke 1:59–63. When a child reaches a certain age, he learns an occupation. This has been and is still practiced by the Jews. In order then to discriminate this particular person from all others by the same name, he was called by his name and occupation. For example:

John was known as the Baptist. Why?—Because the Jews regarded that his occupation was to baptize. Luke was known from all others as the physician. Col. 4:14. Alexander was recognized as the one from all others, with that same name, as the coppersmith. 2 Tim. 4:14. The Prophet Amos was known from all others who lived in his community with a similar name, as the herdman, or keeper of sheep. Amos 1:1; 7:14, 15. And so on.

This custom of naming children in this way is still practiced by the orthodox Jews, and for this reason:

In the European countries, as Russia, Germany, Austria, Hungary, Galicia, Prussia, Poland, etc., as well as in Palestine, where the Jews are very thickly populated, and where the customs and manners of the people do not bring them into much prominence in a commercial way, the Jews are usually known by this first name; as Abraham, Joseph, Isaac, etc. Then to identify this particular Abraham, Joseph, etc., from all others in that same community, with the same name, his occupation would be mentioned.

But when the Jews emigrated to England, America, and to other civilized, Protestant, Anglo-Saxon communities, this was an insurmountable obstacle in their path of progress in not having a family name. So some of the Jews who traditionally professed to descend from the priestly tribe took the Hebrew tribal name, *Co-hen*, *priest*, and Anglo-Saxonized it; and the family name became Cohen. This is also true of the name *Levy*, and of *Israel*.

Still others who found similar difficulties, would adopt a family name from their ancestral occupation in Europe; as for example: Silverman. This name would indicate that some father of this family was once a dealer in silver. This is equally true of the name of Goldman, Silverstein, etc.

The object of this note, however, is to explain to the reader the meaning of the word, כֹּהֵן=*Co-hen*, *priest;* why the priesthood has been done away, and yet the name *Cohen*, or *priest*, is so popularly known.

Paragraph 23. •

(*c*) The word translated " laid " in Isa. 53 : 6, does not express fully the thought that is contained in the original. The margin of the text is much nearer the true meaning. We will insert the last clause of the verse, in the Hebrew, and render as near a literal translation from the Hebrew, as thought from one language to another can be expressed :

Va-yeho-vah hif-ge-a bow eth a-voun koo-lo-noo=וַיהוָה הִפְגִּיעַ בּוֹ אֵת עֲוֹן כֻּלָּנוּ

" And Jehovah *has focussed* in Him the sins of all of us."

The Hebrew word הִפְגִּיעַ is a rare Hebrew word. It expresses the thought of centralizing, compassing to one point, causing to meet in one place, focussing. Leeser's translation renders it " befall." The thought seems to be like this : Just as a photographer would gather all of the sun's rays and focus them, in order to secure the best results for a photograph, so the Lord gathered up all the sins of a lost world, of every sinner in the world, and caused them all to be centered in Jesus Christ. All of them were focussed in Him. He allowed Himself to be thus treated, and thus took upon Himself, and in Himself, all the sins of a lost world.

In the light of these truths, the words of Peter are certainly precious; " Who His own self bare our sins in His own body on the tree." 1 Peter 2 : 24. What volumes these words express. Yes, the blessed Christ had upon Himself confessed every sin of every sinner. Then certainly it is true that where sin abounds, grace doth much more abound. Rom. 5 : 20. Do *you*, dear reader, appreciate the gift ?

CHAPTER XIV.

The Festivals and the Feasts.

"In the last day, that great day of the feast, Jesus stood and cried, saying, If any man thirst, let him come unto Me, and drink. He that believeth on Me, as the Scripture hath said, out of his belly shall flow rivers of living water." John 7:37, 38.

WHY THE FESTIVALS WERE GIVEN.

IN order ever to keep the fact before the minds of the Israelites that they were a separated and peculiar people [1] unto the Lord, a people through whom He wished to reveal to the world the Messiah, and the many experiences connected with His life,—a number of festivals were given to them, which were to be observed at different seasons of the year, and at a specially appointed place. [2] A fast day was also set apart by the Lord, [3] which was intended to teach precious truths concerning the work of the Anointed of God.

2. It never was the intention of the Lord that no other people save the Israelites should observe these feasts; everyone could keep them, who would conform to the laws governing the same. [4] If they did this, however, they would then be as one of them, as one born of the people; [5] and in every respect would constitute similar worshipers of the Lord as were the Israelites.

3. The one feature in all these feasts was to keep before the people the real purpose which God had toward them. If they would see what was intended by these services they would not only be blessed themselves, but others would be brought into the fold, and learn of the great saving plan of God for a lost and sinful world.

[1] Ex. 19:5, 6. [2] Deut. 16:16. [3] Lev. 16:29, 30; 23:26-32; Num. 29:7.
[4] Num. 15:15, 16. [5] Ex. 12:48.

[228]

4. The first feast and festival which the Lord instituted was the Passover.[6] This one was not only the first, but perhaps the most sacred of all; and was designed to teach them some of the strongest and most forcible lessons concerning the Messiah.

5. This festival was introduced before the Israelites left their slavery in Egypt;[7] and it was ever to be associated with the thought of their freedom from slavery. Closely connected with this festival, and part of it, was the offering up of sacrifice;[8] in fact this was the basis of all the feasts. If there were no sacrifice or offering, the entire season of its observance would be useless, as far as the real lesson which God intended to teach thereby. (*a*)

THE PASCHAL LAMB.

6. While there were many offerings during the Passover feast,[9] the special and most prominent of them all was the passover, or paschal lamb.[10] The first instruction given is found in the twelfth chapter of Exodus; and little in addition was afterward given concerning the offering of other sacrifices.[11] There were at least six prominent things to be remembered in the offering of this lamb, every one of which was to teach some truth concerning Him who is "the Lamb of God that taketh away the sin of the world."[12]

1. There was to be a lamb for every household.[13]

2. This lamb must be without blemish.[14]

3. The lamb must be killed in the evening[15] (margin, between the evenings). Hebrew, בֵּין הָעַרְבַּיִם=*Ba-an ha-ar-ba-yim.*

4. The blood of the lamb must be sprinkled upon the side posts and upper door-post of the house, in which the lamb must be eaten.[16]

---

[6] Ex. 12:1-11; 1 Cor. 5:7.   [7] Ex. 12:1; Deut. 16:1.   [8] Num. 28.
[9] Num. 28:11-25.   [10] Ex. 12:3.   [11] Lev. 23:8; Num. 9:2,3; 28:16-20; Deut 16:1-6.
[12] John 1:29.   [13] Ex. 12:3, 4.   [14] Ex. 12:5.   [15] Ex. 12:6.   [16] Ex. 12:7.

EATING THE PASSOVER IN HASTE.

5. The lamb must be eaten the night it was killed; and under no circumstances must any part of it remain till morning; if so, it must not be eaten, but must be burned. [17]

6. Not a single bone of the lamb must be broken. [18]

7. While there are other matters of interest in connection with the paschal lamb, these mentioned are the most prominent, and contain the essence of the truth to be taught.

THE LESSON OF THE PASCHAL LAMB.

8. In instituting this service while the people were yet in the land of their slavery, the Lord evidently intended they should learn from this experience the real meaning of freedom from servitude. Concerning their deliverance and the manner it was to be performed, the Lord said :

" For I will pass through the land of Egypt this night, and will smite all the first-born in the land of Egypt, both man and beast ; and against all the gods of Egypt I will execute judgment: I am the Lord. And the blood shall be to you for a token upon the houses where ye are : and when I see the blood, I will pass over you, and the plague shall not be upon you to destroy you, when I smite the land of Egypt." [19]

9. After they sacrificed the lamb, they were to take of its blood and to sprinkle it upon the two places previously mentioned.[20] When the Lord would pass over the land to smite the Egyptians, then the house which He would observe had the blood sprinkled, that house would be freed from death. It made no difference what the man might have thought or believed ; it made no distinction with the Lord how many years the person claimed to be an Israelite ; nor did it differ how long he had been in Egyptian servitude. Neither did it make any difference to what wing of the twelve tribes he belonged. The one thing necessary for the man of the house, or for the entire people of that house, or for all the people in all the houses of the Israelites, to escape having death in the house that night was to have the *blood* sprinkled in its proper place. Nothing but the

[17] Ex. 12:10.   [18] Ex. 12:46.   [19] Ex. 12:12, 13.   [20] Ex. 12:7.

blood of the lamb could save a person from death. To do this, however, was efficacious, and brought salvation to the individuals who lived in that house.

DELIVERANCE ONLY THROUGH THE BLOOD.

10. It would have been as easy for the Lord to have brought the people from Egypt without having this ordinance performed, if the deliverance were designed merely as a temporal affair, or a deliverance from physical servitude only. But the deliverance of the children of Israel was not alone intended to be a freedom from physical slavery, it was the intention of God to teach the people that Egypt was a synonym of the darkness of sin; their deliverance from Egypt was to be to them a deliverance from the slavishness of sin, since they were set apart as a spiritual people. The only means which God had or has to deliver people from the slavery of sin is the blood.[21] This the people must see at the very beginning of their exode. They must recognize that the only way of deliverance from evil was through the blood of the great Lamb, who should sacrifice His life for them and for the world. They should learn their deliverance from spiritual Egypt was fully as great, if not greater, than their deliverance from the physical slavery of the literal Egypt.

SPIRITUAL EGYPT.

11. That the Lord intended to use Egypt as a figure, and that there was as real a spiritual Egypt as there was a literal one, is evident from what we read in the Revelation:

"And their dead bodies shall lie in the street of the great city, which spiritually is called Sodom and Egypt, where our Lord also was crucified."[22]

Now it is known that the Lord Jesus was not crucified literally, either in Egypt or Sodom;[23] but it is known that these two places were particularly noted for their cruelty and sins,

[21] Ex. 17:11; Heb. 9:22.　　[22] Rev. 10:8.　　[23] Luke 23:33.

which called down the wrath of God upon them.[24] It is also true that it was sin which crucified our Lord of glory ; [25] hence these two places are used as illustrations of sin. This was what the Lord wanted the Israelites to learn concerning their deliverance from Egypt.

EVERYTHING FULFILLED IN CHRIST.

12. Now *every one* of the laws connected with the lamb and its offering at the Passover, was fulfilled in Christ. This was true with no exception. We will, therefore, now consider their fulfillment in the same numerical order as we considered the distinctive features of the typical lamb.

THE PASSOVER LAMB IS CHRIST.

13. 1. The Prophet Isaiah, when speaking of the death of Christ, said :

" He was oppressed and He was afflicted, yet He opened not His mouth : He is brought *as a lamb to the slaughter*, and as a sheep before her shearers is dumb, so He openeth not His mouth." [26]

Soon after the baptism of Christ, He was introduced by John the Baptist to the multitudes as follows :

" Behold the Lamb of God, which taketh [margin, beareth] away the sin of the world." [27]

"And looking upon Jesus as He walked, he saith, Behold the Lamb of God !" [28]

And again, John the beloved says of Him :

"And when He had taken the book, the four beasts and four and twenty elders fell down before the Lamb," . . . [29]

"And I beheld, and, lo, in the midst of the throne, . . . stood a Lamb as it had been slain." [30]

And that He was directly called the Lamb, the Passover sacrifice, Paul says :

" For even Christ our Passover, is sacrificed for us." [31]

[24] Ex. 1: 13, 14; 6:9; Gen. 18: 20.   [25] 1 Cor. 15:3.   [26] Isa. 53: 7.   [27] John 1:29.
[28] John 1:36.   [29] Rev. 5:8.   [30] Rev. 5:6.   [31] 1 Cor. 5:7.

HIS LIFE WITHOUT BLEMISH.

14. 2. Nowhere in the history of the life of Christ can we find where it ever was marred by the least performance of sin.

"Forasmuch as ye know that ye were not redeemed with corruptible things, as silver and gold, . . . but with the precious blood of Christ, as of a Lamb without *blemish* and without spot." [32]

HE DIED BETWEEN THE EVENINGS.

15. 3. The great paschal Lamb, Jesus, died at the very hour the lamb was to be offered, between the evenings; about three o'clock in the afternoon. (*b*) The Scripture saith He was crucified, beginning at the sixth hour; and at the ninth hour he died, [33] which was three o'clock, (*c*) the very time they sacrificed the paschal lamb.

HIS SPRINKLED BLOOD ONLY SAVES.

16. 4. Soon after the Apostles began the preaching of the crucified and risen Savior, they told the people everywhere that it was only through the blood which Jesus shed that they could have the forgiveness of sins; because the blood of Jesus only cleanses from all sins. [34] And Peter, in his first epistle, evidently using the figure spoken of in the sprinkling of the blood of the lamb, says:

"Elect according to the foreknowledge of God the Father, through sanctification of the Spirit, unto obedience and the *sprinkling of the blood* of Jesus Christ." [35]

Thus we see that the sprinkled blood refers to the sprinkling of the blood of the Son of God which saves and purifies the hearts of men and women. [36]

CHRIST'S BODY NOT ALLOWED TO REMAIN OVER NIGHT.

17. 5. When Christ was crucified, it being on Friday, the sixth day, the preparation day for the Sabbath, [37] the Jews came

[32] 1 Pet. 1: 18, 19; 2: 22.   [33] Matt. 27:45, 46; Mark 15: 33–37; Luke 23: 33, 44–46.   [34] Acts 20: 28; Heb. 9: 14.   [35] 1 Pet. 1: 2.   [6] 1 John 1: 7.   [37] Luke 23: 54.

to Pilate and asked that the body of Jesus, and those of the thieves, might not be allowed to remain over the Sabbath as that was a high Sabbath [Hebrew, שַׁבָּת הַגָּדוֹל=*Shabbath-Ha-go-dol=the great Sabbath*] day;[38] (*d*) and it was not allowable to have bodies hanging over night, as this would be defiling to the people, to the Sabbath, as well as to the festival.[39] Hence Pilate gave orders to have them taken down, and it was done Thus we have the fulfillment of the prophecy concerning the lamb that it should not be kept over night. Yes, in Christ we find the Scriptures all fulfilled.[40]

NOT A BONE IN CHRIST'S BODY BROKEN.

18. 6. When the soldiers came to the bodies of the thieves, finding them still alive, they broke their legs, in order to kill them quickly before the sun should set. But when they came to the body of the Savior, supposing that He was not dead, they were ready to treat Him the same as they had done to the thieves. But to their surprise they found Him dead.[41] In order to be certain that all life had departed, they took the sword and pierced His side, whence flowed blood and water.[42] Hence the Scripture was truthfully and literally fulfilled that *not a bone of Him should be broken.*[43] The real lesson of the paschal Lamb was Jesus Christ. Not only as a whole was it fulfilled in Him, but every specification met its completeness in Him, the Lamb of God. Yet strange as it may seem the Jews did not see this. Are there not many at the present time who act as did the ancient people?

THE ORIGINAL COMMANDMENT.

19. When the command was given originally to observe the Passover with its ceremonies, it was in substance as follows:

20. In the first month, the month of Abib or Nisan, on the tenth day of the month, they were to take a lamb for every family. If the family were not large enough, more than one

---

38 John 19:31.   39 John 18:28; 19:31.   40 Luke 24:44.   41 John 19:33.
42 John 19:34.   43 John 19:36.

family would share in this.[44] This number, in the time of Christ, according to the Mishna, must not be less than ten, nor more than twenty. Hence Christ came within the required demand, there being thirteen who sat down to the last Passover supper.

21. This lamb must be kept till the fourteenth day of the month; then between the evenings it must be killed. The night following was to be a gathering of the family, when they were to eat this supper, and when the children were to learn from the father the story of the slavery, and deliverance from Egypt.[45] In connection with the eating of the lamb, unleavened bread was to be eaten; and for seven consecutive days, beginning with the night of the fourteenth, no leaven of any description must be found in any part of an Israelitish dwelling.[46] In addition to the eating of the unleavened bread the people were to have bitter herbs,[47] which were to remind them of the bitterness of the Egyptian servitude.

22. Then the first and last days of the festival were to be rest days, [48] שַׁבָּתוֹן=*Hebrew*, *Sabbaths*, in which no labor was to be performed, save that which was absolutely necessary. These days were not to be observed quite so strictly, from all labor, as was the Sabbath of the Lord, the weekly Sabbath, the seventh day of the week.

ONLY THE CIRCUMCISED TO EAT OF IT.

23. This in detail was the manner which God provided for the observance of the Passover. One thing more it might be well to mention in this connection: No person was allowed to eat of it who was not circumcised.[49] If a man, a stranger, lived in the family, he would either have to be absent from the Passover supper, or if he chose to partake of it, he must be circumcised; then he would be considered as one of the people.[50] Not under any consideration was a person allowed to eat the Passover if he were not circumcised.. This illustrates why the

---

44 Ex. 12:3, 4.   45 Ex. 13:6–8, 14, 15,   46 Ex. 12:15, 18–20; 13:6, 7.
47 Ex. 12:8.   48 Ex. 12:16; Lev. 23:7, 8.   49 Ex. 12:48.   50 Ex. 12:43–49.

children of Israel, during their sojourn in the wilderness, partook of only one Passover.[51] On account of their murmurings against the Lord they were refused admission into the promised land, hence were to die in the wilderness. During the remainder of their thirty-eight years' wandering, not one of their children was circumcised. When they came into the land and were circumcised, then they kept the feast.[52]

THE PERVERSION OF THE PASSOVER.

24. When the Savior came to earth, instead of finding the Passover as it was originally given, He found it to quite an extent perverted, and the meaning of the service largely lost. True, they kept the Passover festival, but now it had become really Jewish.[53] God gave it as *His Passover*;[54] but they had turned it into an institution largely according to their own liking. True, the basis of the festival, the offering of the lamb, they still observed, but so much had been added, and so many burdens at that, that it was really a heavy load to the people. As the Jews observe it at the present day, it is very nearly the same as it was kept in the days of the Savior; hence we will give a description of the Passover as it is now observed, which also will shed some light on a few passages of Scripture in this connection.

THE REMOVING OF THE LEAVEN.

25. On the evening of the fourteenth of Nisan, the master of the house with one of his boys, generally the youngest, searches the house for leaven.(*e*) Some time earlier in the day small pieces of bread are scattered in different rooms and halls of the house, wherever leaven of any kind has been used during the year. In the evening the man of the house generally takes a lighted candle, and goes in search of the leaven. The son carries the candle, while the parent has a feather and a wooden spoon. Each place or corner is very carefully scrutinized, and every piece is gathered up with great precision, so that not a

[51] Num. 9:1-5.   [52] Josh. 5:2-10.   [53] John 2:13.   [54] Ex. 12:11.

PURGING THE LEAVEN.

particle of leaven may be left anywhere in the house. Before this is done all work and study must be put aside, and necessary preparations made. When this is finished the pieces of leaven are securely tied, and placed somewhere in an unused part of the house ; they are removed the next morning about ten, and burned. This is known as "removing" or "purging" the leaven. It is very punctiliously observed, and great care is taken that not one particle of the leaven remains.

26. No doubt this was what Paul had in mind, when in writing to the Corinthian church upon the subject of the Passover, He said :

"*Purge out*, therefore, *the old leaven*, that ye may be a new lump." [55]

Just previous to this search the following prayer is offered :

"Blessed art thou, O Lord our God, King of the universe, who hath sanctified us with His commandments, and hath commanded us to remove the leaven."

Then the following is said after the search has been made :

"All manner of leaven that is in my possession which I have not seen nor removed, shall be null and accounted as the dust of the earth."

After the leaven has been burned the next morning, the following is said :

"All manner of leaven that is in my possession, which I have seen and which I have not seen, which I have removed and which I have not removed, shall be null and accounted as the dust of the earth."

The reason no doubt why in this latter saying these words are inserted, "which I have not seen," "and which I have not removed," is because of the possibility of a mouse having carried in during the night some piece or pieces of leaven and secreted them where the master has not observed them. Should this really be so, the house would have to be searched again. But by inserting this statement, the leaven in the house is null and void, and the man can feel he has a clear conscience. This

[55] 1 Cor. 5: 7.

reminds one of what the Savior said concerning the straining at gnats. After the leaven is burned, food and dishes of every description in the house used during the year must be hid from view.

PREPARATION FOR THE PASSOVER.

27. On the night of the fourteenth day the Passover proper begins. It is then that the Passover supper is observed. Not now having any lamb, substitutes are used in the form of a roasted egg, boiled hard, and the shankbone of a lamb. In addition they use celery, parsley, lettuce, and horseradish for bitter herbs, and a mixture called haroseth, a sort of sauce, to represent the mortar of which the brick was made when the ancestry were in Egypt. See illustration.

28. The table is always prepared before the evening, so that when the people return from the synagogue service they are ready to sit down to supper. This no doubt is the reason why the disciples inquired where they should go and *prepare* the Passover. [56]

EACH PERSON MUST HAVE FOUR CUPS OF WINE.

29. Soon after the family is gathered around the board the man of the house will take a glass of wine, over which a blessing is pronounced. Each person at the table also has a glass at the same time. This wine is made of raisins. It is absolutely necessary to have this wine at the Passover. In fact the importance attached to it is so great that the rabbis taught that if a person had no wine for the feast he must sell or pawn some of his goods and secure it. Or if he had nothing to dispose of, he must secure it from the poverty fund kept for the poor on just such occasions.

30. Not only must they have wine, but they must have sufficient that each member of the family shall have four cups. This is what the rabbis taught even in the time of Christ:

"On the eve of any Passover it is not lawful for a person to eat any-

[56] Matt. 26:17.

thing from the time of the afternoon prayer till after dusk. Even the meanest in Israel shall not eat until they have arranged themselves in proper order at ease around the table nor shall a person have less than *four cups of wine*, even if they must be given him from the funds devoted to the charitable support of the very poor."—*Tract " Pesachim."*

And the Talmud in elaborating upon this subject, says :

" All persons, whether men or women, are obligated on this night to drink four cups of wine, and this number is not to be diminished."—*" Laws of Leaven."*

And again :

" Whosoever has not got wine transgresses a command of the rabbis, for *they* have said, that there is to be no diminution from the four cups. And it is necessary to sell what he has in order to keep the command of the wise men. He is not to depend upon the bread, for if he fulfill the command concerning one cup, he has not fulfilled that respecting the three. Therefore let him sell what he has, and furnish the expense, until he procure wine or raisins."—*" Ways of Life."*

We can appreciate more what the Savior evidently meant when He said that the Pharisees and scribes laid heavy burdens upon the poor people ; too heavy for many of them to bear. [57]

THE SAVIOR TEACHING THE DISCIPLES PRECIOUS LESSONS.

31. Thus when the Savior came to sit down to the last Passover with His disciples He found many things not commanded in the word of God, which of themselves were valueless, even though the rabbis did attach much meaning to them. Yet He could not let the opportunity slip by without teaching them some valuable lesson even from these traditions.

32. These four cups were in existence in the days of the Savior; and during this last Passover service He instituted that beautiful, precious, and helpful reminder of His death and crucifixion.

THE ORDER OF THE SERVICE.

33. When the first cup of wine is drank a blessing is pro-

[57] Matt. 23 : 4.

16

nounced, called the "blessing of the festival." Part of this wine is left in the cup. When this is finished, all the persons at the table are obliged to wash their hands. (*f*) It was no doubt at this stage of the supper that the ranklings in the hearts of the disciples were manifest, and the bitter strife arose who should be the greatest.[58] The Savior then laid aside His garment, took the towel, and washed their feet.[59]

34. The next thing in order is to take some celery or parsley and dip it in salted water, and pass around to each person. This is a sort of preparation for the bitter herbs to follow later. Then the middle cake of unleavened bread is broken. At the present time there are three special passover cakes used, the middle one of which is broken at this period. It is claimed by some that this was observed in the days of Christ, and much significance is attached to this part of the service. If it be so, we can learn several beautiful lessons therefrom.

THE HIDDEN MANNA.

35. It is said that these three cakes represent the three persons of the deity, Father, Son, Holy Ghost. The middle person of the Deity is claimed by the rabbis even, to be the "Mam-re," the Word, the Son of God. (*g*) The breaking of the middle cake represents the breaking of the Son of God, the Messiah. When this custom was adopted, is not generally known, but thus it exists to-day. After the cake is broken in two, one part is hid under a pillow on the couch, the other part is used at the supper. This part that is hidden is called *Aphiko-mon*, meaning *manna secreted or hidden.* After a time this is brought forth, and a small portion is given to each of the persons around the table. This would very naturally suggest a forcible thought upon that text in Revelation:

" To him that overcometh will I give to eat of the hidden manna."[60]

This hidden piece of cake is very precious to the man of the house, and he guards it with great jealousy. So the " Hidden

[58] Luke 22: 24–27. [59] John 13: 4, 5. [60] Rev. 2: 17.

PASSOVER SUPPER-TABLE.

Manna " is very precious to every one of God's dear children, and He should be regarded with great desire.

THE DIPPING OF THE SOP.

36. After the cake is broken, the service proper takes place. The history of the exode is then discoursed upon, and the wonderful dealings of God with His people and with the Egyptians are all gone over. Then the supper proper takes place. During this supper the bitter herbs, in the form of horseradish, are served to every member of the family. One form of this herb is served between two pieces of unleavened bread, then dipped in the sauce previously mentioned. To this evidently Jesus referred, after He had said," One of you shall betray Me," when he remarked :

"He it is to whom I shall give a sop, when I *have dipped* it." [61]

THE CUP OF BLESSING, AND THE LORD'S SUPPER.

37. After this part of the service came the cup of wine, known as the "cup of blessing." It was during this part of the supper that the Lord spoke of the bread and the wine, as emblems of his spilt blood, and broken body. [62]

He instituted that blessed and precious memorial of the Lord's Supper for the church, by which they were to keep Him in mind, till He should come again. This new memorial of the Savior, a pledge that He would come again, was to be regarded by the church as a season of joy, blessing, and appreciation of the great gift of the Lord Jesus, who gave his life a willing sacrifice.

Judas did not stay with the Savior and disciples till the end ; and after He went out, the Lord gave the disciples still further instructions. [63]

38. After this cup was finished and the bread distributed, the " Hallel " was sung, which also explains the expression that after they had sung a hymn (margin, psalm) they went out. [64] The " Hallel " consisted of a number of Psalms. [65] (*h*)

[61] John 13:26.   [62] Luke 22:19, 20.   [63] John 14–17.   [64] Matt. 26:30, margin.
[65] Ps. 115–118.

39. Thus the Savior took the very traditions they had inaugurated, which were in a large degree foreign to the original Passover, and made a most beautiful and sacred institution by which to remember Him in the church, till He come.

TWO DAYS OBSERVED INSTEAD OF ONE.

40. Instead of the people keeping the first and last days [66] of the feast as a sabbath, they observe two days in each case. This addition was of the scribes and Pharisees. The following will explain itself:

"Although the *second holy day* is only of the words of the scribes, everything that is forbidden on the first day is forbidden on it [the second day] also. And every one who professes the second holy day, . . . but by some means violates it, is to receive the beating denounced against rebellion, or to be excommunicated, except he be a learned man."—*The Laws of the Festivals.*

41. Thus we see why the Savior said that they placed heavy burdens upon the multitudes, but they themselves would not lift them with their small finger. Because these men were learned, they considered themselves exempt.

THE TRUE PASSOVER.

42. But the true Passover, and all its meaning, is to be found in Jesus Christ only. He is the Passover; [67] and we are to eat Him with the unleavened bread of sincerity and truth. [68] This is the meaning of the unleavened bread; this is the meaning of the Passover. It was a longing desire on the part of the Savior to eat the Passover with the disciples before He suffered, for then these traditions and burdens would be removed from them, and they would know in all its fullness the meaning of the Passover.

43. If the church of Christ of to-day could only see that instead of the observance of many of the festivals which are being observed as memorials, whether they be Easter, or Christmas, or some other day, which is similar in effect to the

[66] Ex. 12: 16.   [67] 1 Cor. 5: 7.   [68] 1 Cor. 5: 8.

traditions of the Jewish rabbis, they would be more obedient to
His will, they would then enjoy much more of Jesus Christ, the
great Lamb of God, and have a continuous feast in Him who
is the great and blessed Passover.

EXPLANATORY NOTES.

Paragraph 5.

(*a*) There came a time in the history of the Jewish nation that, though
they offered sacrifices and kept the feasts, there was nothing in any of the
service that God could accept. Isa. 1 : 11. The reason why God did not,
and could not, accept their offerings is explained in verses 13–15. If they
had only seen the Christ in all these things, the offerings would have been
precious lessons to them.

Paragraph 15.

(*b*) The words, *between the evenings*, as mentioned in paragraph six,
deserve more notice at this point, to show the remarkable accuracy of the
word of God, and how literally Christ's death fulfilled the prophecy of
the slain lamb of the Passover.

The Jews believed there were two evenings, the evening of the day,
the evening of the night. See Num. 28 : 4, margin. The first evening
began at noon. One writer, on the words בֵּין הָעַרְבַּיִם=*between the evenings*,
says, "We mean by this expression, the dark part of the day, after the
noon hour."

When the first evening began is thus expressed by the commentator
Rashi, a great authority among Jewish writers :

"From the sixth hour [twelve o'clock, see next note] and upward is
called, *ba-an ha-ar-ba-yim, between the evenings;* because the sun inclines
toward his home, which he reaches at evening." The thought evidently
is, that the sun reaching its highest point at noon, begins to decline
toward the west, in which direction it continues till sunset.

And he continues :

"And by the language, *ba-an ha-ar-ba-yim*, we also understand it to be
the hours between the evening of the day, and the evening of the night.
The evening of the day begins with the seventh hour [that is, immediately
after twelve o'clock noon], and continues till the evening of the night.
And the evening of the night begins at night, or sunset."—*Rashi's comment on Ex. 12 : 6.* See also next note.

From this we gather that one evening began at twelve, and the other
began at six. The six hours between these two points being called *between*

the evenings. But the word rendered "between" is of itself extremely significant. It would indicate that the lamb would be killed between the time of the first evening and the time of the second evening. What would be the hour between the first and second evening? between twelve and six? The answer is *three*. And this was *just the hour the Savior expired on the cross.* He was crucified at the sixth hour, He died at the ninth. The Scripture was fulfilled. Jesus Christ was the paschal Lamb. Even Josephus mentions the fact that the paschal lambs were slain from the ninth to the eleventh hours; the time they began to kill them was three o'clock. See Josephus, "Sixth Book of Jewish Wars;" chapter 6, paragraph 3.

(c) The Jews divided the twenty-four hour period into two parts, the day, and the night, each division consisting of twelve hours. See John 11 : 9. Then the two divisions were divided again into sections, or three-hour periods, four periods for the day, four for the night. Those of the night were called watches. See Matt. 14 : 25 ; 24 : 43 ; Luke 12 : 38. Those of the day were divided into the third hour, sixth hour, ninth hour, etc. The first hour of the day began at six in the morning ; therefore the third hour would be nine o'clock. The ninth hour, therefore, would be three o'clock in the afternoon. Thus was the "more sure word of prophecy" fulfilled.

The third hour, sixth hour, and ninth hour, were hours of prayer. See Acts 2 : 15 ; 10 : 3, 9 ; 3 : 1. This custom among the Jews had been in existence for many centuries, and do doubt this is what is referred to in Ps. 55 : 17. Daniel also followed this beautiful method. Dan. 6 : 10. It certainly would be a blessed thing for the children of God to follow at the present time.

Paragraph 17.

(d) The term "high Sabbath" or great Sabbath, was given only to that Sabbath, when the first day of the Passover feast, or Passover sabbath, occurred on the regular weekly Sabbath day, the seventh day of the week.

Paragraph 25.

(e) Should the reader wish to secure further information on the subject of the Passover, he is referred to the Mishna, in the tractate "Pesachim."

Paragraph 33.

(f) For laws concerning the washing of the hands, see appendix.

Paragraph 35.

(g) Scattered through the Talmud, we find stray thoughts from a few of the rabbis, which indicate they believed in a trinity. Their basis for this belief they adduced from the word *E-lo-him*, plural, *Gods*. See notes on chapter 9, paragraph 13, (h).

Paragraph 38.

(*h*) It is certainly strange that at the very time the Jews were singing or chanting this " Hallel," or praise to God, they were fulfilling the same scripture. The closing verses of the Hallel are those which speak of the Jews rejecting the stone that was the head or corner-stone. They were so blinded in the reading of the word of God that they could not discern its fulfillment.

CHAPTER XV.

The Festivals and Feasts.—Continued.

"And thou shalt observe the feast of weeks, of the first-fruits of harvest, and the feast of ingathering at the year's end." Ex. 34:22. "And when the day of Pentecost was fully come, they were all with one accord in one place." Acts 2:1.

THE FEAST OF PENTECOST.

THE feast which came after the Passover was called Pentecost.[1] In fact this latter feast might in a measure be considered the completion of the Passover. The word *Pentecost*, from the Hebrew word, שבעת *She-voo-oth*, means *weeks*.[2] But the word in the Hebrew for weeks comes from the same word, which means *seven* שבע.[3] The word *seven* in the Hebrew is *Shiv-aw*; from the same root word we derive Pentecost and weeks. In other words the feast of Pentecost was a period of seven weeks from the time of the Passover.[4] All this is comprehended in the term, *She-voo-oth*.

THE COMMAND FOR THE FEAST.

2.   The first record we have of this festival is as follows :

"And the feast of harvest, the first-fruits of thy labors, which thou hast sown in the field."[5]

Here it is called the " Feast of Harvest," because at this time the first-fruits of the season were gathered in the land. From the time the wave-sheaf was offered to the Lord, on the second day of the Passover feast, or the first day after the *paschal* sabbath,[6] seven full weeks were to be counted to the Pentecost.(*a*) At this festival, sacrifices and offerings were to be rendered unto the Lord, as was proper on all such occasions.[7] It was

[1] Acts 2:1; Acts 20:16; 1 Cor. 16:8.   [2] Ex. 34:22.   [3] Gen. 29:18.
[4] Deut. 16:9, 10.   [5] Ex. 23:16.   [6] Lev. 23:15, 16.
[7] Lev. 23:16–22; Num. 28:26–31.

TYPES.   ANTITYPES.
1. THE TYPICAL PASSOVER.   2. THE TRUE PASSOVER.
3. TYPICAL FIRST FRUITS.   4. CHRIST, THE FIRST FRUIT.

intended as a beautiful service, one by which the Holy Spirit designed to teach precious truth concerning the Messiah and His work, as was demonstrated in the end, even though the Jewish teachers and rabbis hid the truth.

3. In another place in Exodus we find this statement supplemental to the one already given concerning the feast.

"And thou shalt observe the feast of weeks, of the first-fruits of wheat harvest." [8]

In Deuteronomy we find the following record of this festival:

"Seven weeks shalt thou number unto thee: begin to number the seven weeks from such time as thou beginnest to put the sickle to the corn." [9]

And the time when the sickle was first put to the corn we read was

"The morrow after the Sabbath, from the day that ye brought the sheaf of the wave-offering; seven sabbaths [or weeks] shall be complete." [10]

4. This first putting in of the sickle on that day after the Passover sabbath, not weekly Sabbath, was called the *omer*. From the first day of this omer, on whichever day of the week it happened to fall, till the last day of the omer, was seven full weeks. [11] (*b*) The next day was Pentecost. And strange though it may seem, till this very day, the orthodox Jews adhere to the counting of the omer. The entire period is called the days of the omer.

THE REAL APPLICATION.

5. From what we have thus far observed of this feast, we have a very beautiful lesson concerning the work of the Savior. We read:

"When the day of Pentecost was fully come, they were all with one accord in one place. And suddenly there came a sound from heaven as of a rushing mighty wind, and it filled all the house where they were sitting. And there appeared unto them cloven tongues like as of fire, and it sat

[8] Ex. 34:22.   [9] Deut. 16:9.   [10] Lev. 23:15.   [11] Lev. 23:15, 16.

upon each of them. And they were all filled with the Holy Ghost, and began to speak with other tongues, as the Spirit gave them utterance." [12]

6. We are well aware that as a result of this day's experience, three thousand souls were brought to Christ. [13] What a beautiful "Feast of Harvest." But how did this feast of harvest of souls come about?—As a result of the sowing of the seed by the Son of man. [14] For the original law of the feast was as follows:

"And the feast of harvest, the *first-fruits of thy labors*, which thou hast sown in the field." [15]

7. Let us now see the application in the work of Christ. The Savior Himself said He had come to sow seed. The seed is the word of God. [16] The Son of man is the sower. [17] He sowed His seed in the field; but the field is the world. [18] When He died on the cross there was scarcely a soul who clung to Him, as a result of all His faithful labors of seed sowing. Even His own disciples, save John, forsook Him and fled. [19] With John, remained the mother of Jesus and two other women; that was all. [20]

8. But He Himself said that one person sowed and another reaped, [21] and the results would be shared between them. So for three and a half years He sowed the word of God in this world in the hearts of men; and when the Pentecost had fully come, God being true to His promise of the feast of harvest, gave the Lord Jesus, through His disciples, the first-fruits of His labors. Ah! what a blessed Pentecost that was! What a blessed ingathering harvest of souls! What a precious offering that was to the Lord! And has Pentecost yet realized its climax?

STILL ANOTHER VIEW.

9. However, there is still another view held concerning this Feast of Weeks; that is, that God gave the law to Israel on Mount Sinai, which this feast also commemorates. This

[12] Acts 2: 1-4.   [13] Acts 2:41.   [14] Matt. 13:23; Luke 8:11.   [15] Ex. 23:16.
[16] Luke 8:11.   [17] Matt. 13:37.   [18] Matt. 13:38.   [19] Mark 14: 27, 50.
[20] John 19: 25-27.   [21] John 4: 37, 38.

view of Pentecost was widely believed and accepted by the Jews at the time of Christ. It was observed *also* as the anniversary day of the giving of the decalogue. Jewish tradition teaches that the Lord called Moses up to the mount on the second day of the Jewish Month, Sivan, which is the third month mentioned in Exodus.[22] The Pentecost is observed on the sixth day of this third month.

VARIOUS TRADITIONS CONCERNING THIS FESTIVAL.

10. Many, therefore, are the traditions which have been heaped upon this feast, commenting upon the giving of the law on Sinai. For instance :

" The holy hosts (that is the Israelites) were seized with fear, when thou didst place over them the mountain as a tub; they received the pure law with trembling and with fear."—" *Prayers for Pentecost.*"

This is but a sample, many more might follow.

GOD'S REGARD FOR HIS LAW.

11. If, however, it be true that the Lord did give the law at this time, and it would appear that there was strong inclination toward that belief, it simply shows how much the Lord regarded that blessed law of His which He spake on Mount Sinai, by confirming its truthfulness with fire[23] and with power, that Jesus Christ who died for sin,[24] which is the transgression of the law,[25] did not die in vain.[26] This demonstration on Pentecost then was to reveal to men that when Christ died, the law in its purity and spiritual power, was abundantly magnified;[27] and this glorious power manifested through these servants attested to its eternal and abiding firmness. Surely Jesus Christ did magnify the law, and make it honorable, both on earth and in heaven.

THE NEW YEAR ; THE BLOWING OF TRUMPETS.

12. The next festival in order of time was the " The Blowing

[22] Ex. 19: 1.   [23] Deut. 33: 2.   [24] Isa. 53 :10.   [25] 1 John 3: 4.
[26] Gal. 2: 21; Rom. 3: 31.   [27] Isa. 42: 21.

of Trumpets," [28] sometimes called, "The New Year." (*c*) This festival occurred the first day of the seventh Jewish month, Tishri. The day was to be regarded as a sabbath,[29] in which no ordinary pursuit of labor must be performed ; still certain permissions were granted which were forbidden on the Sabbath of the Lord. This was true of all the festival sabbaths ; certain kinds of labor were permissible, especially those in connection with home duties. Like many of the other festivals, tradition added another day, making the people observe the first two days of this month, instead of just one as the Lord commanded Moses.

THE SIGNIFICANCE OF THIS FESTIVAL.

13. The special feature of this festival or holy day, was the blowing of the trumpets. Here is the command :

"And the Lord spake unto Moses, saying, Speak unto the children of Israel, saying, in the seventh month, in the first day of the month, shall ye have a sabbath, *a memorial of blowing of trumpets*, an holy convocation." [30]

9. That this sabbath or holy day must have been made with some significance in view is self-evident ; but especially do we notice this to be true, when we consider the month in which it occurs. First, it marks the beginning of the civil year. Second, it is just ten days prior to the Day of Atonement, of all days in the year the most sacred and solemn. Third, in this same month occurred the Feast of Tabernacles, one of the most joyful of the year, which no doubt was full of meaning, seeing that it pertained to the gathering of the final harvests. Fourth, in the seventh month the trumpet was blown in the year of Jubilee, announcing to all the people that the year of liberty had come to every person who had been in bondage during the previous fifty years.[31] Fifth, the seventh month, was a type of the seventh sabbatic year, which was a year of rest.

TRADITIONS ADDED TO THIS HOLY DAY.

14. When the trumpet therefore was blown on this first day

[28] Lev. 23: 23-25; Num. 29: 1.   [29] Lev. 23: 24.   [30] Lev. 23: 24.   [31] Lev. 25 :10.

of the seventh month, how much the Lord intended should be known by the people, if they would only ask the meaning of the blowing of the trumpets. In addition to the lessons the Lord intended them to learn, the people themselves have added certain features to this holy day, which make it additionally impressive. An entire tract, called "*Rosh-Ha-shona*," has been written on this sabbatic day. In addition to the multitude of erroneous ideas contained in this work, there are some things full of significance. Like the Passover, despite the traditions, many truths relating to the Christ can be drawn therefrom.

THE IMPRESSIVENESS OF THE BLOWING OF TRUMPETS.

15. The Talmud teaches that the blowing of the trumpets signifies God's loud call to repentance. Since this seventh month closes up the year's work in connection with the sanctuary service, and with the harvest, how appropriate for the trumpet to blow, that the people should turn their attention more to the things of God, and prepare for the final work. Hence this is made one of the most sacred days to the Jews. They also teach that on this day three sets of books are opened,—the book of life to examine the good deeds of the people, the book of death to examine the evil deeds, and a sort of intermediary book to examine into the accounts of those whose cases *are* to be decided at the Day of Atonement, ten days later. The ten days following this sabbath day are called, " The ten days of repentance." The most careless and indifferent during these days devotes his time to the service of God, and seeks for preparation of heart that when the Day of Atonement arrives he may receive a " seal" of life for the year to come.

THE CALL TO REPENTANCE.

16. Thus the blowing of the trumpets was a sort of awakening of the people to examine into their condition, and to see that their sins were all forgiven, and that they repented suffi-

ciently to have that peace and pardon. It was a call to prayer, a call to earnest seeking of the Lord; it was a sort of preparation for judgment. In the prayer for the New Year's day we find the following:

"On the New Year's day it is written, and on the Day of Atonement it is sealed, who shall pass away from the world, and who shall be created into the world; who shall live and who shall die; who shall live the length of his days, and who shall have his days shortened; who shall be given to the sword, who to the fire, who for drowning, who for hunger, who for thirst," etc.

17. Hence the rabbis taught that repentance, prayer, and the giving of alms, would annul the evil decree. Thus this day and the succeeding ten days were days of heart searching and of turning to God, that the Lord would bless and forgive them. Could the Jews only realize that this was what the Savior came to the world for, how they would appreciate the meaning of the Lord's purpose which *they* in a measure placed even upon this day. For we read:

"Unto you first, God having raised up His Son Jesus, sent Him to bless you, in turning away every one of you from his iniquities. [32]

18. It is thought by some that the Apostle Paul evidently had this blowing of trumpets and its significance in mind, when writing to the Romans, [33] Corinthians, [34] and Ephesians. [35] (*d*)

GOD'S TRUMPET NEEDS TO BE SOUNDED.

19. The trumpet of God needs to be blown in Zion, [36] and in the world to-day to call men to repentance, to prepare them for the great judgment day [37] which the world will soon have to meet, when the antitypical Day of Atonement shall have been completed. The prophet says:

"Cry aloud, spare not, lift up thy voice like a trumpet, and show My people their transgression, and the house of Jacob their sins." [38]

THE DAY OF ATONEMENT.

20. As has already been mentioned, the next solemn day

[32] Acts 3:26.   [33] Rom. 12:11, 12.   [34] 1 Cor. 15:34.   [35] Eph. 5:14.
[36] Joel 2:15–17; Zeph. 1:14–16.   [37] Rev. 14:6, 7.   [38] Isa. 58:1.

DAY OF ATONEMENT.

given to the Israelites, was the Day of Atonement.[39] This was the most solemn of all days of the year. Whatever the condition of the people during the year, if they would only come up to *this day*, and seek the Lord while the priest was ministering in the sanctuary, there was hope, pardon, salvation for them.[40] If they *did not come up* to the Day of Atonement they were to be cut off from among the people.[41] The original command for this day is given as follows:

"And the Lord spake unto Moses, saying, Also on the tenth day of this seventh month there shall be a day of atonement: it shall be an holy convocation unto you; and ye shall afflict your souls, and offer an offering made by fire unto the Lord. And ye shall do no work in that same day: for it is a day of atonement, to make an atonement for you before the Lord your God. For whatsoever soul it be that shall not be afflicted in that same day, he shall be cut off from among his people. And whatsoever soul it be that doeth any work in that same day, the same soul will I destroy from among his people. Ye shall do no manner of work: it shall be a statute forever throughout your generations in all your dwellings. It shall be unto you a sabbath of rest, and ye shall afflict your souls: in the ninth day of the month at even, from even unto even, shall ye celebrate your sabbath."[42]

SPECIAL OFFERINGS FOR PRIEST AND PEOPLE.

21. In addition to the regular offerings for all occasions the priest and the people were to have special sacrifices for this most solemn day.[43] First, the priest was to offer sacrifices for himself and his family,[44] then the offerings for the people were to be rendered to the Lord.[45]

THE TWO GOATS.

22. There were two goats to be selected for the people on that day, and to be brought to the high priest.[46] Then lots were to be cast for them; one lot was to be for the Lord (Hebrew, נוֹרָל אֶחָד לַיהוה-*Go-rel Ec-hod La-Ye-Ho-Vah=Jehovah's one lot*), and the other for the Azazel, לַעֲזָאזֵל, or *scapegoat*,[47] as rendered

---

[39] Lev. 23:26-28.   [40] Lev. 16:30.   [41] Lev. 23:29, 30.   [42] Lev. 23:26-32.
[43] Num. 28:7-11.   [44] Lev. 16:3, 6; Heb. 5:3.   [45] Lev. 16:5; Heb. 9:7.
[46] Lev. 16:7.   [47] Lev. 16:7, 8.

in our version. When the lots were cast, that goat which was for the Lord was offered by the high priest.[48] The blood of this animal was then taken into the *most holy place of the sanctuary*, and sprinkled *before* the mercy-seat, and *on the mercy-seat* seven times.[49] He was also to take the censer and fill it with incense;[50] and while he was making the atonement with the blood in the most holy place, the smoke from this incense would cover the mercy-seat, and fill the sanctuary with the sweet fragrance,[51] while the glory of the Lord would fill the place.

23. While this was being done by the high priest, the people without were fasting, praying, and earnestly seeking the Lord for the pardon and obliteration of all their sins. This service was conducted in behalf of *all* the people.[52] When the high priest finished this work on this day, then the *whole camp of Israel* was clean, for the man who did not comply with the command of God by fasting, praying, and affliction of soul on this day was to be cut off.[53] The Day of Atonement to Israel, therefore, involved three things:

THE BLOTTING OUT OF SINS.

24. 1. The blotting out of sins. When the high priest sprinkled the blood on the mercy-seat and before the mercy-seat on the Day of Atonement it was to represent that *all* the people of Israel had transgressed the law of God, which was under the mercy-seat in the most holy place of the sanctuary, and that all were desirous of having these sins entirely removed. The law demanded the sinner's life;[54] but the blood would cleanse *and blot out* the sins;[55] for it was through the blood that pardon was secured. The people having now received the atonement for their transgressions, and the glory of God having filled the house, which indicated that God had accepted the offering, the priest came out from the inner sanctuary with the sins of the people which had been accumulating all the year, as well as

---

[48] Lev. 16:9; Num. 29:11.   [49] Lev. 16:5.   [50] Lev. 16:12.   [51] Lev. 16:12, 13.
[52] Lev. 16:17.   [53] Lev. 23:28–30; Num. 29:7.
[54] 1 John 3:4; Rom. 6:23; Eze. 18:4.   [55] 1 John 1:7; Heb. 9:22.

17

those which had been forgiven that day. Thus all the sins of all the people were removed that day; and the sinful *record* of the year was all cleansed. The blood was also sprinkled upon the vessels of the sanctuary to cleanse them. [56] In other words, the blood on this day cleansed all the people, and removed and blotted out all their sins. It also removed all uncleanness from everything connected with the sanctuary service, which had a part in the ministry for sin during the entire year.

THE AZAZEL, OR SCAPEGOAT.

25. When this work in the sanctuary was finished, the priest came to the door of the tabernacle, and called for the other goat, the Azazel. [57] The priest then laid his hands upon the head of this live goat, and confessed upon it all the sins [58] which had been accumulating in the sanctuary all through the year, and which the priest had brought out with him. All these sins were then transferred to the head of this animal, which was to bear them instead of the people. Then he was led by a proper man into the wilderness,[59] where he was to remain till his death. Jewish writers say the animal was thrown over a steep precipice, and so died.

26. When this day's service was accomplished, the people not only were *forgiven* of their sins, *but in figure, or type*, had them all blotted out. So that from the evening of that day they began as it were a new year's experience with the Lord. Their record was now a clean one; the atonement was completed. They were purged and cleansed from all sin, and so also was the sanctuary.

27. 2. The cleansing of the sanctuary. As has already been mentioned the sanctuary was also cleansed this day with the shed blood of the Lord's goat. [60] The reason for this was that during the year the animals which had been slain for the sins of the people had their blood brought into the holy place,

56 Lev. 16: 16, 18, 19.   57 Lev. 16: 20.   58 Lev. 16: 21.   59 Lev. 16: 22.
60 Lev. 16: 16, 18.

HIGH PRIEST CONFESSING SINS ON SCAPEGOAT.

by which act the records of the sins were kept. Of course this was merely typical and figurative; nevertheless these vessels and furnishings were affected by the blood which was sprinkled upon them during the year. Since the blood of the animal slain, represented the sins of the sinner, as well as the life of the innocent one, these vessels shared in the work of the sins of the people. Therefore on this Day of Atonement, when the work of blotting out of sin for the people was completed, the sanctuary also must be cleansed from sin and its effects. So when the high priest left the sanctuary that day, in type, there would be no more remembrance or thought of sin. (*e*)

THE DAY OF JUDGMENT.

28. 3. The Day of Atonement was also a day of judgment to the people. We found that the Lord commanded that the person who did not observe this day must be cut off from among his people. By his not obeying the command of God this day, and seeking the cleansing from his sins through the blood which was shed for him, he showed himself unworthy of life, and practically sealed his destiny and closed his probation. Whereas the man, though he had sinned during the year, though he had disobeyed and even forsaken the Lord, if he only heeded the command of God and observed this day, and sought pardon through the blood, was forgiven, accepted, and was recognized as one of God's own. This day's actions practically decided the life or death of the man. It was, in other words, a day of judgment. And to this day, the Jews recognize this fact; for many a time in their worship on this day they speak of it as the הדין יום= *Youm-Ha-din=the day of judgment.*

THE ANTITYPE.

29, While such was the command of God to that people concerning the atonement, it is evident the virtue and efficiency of the forgiveness of sins, and of the real blotting out of sin was not in the literal blood of those animals. We are plainly

SCAPEGOAT IN THE WILDERNESS.

told that the *blood of bulls and goats cannot take away sin.*[61] The Savior Himself said that a man is better than a sheep.[62] If no man can redeem his brother under any consideration,[63] it is evident that no animal has sufficient virtue to secure for a man forgiveness.   Then all this was done simply to illustrate what would actually take place through the blood of the Lamb of God, who would be slain in their behalf.   Through all these offerings and services, they were to see the precious Savior, and have faith in the Christ of God, the Redeemer of Israel.[64]

30. No doubt the pious people saw this, and they knew much of the meaning of the services.   But it is evident that the majority of the people saw nothing in this work, save the mere shedding of the blood of the animal, as a literal command, and the laying on of the hands of the priest on the head of the Azazel as a form for the carrying out of the letter of the words of the Lord.   They considered the real virtue in their own deed.

THE DIVINE COMMENTARY ON THE ATONEMENT WORK.

31. In the study of the book of Hebrews we find the blessed and glorious truth of this service very forcibly revealed.   God gave to Paul, after He had opened his eyes to see Jesus as the Messiah, the whole philosophy of the sacrificial system, especially concerning the work of the completed atonement.   What wonderful and precious truths there are revealed in this service of the atonement, not only for the Israelites, but for the people at the present day.

32. It is well known that the Lord's lot, or the Lord's goat, represented Him, who bore the sins of the world.   The other lot, the Azazel, represented him who brought sin into the world, or Satan.[65]   In fact the Jews at the present time use the word *Azazel,* as a synonym for Satan. (*f*)

CHRIST ENTERS THE HOLY PLACE IN THE SANCTUARY.

33. After Jesus shed His blood for the people, He went to

[61] Heb. 10:4.   [62] Matt. 12:12.   [63] Psa. 49:7.   [64] Isa. 49:7.   [65] 1 John3:8.

heaven, and there sat down on the right hand of God.[66] The priesthood had now changed [67] from the Levitical or Aaronic, to the Melchisedec or the everlasting.[68] Christ now was to fully carry out in heaven, with His own blood,[69] what has been done by the priest on the earth with the typical blood. All this work of the Aaronic priesthood was to teach the people what the Messiah would do for them and for the world by His own precious blood. In order then to carry out the antitypical work, Christ, when He ascended to heaven and sat down on the right hand of the throne of God, entered into the *holy place* of the heavenly sanctuary.[70] Or in other words He ministered with His blood in the first apartment of the heavenly sanctuary. This is what the earthly priest did during the three hundred and fifty-nine days of the ministry,[71] (*g*) for it must be remembered that the high priest entered the most holy place of the sanctuary only on the Day of Atonement, *that one day.*[72]

FORGIVENESS THROUGH CHRIST'S BLOOD.

34. As soon as Christ began to minister His blood in heaven, the Apostles preached that the work of the priesthood had been transferred above.[73] The blood of Christ was the only blood that had virtue;[74] they would find forgiveness in Him alone,[75] and in His blood which He was ministering for sin. That He did enter into the first apartment of the heavenly sanctuary, is evident from the vision which Jesus gave to John.[76] These articles of furniture were in the first apartment.

35. Fully to carry out the typical work of atonement Christ would remain in the holy place until the antitypical Day of Atonement, when the people would not only receive the blessing of forgiveness of sin,[77] but also have their sins blotted out. The heavenly sanctuary would then be cleansed, and the great day of judgment would take place.

[66] Heb. 4:14; 8:1; 10:12.　　[67] Heb. 7:12.　　[68] Heb. 7:11, 21, 22, 28.
[69] Acts 20:28; Heb. 9:14.　　[70] Heb. 8:1, 2; Rev. 1:12, 13.　　[71] Heb. 9:6.
[72] Lev. 16:2; Heb. 9:7.　　[73] Acts 2:30, 33.　　[74] 1 John 1:7.　　[75] Acts 13:38.
[76] Rev. 1:12, 13.　　[77] Acts 3:19, 20.

ANTITYPICAL DAY OF ATONEMENT.

According to the word of God this antitypical work is now transpiring; [78] we are *now* living in the time when the Savior has entered into the most holy place of the heavenly sanctuary: [79] He will blot out the sins [80] of those who are seeking Him with all their heart, and who wish to know the fullness of His will, even as the people did anciently on the Day of Atonement. He is to cleanse the heavenly sanctuary, [81] as the scriptures declare the holy places in heaven will be cleansed. [82] The call *has been heralded* to the world, and is even now going forth to every nation, kindred, tongue, and people, announcing that the hour of His judgment is come. [83]

CHRIST'S COMPLETING WORK.

36. Truly we are living, we are dwelling in a grand and awful time, in an age on ages telling, to be living is sublime. Soon the great High Priest will rise up from the seat of mercy; [84] soon He will have finished His work in the heavenly sanctuary, [85] and have blotted out the sins of the people. Soon all His devoted children will have received the seal of the living God, [86] will have wonderfully appreciated the precious meaning of the mercy-seat in the heavenly sanctuary, [87] beneath which is found the great and original copy of God's eternal law. [88]

THE ANTITYPICAL SCAPEGOAT.

37. When all the sins of all of God's people shall have been blotted out through the precious blood of the Lord Himself, as a Lamb without spot, [89] then the Azazel, the antitypical scapegoat, Satan, shall be brought to the heavenly High Priest, who will lay the sins of the redeemed upon his head; and then he shall be shut up for a thousand years in the wilderness of this earth, [90] which becomes desolated at the personal advent of Christ. [91] As a result of transgression and sin, the evil angelic

[78] Dan. 8: 14.   [79] Rev. 3: 7, 8.   [80] Acts 3: 19.   [81] Dan. 8: 14.
[82] Heb. 9: 8, 23.   [83] Rev. 14: 6, 7.   [84] Luke 13: 25.   [85] Rev. 22: 11; 16: 17.
[86] Rev. 7: 3; 14: 1-4.   [87] Zech. 6: 13; Heb. 4: 16.   [88] Rev. 11: 19.   [89] 1 Pet. 1: 19.
[90] Rev. 20: 1, 2; Isa. 24: 1, 3, 19, 22; Jer. 4: 23, 26.   [91] Isa. 2: 19, 21; Rev. 6: 14, 16, 17.

hosts are to abide in this chaotic condition, while the children of the Lord are dwelling during the thousand years[92] in those heavenly mansions,[93] with Him who has bought and redeemed them.[94]

LESSONS FOR THE CHURCH.

38. These are some of the lessons for the church to-day concerning the Day of Atonement. Blessed is that man whose eyes see,[95] and whose heart understands.[96]

The Jews did not understand this; [97] hence to them the atonement meant little. To this day the anniversary of the Day of Atonement is observed with much solemnity, with much devotion, with much heart-searching and weeping; but ah! they have no blood, they have no goat, they have no sanctuary, they have no high priest.

HOW THE JEWS NOW PREPARE FOR THE ATONEMENT.

39. Very few of the Jews of to-day, who have faith in the Bible, will perform any labor on this day. On the afternoon of the day previous to the atonement every kind of work is laid aside. Friends and foes meet; all enmity is put away; wrongs are freely confessed to one another; harmony is once more restored.

40. Before the sunset of this day every family takes a substitute for the Lord's goat which the priests offered while the temple stood, and trusts by *this means*, with an oral repentance,[98] to receive forgiveness. Perhaps we can do no better than give the reader the present

METHOD OF ATONEMENTS.

"It is the custom on the day before the atonement to make *ka-po-rous*, *atonements*. A rooster is taken for the male, and a hen for the female of the family. The head of the family makes the atonement first for himself, as it was the custom of the high priest to first make atonement for himself, then for his family, then for the house of Israel. And the order of the atonement is as follows:

[92] Rev. 20:4.　　[93] John 14:1-3.　　[94] Rev. 1:5.　　[95] Matt. 13:16.
[96] Luke 24:45.　　[97] Matt. 13:14.　　[98] Hosea 14:2.

"He takes the rooster in his hand and says the following verses : 'The children of men that sit in darkness and in the shadow of death, being bound in affliction and iron ; He brought them out of darkness and the shadow of death, and break their bands in sunder. Fools, because of their transgressions, and because of their iniquities are afflicted. . . . O that men would praise the Lord for His goodness and for His wonderful works to the children of men.' 'If there be for him an angel, an intercessor, one among a thousand, to show unto man his uprightness, then He is gracious unto him, and saith, Deliver him from going down into the pit ; I have found a ransom.'

"He then moves the atonement around his head, whilst saying : '*This is my substitute ; this is my offering ; this is my atonement ; this rooster goeth before me to death*, and I be made free, and will walk in long life, in happiness, and in peace.' "

41. When the person is through with this service, he places his hands upon the head of the fowl, as did the high priest when he laid his hands upon the head of the scapegoat ; and the bird is then slaughtered.

FORMAL REPENTANCE.

42. In addition to this custom the Jews do a great deal of apparent repenting ; as they hope, by so doing, to compensate for the loss of the true work. So it is written :

"At this time when there is no temple in existence, when there is no altar, there is *no atonement, only repentance.* Repentance atones for all transgressions. Even a very wicked man, who all the days of his life, has committed great wickedness, and repents at the last, not the least of all his evil deeds will ever be mentioned to him ; for it is said : 'As for the wickedness of the wicked, he shall not fall thereby, in the day that he turneth from his wickedness.' The *Day of Atonement* itself also atones for them that repent, for it is said : *For on that day he shall make an atonement for you.*' "—"*Laws of Repentance.*"

43. Thus we see when the light which has been given is refused, how terrible is the darkness which ensues. All manner of substitutes are offered ; the day is spent in fasting, in weeping, in lamenting, in repenting, in praying, in doing most everything, if only their sins can in some way be forgiven. For nearly twenty-seven hours not even a single drop of water is

II
TYPES AND
ANTITYPES

TYPES.	ANTITYPES.
5. THE TYPICAL PENTECOST.	6. PENTECOST, THE ANTITYPE, HOLY SPIRIT DESCENDED.
7. TYPICAL DAY OF ATONEMENT.	8. ANTITYPICAL WORK OF ATONEMENT.

put to the lips. The most of the time is spent in stocking feet at the synagogue. Scores and hundreds of pages of prayers are read and recited. The feeling of the people is that the day of judgment has come to them; and they must do all in *their power* to receive a favorable decision.

A SEALING WORK.

44. As the day draws to its close, the earnestness and intensity increases. It is generally believed that the close of this day is regarded in heaven as a "sealing time." If the people have done sufficient repenting, they will receive a "good seal," which means that they have stood the test in heaven. If not, then they fear they are lost, and may die at any time. Hence in their closing prayers of the day, instead of saying, "Our Father, our King, *write* our name in the book of life;" "Our Father, our King, *write* our name in the book of remembrance," etc., they say, "Our Father, our King, *seal* our name in the book of remembrance." "Our Father, our King, *seal* our name in the book of life." And when the service is ended, they greet each other with the salutation, "I hope you have received a good seal."

THE DAY OF ATONEMENT FOR CHRISTIANS.

45. If Israel had only known the things which belonged to her peace, but they were hid from her eyes.[99] The freedom they needed is in Him, [100] in His atoning work, in His atoning blood, in His repentance. And whatsoever things were written aforetime were written for our learning, upon whom the ends of the world are come.[101] In this antitypical "Day of Atonement," when our great High Priest is completing the work for His people, how earnestly all should seek Him, the Lamb of God; should learn all He wishes each to know from His blessed word; should follow Him in the most holy place of the heavenly sanctuary; should know that they shall be sealed with the "seal of God." This is the privilege of all.

[99] Luke 19:42.   [100] John 8:36.   [101] Rom. 15:4; 1 Cor. 10:11.

EXPLANATORY NOTES.

Paragraph 2.

(*a*) In Lev. 23 : 15, 16, the record states that the people were to count seven sabbaths from the time of the offering of the wave-sheaf, till the Feast of Weeks. The count was to begin the day after the first day of the feast, which was a festival sabbath. Num. 28 : 26. This festival *might* occur on a weekly Sabbath; if so, then the feast would be observed just the same, with this exception, that the works which were permitted on the festival sabbath, were not to be done on this Sabbath of the Lord. Preparation must be made the previous day. Mark 15 : 42. It should be borne in mind, however, that the Sabbath of the Lord, the seventh day, and the festival sabbaths, were entirely different, and were quite distinct. Lev. 23 : 37, 38.

Paragraph 4.

(*b*) The seven sabbaths mentioned in these verses are the same as though it said seven weeks. While the word *sabbath* means *rest*, the word also means *seven*. But the word *seven* is the same word as is translated *week*. Therefore the word *sabbath* is the term which comprehends the entire week.

To make this still more plain, we will cite a custom which still prevails among the orthodox Jews. Each morning at the synagogue, just as the service is to close, a Psalm is selected and read for this particular day. For example: On the first day of the week, the same as Sunday, they would repeat the twenty-fourth ; the second day, the forty-eighth; the third day, the eighty-second; the fourth day, the ninety-fourth, etc. Each one of these Psalms has this heading: " For the first day, this is the first in the Sabbath, in which the Levites in the temple would say the twenty-fourth Psalm." " This is the second in the Sabbath," etc. " This is the third in the Sabbath," etc. And thus it would continue till the sixth in the Sabbath, then would come the Psalms for the Sabbath. That is, every day of the week was tributary to the Sabbath. The Sabbath was the goal; each day wended toward that day. Therefore each day was one day in the Sabbath. But it can easily be understood that after the Sabbath was past, and the first day again came, the same Psalm for the first day would be repeated.

This makes it clear that the week consisted of seven days ; the last day was the Sabbath. Each day was simply an integral part of the last day. Then when the Sabbath came, the week terminated; for all the days had been swallowed up in this. And thus the Sabbath had come to stand in the place of the week.

So that on whatever day the Passover occurred, the day after this festival sabbath was the commencement of the fifty days. Then fifty days from *this day* would be Pentecost, or the day after the completed seven sabbaths. See Lev. 24 : 15, 16.

The year that the Savior was crucified the Passover sabbath fell on Friday, from Thursday evening sunset to Friday evening sunset. The first day of the omer, therefore, would be the Sabbath of the Lord. This day was then the first day after the Passover sabbath; therefore, fifty days from this day would again bring us to the seventh day of the week, or the Bible Sabbath. It is thus evident that the Holy Spirit fell on the Sabbath of the Lord, the seventh day of the week. See Lightfoot, Edersheim, and other Hebrew Christian writers.

Paragraph 12.

(c) In the Mishna, treatise ראש השנה=*Rosh-Ha-shona=New Year*, we find the following concerning this festival of New Year's:

"There are four periods of commencement of years, viz., on the first of Nisan (Esth. 3 : 7), is a new year to compute the reign of kings and festivals; the first of Elul (This was the sixth Jewish month. Neh. 6 : 15) is a new year for the tithe of cattle. . . . The first of Tishri (the seventh Jewish month) is New Year's for the ordinary or civil year, for the computation of the seventh years, and of the jubilees (Lev. 25 : 1–16) ; also for the planting of trees and herbs."—*Chapter 1.*

Paragraph 17.

(d) In paragraph sixteen attention was called to the fact that the Jews regarded the blowing of the trumpets as a means of awakening the people from their sins to repentance. One writer, commenting on the meaning of the blowing of the horns, says:

"Rouse ye, rouse ye from your slumber; awake from your sleep, you who mind vanity, for slumber most heavy has fallen upon you." Quoted from Edersheim.

This Jewish writer gathered this idea from the sayings of the rabbis. Paul understood well the general teachings of the Mishna on this point; and it would seem that he had reference to this idea of the "Feast of Trumpets" and its significance, when writing to the churches.

Paragraph 28.

(e) It should be remembered that all this work of the priestly ministrations was designed to teach the people the truths of the real Lamb, offering, and shed blood, which was to be fulfilled in the Messiah. For the apostle plainly states that in the performance of this work there was still a remembrance of sin. Heb. 10 : 5.

Paragraph 32.

(*f*) The author appreciates the fact that the unanimous opinion of writers is that the scapegoat represents one other phase of the work of Christ's atonement. But the type, the Scripture, the plan of redemption, will not admit of such conclusion, and for these reasons :

1. The Lord's lot, or the Lord's goat, typically accomplished everything which was necessary to save and redeem completely the sinner and the world. For this goat was to be offered as a חטאת=*sin offering*. In the fourth chapter of Leviticus, where the sin offerings are introduced, they are all sacrificed to bear the *sins* of the people, and they are all offered as חטאת=*cha-tos, sin offering*. When the penitent saw in this animal his typical substitute, he was forgiven of his sins, and there was an atonement made. Lev. 4 : 20, 26, 31. Hence the חטאת, or *sin offering*, was sufficient to fully meet the requirements of the sinner.

Therefore the *cha-tos*, or *sin offering* which was offered on the Day of Atonement, was ample to do all that was necessary for the blotting out of the sins of all the people.

2. The real virtue in this Lord's goat was the shedding and the sprinkling of its blood for the people as well as for the sanctuary. Lev. 16 : 15. But without the shedding of the blood there can be *no remission of sins.* Heb. 9 : 22. The reason is because it is the *blood*, or the life, that makes the atonement. Lev. 17 : 11, last clause. There was nothing, however, about the Azazel that had any blood shed or sprinkled. It was not offered as an offering for sin, neither was its blood used for any remission of sin. Now Christ, the antitype of the Lord's goat, accomplished all this for man, as has been clearly shown thus far in the work. He was the חטאת, *sin offering*, and bore the sins of the people in His own body. Through His blood only there can be forgiveness or remission, or blotting out of sin. Hence there was nothing about the Azazel that assisted in illustrating Christ's work of atonement for man.

3. That the Azazel, or scapegoat, does represent the devil and Satan is evident, as all the sins of the righteous will have to be borne by him, because he is the originator of sin. Christ put Himself in the place of man and bore man's sins (see 2 Cor. 5 : 21) that man might not die for his own penalty. In other words Christ became man's substitute. But the wicked who do not accept of Christ's shed blood and of His righteous life will have to bear their own sins. Rom. 6 : 23 ; Ezek. 18 : 4, 20. And so the devil, who is the cause of all the sins of the righteous who have been pardoned through the blood of Christ, will have to bear the responsibility of those sins, even as those sins on the Day of Atonement which were forgiven and blotted out, were placed upon the head of the scape-

goat. This thought makes the typical, the scriptural, and redemptive plan, all in harmony. See also paragragh thirty-six of this chapter. Thus we see that the Lord's goat represented Christ, and the Azazel, or scape-goat, represented Satan, the devil.

Paragraph 33.

(*g*) The Bible computation of months is thirty days to the month. In Gen. 7 : 11 it states that the flood began on the seventeenth day of the second month; it began to abate the seventeenth day of the seventh month, where it rested on Mount Ararat. Gen. 8 : 4. This would make the time from the beginning of the flood till it began to subside, just five months. For example:

Month 7	Day 17, waters diminish.
Month 2	Day 17, flood begins.
Months 5	Days 0

But we read that the flood prevailed upon the earth one hundred fifty days. Gen. 7 : 24. And after the one hundred fifty days it began to abate. Gen. 8 : 3. This would therefore make the one hundred fifty days equal to the five months, they both teaching the same thing. By dividing the one hundred fifty days by five, we would have thirty days to the month. Thus:

150 days=5 months. 150 days÷5=30 days=1 month.

Paragraph 35.

(*h*) See for further information upon this subject paragraph thirty-seven, and chapter seventeen.

Paragraph 38.

(*i*) The following is part of a prayer they offer on the Day of Atonement in their synagogue worship :

"And because of the abundance of our sins, we have no burnt offering nor sin offering, no staves for the holy ark, no peace or meat offerings, no lot nor any of the heavenly fire, . . . *no sanctuary nor any sprinkling of the blood*, no trespass offering nor any sacrificing, no purifying with ashes nor any red heifer, no Jerusalem nor any Lebanon, no laver nor any bread of the presence, no altar nor evening sacrifice, . . . no vail nor any atonement. . . . And all this because of our sins and the sins of our forefathers; we are diminished, and have not these things; and since that time have we been destitute of these things.—" *Prayers for the Day of Atonement, Section Mu-saph.*" מוסף ליום כפור=*Mu-saph la-joum kippur.*

CHAPTER XVI.

The Festivals and the Fasts.

"In the last day, that great day of the feast, Jesus stood and cried, saying, If any man thirst, let him come unto Me, and drink. He that believeth on Me, as the Scripture hath said, out of his belly shall flow rivers of living water." John 7:37, 38.

THE FEAST OF TABERNACLES.

IT was said by one, on a certain occasion, that the best of the wine was saved for the last of the feast.[1] This saying has significance when applied to this feast of the Lord. While all the festivals were designed to mean much to the people, as viewed in the light of the Lord Jesus, if they only understood them, the Feast of Tabernacles was the crowning one of all, especially so from the standpoint of outward joy and happiness.

THE PURPOSE OF THIS FEAST.

2. This feast, as has already been mentioned, was observed in the seventh Jewish month,[2] beginning on the fifteenth day, and lasting for seven days,[3] although there was an eighth day connected with this,[4] upon which no work should be done. The first and the last days were to be festival sabbaths.[5] Many were the offerings to be sacrificed to the Lord during these days,[6] in addition to the regular offerings. This festival was to commemorate the ingathering of the harvests of the field, hence was called "The Feast of Ingathering."[7] It was sometimes called "The Feast of Booths," because during these days the people were commanded to dwell in booths.[8] (a) It was this command that was lost sight of for nearly a thousand years, and was not discovered until after the restoration from Babylon, when Ezra read it to the people from the book of the law.[9] (b)

[1] John 2:10.   [2] Lev. 23:33, 34.   [3] Num. 29:12.   [4] Lev. 23:39.   [5] Lev. 23:35, 36.
[6] Num. 29:12-39.   [7] Ex. 23:16, second clause.   [8] Lev. 23:42.   [9] Neh. 8:13-17.

3. This feast was intended to keep before the minds of the people the completed work of the Messiah. When His labors will be finished, what a great joy and gladness will take place, both in earth and in heaven![10] His labors will be rewarded;[11] His redemptive work will be completed; His salvation gloriously triumphant. Hence in a special manner was this festival to be one of joy and happiness.[12]

CHRIST'S APPLICATION OF THE FESTIVAL.

4. With the passing of each day the joy was intensified; the services and sacrifices were attended with a great deal of pleasure and happiness; and every one who was at Jerusalem and who attended this feast realized a large measure of joy. This state of affairs had grown remarkably till the time of Christ, especially since its discovery in the days of Ezra; and the Savior, always ready to have people see that all things in Moses and in the prophets were fulfilled in Him, while in the temple on the last day of this feast, which was called the " Rejoicing of the Law," made a remarkable application of the festival to Himself.

JESUS' APPEAL TO THE PEOPLE.

5. While the sacrifice was being prepared on this day, a priest went to the Pool of Siloam, amid a great procession of musicians and singers, and took therefrom about a quart of water. This he carried in a golden pitcher. The water then was carried up to the altar, and placed in a basin at the base of the altar. (*c*) While this procession was passing, and all the people were rejoicing in what was being done, amid all the demonstration of joy, Jesus cried aloud to the multitudes:

" If any man thirst, let him come unto Me, and drink. He that believeth on Me, as the Scripture hath said, out of his belly shall flow rivers of living water." [13]

6. How this must have arrested the attention of the people;

---

[10] Deut. 16: 13, 14; Rev. 7:9–12; Rev. 5: 13.　　[11] Isa. 53: 11, 12.
[12] Deut. 16:14.　　　　[13] John 7: 37, 38.

for He referred to certain scriptures as its fulfillment.   And of
these scriptures we find the following :

"Behold, God is my salvation ; I will trust, and not be afraid : for the
Lord Jehovah is my strength and my song ; He also is become my salva-
tion.   Therefore with joy shall ye draw water out of the wells of salvation.
And in that day shall ye say, Praise the Lord, call upon His name, declare
His doings among the people, make mention that His name is exalted." [14]

THE PEOPLE IMPRESSED AT CHRIST'S INVITATION.

7. If the Jews had only then seen the meaning and intent
of that whole service as the Savior brought it to their attention,
what a wonderful feast they would have had, and what great
rejoicing !   Certainly this must have made a great impression
upon the people.   Right in the midst of all the vast multitudes,
and when the priests and leaders had them under their entire
control, for Christ to make this ringing announcement which
was echoed and re-echoed through that entire temple building,
must have struck terror to the hearts of these leaders.   It also
had the tendency to draw from many of the people the saying :
"This is the Christ."   "Of a truth this is the Prophet." [15]

8. Had they only opened their hearts to believe and receive
this announcement, how many might have drawn from the great
Siloam, He who was the Sent (*d*) of God, the River of living
water, and would have received the fullness of the blessed
Spirit.

ANOTHER LESSON.

9. In order still to impress upon them precious lessons
which they might learn from this feast, another incident happened by which He sought to make clear that this feast found
its fulfillment in Him.   One pleasing characteristic of the occasion in the days of the Savior was the way the temple was illuminated.   Everything was illuminated in the temple, and the
light shone most gloriously. (*e*)   This was to add to their joy
and happiness.   So the day after the incident previously men-

<hr />

[14] Isa. 12:2-4; see 44:3.   [15] John 7:40, 41.

tioned, He called the attention of the people to the lights that were yet burning in the sacred house, and said : " I am the light of the world. He that followeth Me shall not walk in darkness." [16] And before the feast was completed Jesus opened the eyes of the blind man,[17] to demonstrate to them that He was the light of the world. If they would only in those lights recognize Him, then the feast would be blessed light to their hearts. It is not surprising then that John should have heard from the lips of Jesus :

" I am Alpha and Omega, the beginning and the ending," " the first and the last." [18]

Yes, He is the all in all. Blessed be His name.

THE COMPLETED FEAST.

10. While many things in this festival revealed Jesus as the Christ, and showed His salvation to the thirsty and darkened soul, its completeness will be realized at His glorious appearing. The festival was to commemorate the ingathering of the harvest.[19] When the crops had ripened, and the field had brought forth an abundant harvest, the sickle had been put in, and the fruits gathered into the garners, the people could surely have reason to be glad and rejoice.[20]

ITS PRECIOUS APPLICATION.

11. So the Son of man, the Messiah, the Deliverer, who came to this earth to sow seeds of truth in the hearts of men, when He shall send forth His angels with the sound of a trumpet [21] to reap the harvest of the earth,[22] to gather into His garner the fruits of His toil and effort,—shall have great occasion to be glad and to joy in great abundance.[23] Then the first-fruits and the gathered harvest shall, together with the Sower, cause the arches of heaven to echo and re-echo with songs of gladness, praise, honor, and glory,[24] as the song of

---

[16] John 8:12. [17] John 9:3-10, [18] Rev. 1:8, 11. [19] Ex. 23:16.
[20] Deut. 16:14. [21] Matt. 24:31. [22] Matt. 13:39; Rev. 14:14-17; Matt. 3:12.
[23] Isa. 53:11. [24] Rev. 5:13; 7:9, 10.

Moses, the servant of God, and of the Lamb,[25] shall be sung by every person in earth, under the earth, in the sea, ascribing praise, glory, and honor to Him who sitteth on the throne and to the Lamb.[26]

THE GREAT HARVEST GATHERED.

12. What a blessed thought to know that that day is hastening;[27] that even now the reapers are getting ready to gather the harvest of souls. Soon the Master will descend with all the holy angels,[28] and gather His elect from the four winds, from one end of heaven even to the other. Then with Abraham, Isaac, and Jacob,[29] with all the true and faithful servants of God[30] we shall observe the great Feast of Tabernacles. Oh what a blessed rejoicing that will be!

FEAST OF DEDICATION.

13. Thus far we have considered the feasts, festivals, and the fast which were given to the people by the mouth of Moses. But later as circumstances arose among the Jews, other feasts and fasts were introduced. Not all of these, however, are spoken of in the Scriptures. Two other feasts are spoken of in Scripture: "Feast of Dedication,"[31] and the "Feast of Purim."[32] The former is observed about December, in the month Chisleu. It was instituted about 164 B. C. by Judas Maccabæus, after the Greeks were conquered, the temple recovered by the Maccabees, the polluted altar restored to its proper place, and the worship of God properly conducted.

HOW AND WHY OBSERVED.

14. The real significance of the feast, however, is not generally known. Such men as Josephus as well as other notable writers differ as to the origin of the feast, though tradition has it that when the temple was restored there was found only one jar of oil on hand, sealed with the high priest's signet, with which to feed the candlestick. This, it is true, was pure oil, but insuf-

---

[25] Rev. 15: 3.   [26] Rev. 5:13.   [27] Zeph. 1:14.   [28] Matt. 25:31.
[29] Matt. 8:11.   [30] Luke 13:29.   [31] John 10:22.   [32] Esther 9: 20–22, 32.

Feast of Purim.

ficient to carry on the work for one single day. To the surprise of all, the flagon never failed for eight days, the length of time it took to secure a supply; and thus the lamps were continued undiminished. In order to commemorate this wonderful miracle the people were commanded to illuminate the temple for that length of time, and also to do the same thing in all private houses, as well as in the synagogues. Hence the custom is on the first night of the festival to light one light, the next night two; and so on every night till the eighth night, when the whole eight were to be lighted. During these days no public fasting was allowed, and the people in general were given over to joy and gladness.

15. It was on one of these occasions that we have the Savior's experience in the temple with the Jews, when they inquired of Him if He were the Christ. [33] If they could have only seen Him as the One who was ready to pour the oil of His grace into their souls, even as they believed the miraculous supply of oil was given with which to feed the candlestick, they then would have received Him as the Anointed One, whom God anointed [34] with His holy oil, [35] and who in turn would have anointed them with the Holy Ghost and with power. [36]

FEAST OF PURIM.

16. These are all the feasts spoken of in the Bible, except the Feast of Purim, though there were others that the Jews celebrated in Christ's day, and which are still observed. The Feast of Purim was to commemorate their deliverance from the wicked Haman, [37] who desired to destroy all the Jews in the Persian realm. This day to the Jews is a day of feasting and mirth. Banquets, parties, and receptions are held everywhere.

FEAST DURING THE OMER.

17. Then there is one day during the omer,—the time from

33 John 10: 22–24.   34 Ps. 2: 6, margin.   35 Ps. 45: 7; Heb. 1: 8, 9.
36 Acts 2: 38.   37 Esther 3: 5, 6.

the Passover to the Pentecost,—the thirty-third day, called
לג לעומר*=Lag-La-Omer;* the word *Lag,* being a combination of
two Hebrew letters, *Lamed,* equivalent numerically to *thirty;*
and *Gimel,* equivalent numerically to *three;* hence it is known
as the thirty-third day of the counting of the omer.

18. On nearly all these feasts the orthodox Jew ceases
from labor, and considers the observance of the feast a religious
devotion. To many of the people they are burdens, heavy to
be borne, as it means a loss of labor and means. " If the Son
therefore shall make you free, ye shall be free indeed." [38] In
Christ there is a continuous feast; He satisfies the desires of
every longing soul. [39]

THE FASTS.

19. The Lord only commanded originally the one fast, the
Day of Atonement. But there were a number added later, on
account of conditions which arose at different times. It was
generally true in the experience of Israel that when they
reached a place where they were brought into great straits, they
spent a season in fasting and prayer, and the Lord always sig-
nally answered their desires, in giving them victory. [40] But we
find there are several fasts mentioned in the Bible, which have
at least some significance, and might be of interest to the reader.

FAST OF THE FOURTH MONTH.

20. The first time we meet with this fast is in Zechariah's
prophecy. [41] This fast was observed on the seventeenth day of
the month. It originated in Babylon during the captivity. The
cause for the fast was the besieging of the first temple, by
Nebuchadnezzar on the ninth day of the month, and the siege
of the second temple by Titus on the seventeenth day of the
month. Should the seventeenth day fall on the Sabbath, the
fast is observed the next day. The only fast day in the year
that the Jews observe on the Sabbath is the Day of Atone-

---

[38] John 8:36.   [39] Hag. 2:7; Ps. 37:4.   [40] 2 Chron. 20:3; Ezra 8:21; Jer. 36:9.
[41] Zech. 8:19.

ment. No other fast is allowed to be observed that day. The reason for this is that the Lord said that the people should call the Sabbath a delight, the holy of the Lord, honorable. [42] And the people regarded a day of fasting as a matter of distress and sadness rather than of delight.

THE FAST OF THE FIFTH MONTH.

21. Soon after this fast was inaugurated, or about the commencement of the Babylonian captivity, the fast of the fifth month was instituted. [43] On this day, *it is said*, that five things occurred, as reasons why the people should fast.

1. The temple at Jerusalem was destroyed by Nebuchadnezzar on this day. [44]

2. The temple was also destroyed on this day by Titus, the Roman general.

3. On this day it was decreed in the wilderness that the children of Israel should not enter into the promised land, but that their carcasses should fall in the wilderness. [45]

4. On this day the Scripture was literally fulfilled which said that "Zion shall be ploughed as a field." [46] One, Turnus Rufus, a Roman centurion, passed over the site of Mount Zion with the plowshare.

5. On this day Bar-Cochba, the false Messiah of the second century, whose cause was espoused by Rabbi Akiba, one of the greatest and most scholarly of rabbis, was driven to the city of Bither, where he was killed. About four hundred thousand persons lost their lives with him and many more thousands were taken captives.

HOW THIS FAST IS OBSERVED.

22. During this day the Jews spend most of their time in mourning at the synagogue service on account of their sins and those of their fathers, and of visiting the dead at the cemeteries, and in a general penitent manner. Everything in the

[42] Isa. 58: 13.   [43] Zech. 7: 3; 8: 19.   [44] Jer. 52: 12-14.   [45] Num. 14: 28-33.
[46] Jer. 26: 18; Micah 3: 12.

synagogue is stripped of its adornments; the minister in the evening of the day, reads the book of Lamentations, while seated on a very low stool, with a lighted candle by his side; the same reading is repeated the next morning. Save the Sabbaths, this is the only morning in the year when the talith, scarf, or garment, with phylacteries, are not worn, as mentioned in the twelfth paragraph of chapter six.

23. Instead of the people observing those days of fasts to commemorate the sins of their fathers, how much better it would be for them, if they considered what those sins were, and then turned into the path of righteousness, by breaking away from the wicked course of their fathers. This is no doubt the reason why Jesus said to the Jews, ye are partakers of the sins of your fathers. [47] By doing as their fathers did, when they knew their fathers sinned, and not repenting of their own course, the people showed that had they lived in those days they would have done the same. If they had only believed in the Lord Jesus, and accepted Him as their Savior, then Jerusalem would never have been destroyed. [48] But Jesus said that not a stone would be left of the temple, that would not be thrown down. [49] Then every time that the Jew fasts on this day, he is simply proving that Jesus is the Christ.

FAST OF THE SEVENTH MONTH.

24. This month contains two fasts, the one on the tenth day, the Day of Atonement, and the one on the second day. The reason for the observance of this latter fast was said to be the death of Gedaliah and his companions at Mizpah. [50] It is not generally observed, save by the most strict and pious of the people.

OTHER FASTS.

25. In addition to these public fasts there were more than twenty other fasts during the year, both public and private. Of these we might especially note the ones the Pharisee speaks

[47] Matt. 23:30, 31.   [48] Jer. 17:25.   [49] Mark 13:1, 2.   [50] Jer. 41:1-3.

of : " I fast twice in the week." [51]   These were on Monday and Thursday.   The tradition says that Moses went up to Mount Sinai the second time to receive the tables of the law on Thursday, and came down on Monday; and because of this these Pharisees fasted.   But it was rather done because of what merit they thought they received therefrom; all of which serves to illustrate the Savior's words :

" And He spake this parable unto certain which trusted in themselves that they were righteous, and despised others." [52]

By performing these things the Pharisees thought they were gaining righteousness, and were thereby greater favorites than others in heaven.   But the Lord says He looks not on the outward person, but on the heart. [53]   And the blood of Jesus Christ His Son cleanses from all sin. [54]

HOW THE CHURCH MAY GET POWER.

26. The Savior said that the time would come when His disciples would fast after He left them; [55] but the object of these fasts was to seek for purity of life through Jesus only, and better to know and understand the will of Christ Jesus. [56]

27. If the church of to-day were to do more of this kind of fasting, the Holy Spirit would be poured out in greater measure; God's work in the world would be blessed and prospered; and many souls would be brought to King Jesus, who fasted many a day for His followers.

[51] Luke 18:12.   [52] Luke 18:9.   [53] 1 Sam. 16:7.   [54] 1 John 1:7.
[55] Matt. 9:15.   [56] Acts 13:2; 14:23.

EXPLANATORY NOTES.

Paragraph 2.

(*a*) In the tractate, " Succah," of the Mishna, we find the following on the making of the booth, or succah, as it is called :

" A succah which is above twenty *amoth* [about thirty feet] high, is not according to law.   Rabbi Jehudah declares it is allowable.   One which is not ten hands high [about three feet], which has not three walls, or which is more exposed to the sun than to the shade, is not valid. An old succah, the school of Shammi holds not lawful; but the school of Hillel permits it. What is considered an old booth?—One that has been built thirty days before the festival; but if it was constructed on purpose for the festival, even though it were a year old, it is lawful.

"If a man build his succah beneath a tree, it is as though he had built it in a house. Should he construct one booth above another, the upper one is lawful, but the other is invalid. Rabbi Jehudah said, 'Should the upper one not be habited, the lower one is valid.'"—*Chapters 1 and 2.*

(*b*) It certainly seems remarkable about this festival. It was not known for over one thousand years, from the days of Joshua the son of Nun, till after the return of the Babylonian captivity. This was a period of nearly eleven hundred years. During this period some of the greatest men of God lived and died—Samuel, David, Elisha, Elijah (The latter was translated without tasting death. 2 Kings 2:11), all the greater prophets, and the lesser prophets, save two. Yet none of them had ever observed this feast. But when the Lord revealed this lost truth to them, how glad and rejoiced they were at its discovery. No doubt this was to teach God's people in future times the importance of personally believing and obeying everything the Lord says, even though many of the pious men of God in days gone by, had acted differently. The word of the Lord only is what is to be followed.

Paragraph 5.

(*c*) A few statements from the Mishna concerning the carrying of the water, might be of interest to the reader:

"How was the pouring of the water? A golden pitcher that held three lugs [about a quart], was filled from the brook Siloah [Siloam]. When they came with it to the water gate, they blew a blast, a long note, and another blast. The priest then ascended the stair of the altar, and turned to the left; two silver basins stood there. . . . Each was perforated with a small hole, like a nostril, at the bottom. The one for the wine was somewhat wider, the other for the water, narrower, that both might get empty at once. The one to the west, was for the water; the other, to the east, for wine. . . . The music played during the drawing of the water. . . . The rabbis said, 'He who has not witnessed the rejoicings at the water drawing, has, *throughout the whole of his life*, witnessed no real rejoicing.'"

From these statements one can appreciate the crowds that must have thronged the temple at this period, and how intensely every heart must have throbbed as the water was being carried to the altar. The Savior understanding its meaning so well, as the people understood it, must have caused considerable stir as He called their attention to Himself in all this service.

Paragraph 8.

(*d*) The word *Siloam* is an intensely interesting word, and is full of meaning. The word originally was *Shiloh*, Hebrew שׁילֹה=*Shi-loh*. This is first found in Gen. 49 : 10. The great Onkelos, who wrote his famous Targum on the Pentateuch, says that this term "*Shiloh*" means *Messiah*. He says on Gen. 49 : 10, on this expression, כִּי יבֹא שׁילה=*Kee-yo-vou-Shiloh=* "*till Shiloh come*," the following : עַד דְּייתי משׁיחא=*Ad d-ya-tha M-she-cho=* "*to the coming of the Messiah*." He is sustained in this position by such learned men as Kimchi, Ben Ganach. Then the word is also called Shiloah, Neh. 3 : 15; Isa. 8 : 6. This time the term is used for the brook. But the word *Shiloah* is in the Hebrew שׁלֹה=*She-lo-ach*. But *She-lo-ach* means *sent*, or messenger. Hence the Shiloh of Gen. 49 : 10; the Shiloah of Nehemiah and of Isaiah originally come from the same word. But the pool of Siloam, whence the water was taken, is the same as the waters of Shiloah. John 9 : 7.

Therefore when the Savior called the attention of the people to drink of Him it was practically telling them He was the *Shiloh*, the *Messiah;* in Him were the waters of the *She-lo-ach*, the Sent of God. Thus the truth must have been a beautiful one if they only could have seen it; that is the truth of the scripture He referred to, as being fulfilled in Him.

Paragraph 9.

(*e*) Concerning the lighting of the temple during this festival in the days of the Savior, the Mishna has the following :

"At the expiration of the first holy day of the festival they descended into the women's court, where great preparations were made for the rejoicing. Four golden candelabras were placed there, with four golden basins to each candelabra. Then a ladder was placed to each candelabra, on which stood a youth of the priestly tribe, holding a jar of oil, containing one hundred twenty lugs [forty quarts], with which he replenished the basins."

"The cast off breeches and belts of the priests were torn into shreds for wicks, which they lighted. There was not a court in Jerusalem that was not illuminated by the lights of the water-drawing."

"Pious and distinguished men danced before the people with lighted flambeaux in their hands, and sang hymns and praises before them ; and the Levites accompanied them with harps, psalteries, cymbals, and numberless musical instruments."—*Tractate "Succah," chapters 1 to 3.*

How beautifully appropriate for the Savior to present Himself to

them as the real and true Light, under such circumstances. Of course
the people in a measure appreciated that when the Messiah did come He
would be the light both for Jews and Gentiles. See Isa. 60:1; 9:12.
This then was but an added testimony to them that He was the Messiah.

Paragraph 16.

(*f*) There is an entire tractate of the Mishna with a number of chapters devoted to the way this feast should be observed. It contains scores
of laws and observances. The treatise is entitled, " Megillah," or the
" Scroll of Esther."

CHAPTER XVII.

A Remarkable Prophecy, and Its Fulfillment.

" We have also a more sure word of prophecy; whereunto ye do well that ye take heed, as unto a light that shineth in a dark place, until the day dawn, and the day-star arise in your hearts: knowing this first, that no prophecy of the scripture is of any private interpretation." 2 Peter 1:19, 20.

WAITING FOR THE MESSIAH.

EVERY pious and devoted Israelite that lived before Christ came to the earth, longed for the privilege and the opportunity of seeing Him. Whether he were a prophet, priest, or king, his one desire was to set his eyes upon the Messiah. [1] That this was so is evident from the Savior's own words:

" But blessed are your eyes, for they see: and your ears, for they hear. For verily I say unto you, That many prophets and righteous men have desired to see those things which ye see, and have not seen them; and to hear those things which ye hear, and have not heard them." [2]

And the Apostle Peter speaks a little later in this manner:

" Receiving the end of your faith, even the salvation of your souls. Of which salvation the prophets have inquired and searched diligently, who prophesied of the grace that should come unto you: searching what, or what manner of time the Spirit of Christ which was in them did signify, when it testified beforehand the sufferings of Christ, and the glory that should follow." [3]

GOD PROPHESIED THE TIME.

2. God, however, had made a prediction that the Messiah in person should come at a definite time; and this all the people might have known. [4] Had they only studied the word of God as diligently as they heeded the traditions of men, they

[1] Luke 2:25–30, 38.   [2] Matt. 13:16, 17.   [3] 1 Pet. 1:9–11.   [4] Luke 19:44; 1:68–70.

[285]

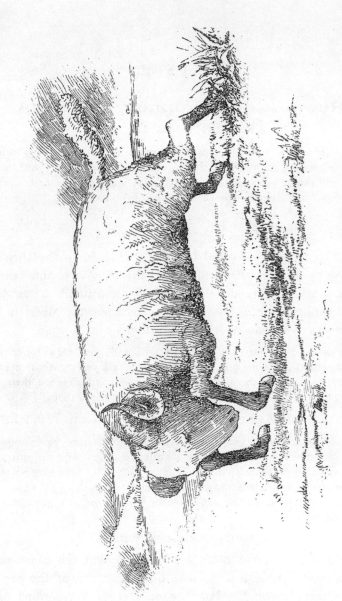

THE RAM WITH THE TWO HORNS.

would have learned of this, and then would have been prepared to meet Him.

3. Strange as it seemed to the Jews, and strange as it may seem to the people of the present time, nearly five hundred years before Christ appeared in the flesh, as the Messiah, there was a prediction made that He would come; the very year, yes, even the month, of His coming was announced. [5] Certainly, a remarkable incident, and in a measure the Jews appreciated it, but its full force and significance they never understood.

A SINGULAR STATEMENT.

4. After the Savior was baptized, and John was imprisoned, Jesus came into Galilee, preaching the gospel of the kingdom of God; [6] and He said:

"*The time is fulfilled*, and the kingdom of God is at hand: repent ye, and believe the gospel." [7]

5. This no doubt has been considered by many at the present time as a singular statement, even as it was thought to be by the people in Christ's day. Yet it need not have been, had they only studied the word of God. From the expression itself and the manner it was told, it is evident that the people should have known what He meant, even as He asked Nicodemus, when speaking to him of the new birth, "Art thou a master of Israel, and knowest not these things?" [8] clearly indicating that he ought to have known, and his ignorance was without excuse.

6. "The time is fulfilled." [9] What time? This no doubt was the question that many must have asked. Yet it must have been clear to them that *the time* had something to do with the kingdom of heaven, and with the Messiah, in bringing the kingdom to men. Is there then a prophecy that the Jews might have known concerning this time, and thus have been definitely prepared for the Messiah? If so, we can better appreciate the meaning of their stumbling over Him as the Christ. [10] Possi-

---

[5] Gal. 4: 4. [6] Matt. 4: 12-23. [7] Mark 1: 14, 15. [8] John 3: 10.
[9] Mark 1: 15. [10] Isa. 28: 16; Rom. 9: 32, 33; 1 Pet. 2: 6-8.

bly too, we may discover that the Lord has included in this great prophecy certain predictions which affect the church of to-day, in connection with Christ's second advent.

THE WONDERFUL PROPHECY OF THE TIME.

7. That such a prophecy should have been given, we might expect, for God had told the people several centuries before, that He would do nothing but what He revealed His secrets unto His servants the prophets.[11] What *greater event* could take place in this world than the coming of the Messiah,[12] the " Desire of all nations; "[13] "the Hope of the world "?[14] We would then naturally expect that the Lord would reveal to some of the prophets, not only that the Messiah would appear,[15] but the time of his appearance, so that the people might be in expectation of Him.

8. Such a prediction we find in the prophecy of Daniel, which, after a brief consideration, will enable us to see clearly the force of the Savior's statement, " The time is fulfilled," as well as that other scripture, " *This day is this scripture fulfilled in your ears.*"[16]

A REMARKABLE VISION.

9. In the eighth chapter of the book of Daniel, we find that the prophet was given a vision.[17] While in this vision several things were presented to him. He saw first a ram with two horns, one of which was higher than the other.[18] After this he beheld an he-goat, or shaggy-goat, coming from the west, directing his aim at this ram.[19] He ran into the ram with the fury of his power, smote him, brake his two horns, and completely crushed him.[20] This he-goat had a remarkable horn between his eyes;[21] and when the goat became great, this notable horn was broken; and in its place there arose four others, which were scattered to the four winds of heaven.[22]

[11] Amos 3:7. [12] Gen. 49:10. [13] Haggai 2:7.
[14] Eph. 2:12; Ps. 71:5; Col. 1:27; 1 Thess. 1:3; 1 Tim. 1:1. [15] Mal. 3:1.
[16] Mark 1:15; Luke 4:21. [17] Dan. 8:1. [18] Dan. 8:2-4. [19] Dan. 8:5, 6.
[20] Dan. 8:7, 8. [21] Dan. 8:5. [22] Dan. 8:8.

THE HE GOAT, WITH NOTABLE HORN.

19

10. Out of one of these four horns there came another little horn, which waxed exceeding great, southward, eastward, and toward the pleasant land. [23] This little horn destroyed everything that came in its way, and finally became exceeding great, even to the host of heaven; and he also magnified himself to the Prince of the host. [24]

11. After this scene, Daniel, while still in a vision, overheard a conversation. One saint asked another saint a certain question, [25] to which, when the reply was made, Daniel received this answer:

"And he said unto me, Unto two thousand and three hundred days; then shall the sanctuary be cleansed." [26]

12. At this point Daniel awoke, and seemed desirous to understand what he had seen and heard. [27] He then overheard some one calling to the Angel Gabriel to make Daniel understand the vision. [28] The angel immediately proceeded to carry out the instruction, informing Daniel, however, that this vision would not be completely fulfilled till the time of the end. [29]

THE EXPLANATION OF THE VISION.

13. The prophet was then informed that the ram which he saw having the two horns represented the kings of Media and Persia. [30] The he-goat represented Grecia. [31] The notable horn that was between its eyes was the first king. [32] This was of course Alexander the Great. The four horns, [33] which arose in that kingdom after Alexander died, or was broken [34] as the text says, were the four leading generals of Alexander, who separated the kingdom into four parts. These generals were Cassander, Lysimachus, Seleucus, and Ptolemy.

14. The angel further said that in the closing days of their kingdom there should arise another power, represented by the little horn, which should be strong and mighty. This we are

[23] Dan. 8: 9.   [24] Dan. 8: 10–12.   [25] Dan. 8: 13.   [26] Dan. 8: 14.
[27] Dan. 8: 15.   [28] Dan. 8: 16.   [29] Dan. 8: 17–19.   [30] Dan. 8: 20.
[31] Dan. 8: 21.   [32] Dan. 8: 21.   [33] Dan. 8: 22.   [34] Dan. 8: 8.

aware, represented the iron monarchy Rome, which succeeded Grecia, as a universal power. [35] This power would also stand up against (oppose) the Prince of princes [36] who is Jesus Christ. [37] This certainly the Bible declares Rome did, when Pontius Pilate, the Roman governor, passed the death sentence upon the Lord Jesus Christ, and gave the authority to the Jews to put Him to death. [38]

ONE PORTION UNEXPLAINED.

15. So far everything of the vision was explained, except the verse, " Unto two thousand and three hundred days, then shall the sanctuary be cleansed." [39] The angel then told Daniel that the vision, concerning the evening and the morning which was given, is true. This vision of the " evening and morning " referred to meant the two thousand and three hundred days. For the literal translation of the Hebrew reads thus :

"And he said unto me, Until evening and morning two thousand three hundred, and the sanctuary shall be cleansed, or justified."

In the margin of Dan. 8 : 14 we find the words, *evening and morning*, instead of the word, *days*. (*a*) Hence it is evident that this is what the angel had in mind when he told Daniel that the " vision of the evening and morning " which he had seen was true; [40] but it was to be closed up for many days.

DANIEL SEEKING LIGHT.

16. When the angel closed with these words, Daniel was perplexed and astonished. [41] This was the part of the vision which he particularly wished to know; but here he was left without information. This further knowledge was not granted to him on this occasion, because what he had seen made such an impression upon his mind, especially as He beheld the crucifixion of the Lord Jesus Christ by the hands of those wicked men who slew Him, [42] that it caused him to be ill, and he was obliged to leave his duties for a time. [43]

35 Dan. 8: 23, 24; Luke 2: 1.　　36 Dan. 8: 25.　　37 Acts 3: 15; 5: 31; Rev. 1: 5.
38 John 19: 15, 16; Acts 4: 25, 26.　　39 Dan. 8: 14.　　40 Dan. 8: 26.
41 Dan. 8: 27.　　42 Dan. 8: 25.　　43 Dan. 8: 27.

17. However, the desire to understand that part of the vision never left him; he knew there were some matters connected with that in which he was interested. Hence like a true man of God, with a burning and a yearning to know the will of God and to receive all that the Lord had for him, he began to study the Bible,[44] hoping if possible to receive light, that the cleansing of the sanctuary and the time might be made clear to him.

HIS SEARCH REWARDED.

18. In the course of his study of the Scriptures, he came across some texts in Jeremiah, which impressed him that there existed some relation between the two things, the time—the twenty-three hundred days—and the event—the cleansing of the sanctuary. Since Jerusalem was desolate and defiled by the hands of the Gentiles under Nebuchadnezzar, who burned the house of God and removed the vessels to Babylon,[45] he concluded that this vision had something to do with the restoration and return of the temple and the people. And since he found in Jeremiah's prophecy a certain time promised, after which they should be reinstated into the favor of God, his conclusion was no doubt irresistible that he had found what he sought. Here are the texts:

"For thus saith the Lord, That after seventy years be accomplished at Babylon I will visit you, and perform My good word toward you in causing you to return to this place. For I know the thoughts that I think toward you, saith the Lord, thoughts of peace, and not of evil, to give you an expected end. Then shall ye call upon Me, and ye shall go and pray unto Me, and I will hearken unto you. And ye shall seek Me, and find Me, when ye shall search for Me with all your heart. And I will be found of you, saith the Lord: and I will turn away your captivity, and I will gather you from all the nations, and from all the places whither I have driven you, saith the Lord; . . .[46]

"And it shall come to pass, when seventy years are accomplished, that I will punish the king of Babylon, and that nation, saith the Lord, for their iniquity." . . .[47]

[44] Dan. 9: 2.   [45] 2 Kings 25: 8-10; Dan 1: 1, 2.   [46] Jer. 29: 10-14.
[47] Jer. 25: 12.

19. Then taking God at His word, he immediately began to carry out the instruction, in earnestly seeking the Lord with fasting and praying; [48] and continued thus till the answer came. The burden of his prayer [49] was that the Lord would remember how kind and merciful He was, how sinful the people were, and that He would carry out the promise contained in that message of the sanctuary to be cleansed. He prays:

"O Lord, according to all Thy righteousness, I beseech Thee, let Thine anger and Thy fury be turned away from Thy city Jerusalem, Thy holy mountain: because for our sins, and for the iniquities of our fathers, *Jerusalem and Thy people* are become a reproach to all that are about us. Now therefore, O our God, hear the prayer of Thy servant, and his supplications, and cause Thy face to shine upon Thy *sanctuary that is desolate*, for the Lord's sake." [50]

HIS REQUEST GRANTED.

20. While in this earnest, prayerful attitude, about the time of the evening sacrifice, [51] (*b*) he received a visitation from the same angel who had partially enlightened Him previously. [52] The angelic hand being placed tenderly upon the faithful and devoted prophet, the heavenly messenger informed him that he had come to answer his request, [53] and give to him the desires of his heart, because he was dearly beloved in heaven. [54] What a beautiful testimony to receive from the heavenly visitant, who had just come from the very presence of God. [55]

21. He immediately began where he left off with the previous explanation, found in the closing part of the eighth chapter. [56] He said:

"Seventy weeks are determined upon Thy people and upon Thy holy city, to finish the transgression, and to make an end of sins, and to make reconciliation for iniquity, and to bring in everlasting righteousness, and to seal up the vision and prophecy, and to anoint the most holy." [57]

THE TIME.

22. Thus we see that the Angel Gabriel begins at the very

[48] Dan. 9:3.　　[49] Dan. 9:5-19.　　[50] Dan. 9:16, 17.　　[51] Num. 28:4.
[52] Dan. 9:21.　　[53] Dan. 9:22.　　[54] Dan. 9:23.　　[55] Luke 1:19.
[56] Dan. 8:26.　　　　　　[57] Dan. 9:24.

point that Daniel wishes to know, namely, the time shown by the twenty-three hundred days. [58] No other time is mentioned in the vision of the eighth chapter. No other vision had been given to the prophet since he received that one. No explanation had been given to him since he received the vision; his prayer was that he might know the meaning of the unfulfilled portion of the heavenly scene. When then the angel comes to him, and informs him he is to give him the wishes of his heart, and commences by announcing a period of time, the evidence is most conclusive that he refers to that period, or to a portion of that period with which Daniel was familiar. The only period of time being that in the previous chapter, the prophet at once recognizes the relation of the two.

WHAT WAS INVOLVED IN THE SEVENTY WEEKS.

23. Here then we have a period designated as "seventy weeks," which were determined, or cut off, (c) or decreed, upon Daniel's people, the Jews. During this period eight specific events were to take place, every one of which would be connected with the time specified.

24. First, the seventy weeks were cut off, or decreed upon this people; that is, this period of time was allotted to the Jews, at the end of which the Jews, as a nation, would be cut off.

25. Second, during this period, or ending with this period, the holy city would be cut off. The temple, the house of God, the land, the city of the people, would no more bear that relation to God which they formerly did, when the Jews were the chosen people of God.

26. Third, the transgressions of the people would be finished, or as the Hebrew renders it, closed up, or completed; that is, during this period the Jewish people would reach the climax of their sins and wickedness, which would close their probation as a nation. On account of their wicked course

[58] Dan. 8:14.

during this period their transgressions would be beyond any remedy. [59]

27. Fourth, to make an end of sins; or as the margin renders the thought, "to seal up," which is the Hebrew expression, וּלחתם=*Ool-cho-sam.* The word rendered *sins* in this phrase, is the same Hebrew word as "sin offering," חטאות=*Cha-tos*; that is, during this period of seventy weeks, the sin offerings would be sealed, completed, finished. The method also of the forgiveness of sins, through the blood of the animals, would therefore come to an end, because of the abolition of these sin offerings. This certainly is the thought in the text, concerning the word *Cha-tos.* The words of this expression in the Hebrew, *Ool-cho-sam-Cha-tos*, are literally, "and the sealing up of sin offerings."

28. Fifth, to make reconciliation for iniquity, or as the Hebrew word renders the thought, "the atonement for sins," "the forgiveness for sins." The Hebrew word, כפר=*Cha-par*, is the word which means *atonement*, or *forgiveness*; (*d*) that is, during this period of seventy weeks, atonement would be made for sins, by which men would have the forgiveness of sins.

29. Sixth, the bringing in of everlasting righteousness; that is, during this time everlasting righteousness would be brought in, righteousness of eternity. On this expression the great and scholarly rabbi and commentator, Rashi, says that this everlasting righteousness will be brought to the people through the *Messiah* who is to live forever.

30. Seventh, to seal up the vision and the prophecy; that is, the vision concerning the twenty-three hundred days, and concerning the prophet through whom the vision came, would be sealed up, certified, demonstrated, during the seventy weeks. (*e*) In other words, something would occur during this period that would prove conclusively that this vision was of God, as well as was the man who gave it.

31. Eighth, the anointing of the most holy; that is, the

[59] 2 Chron. 36: 16.

"holy of holies," the holiest of holy things and places would be anointed during this period.

WHY DANIEL RECEIVED HIS TESTIMONY.

32. All these things were to transpire during these seventy weeks. Surely then this is a most remarkable prophecy, one that should have stirred every Israelite to make investigation, one that deserved most profound and thoughtful search. It is not at all surprising then that to the Prophet Daniel should be brought that sweet testimonial from heaven, that he was a man greatly beloved, [60] because he was so desirous of ascertaining what was intended by that time and event spoken of by the angel.

THE BEGINNING OF THE TIME.

33. While Daniel had revealed to him, in part, the thing he wished to know concerning the time, he was still left in the dark when the time was to begin. If the angel would leave unexplained this important part, then mystery would still be enshrouding this great truth. The angel, however, knowing Daniel's desire, proceeds to explain the commencement of this time by saying:

"Know therefore and understand, that from the going forth of the commandment to restore and to build Jerusalem unto the Messiah the Prince shall be seven weeks, and threescore and two weeks: the street shall be built again, and the wall, even in troublous times. And after threescore and two weeks shall Messiah be cut off, but not for Himself; and the people of the prince that shall come shall destroy the city and the sanctuary; and the end thereof shall be with a flood, and unto the end of the war desolations are determined. And He shall confirm the covenant with many for one week: and in the midst of the week He shall cause the sacrifice and the oblation to cease, and for the overspreading of abominations He shall make it desolate, even until the consummation, and that determined shall be poured upon the desolate." [61]

34. Here then we have the heavenly messenger giving to the prophet, directly from the court of glory, the definite and

[60] Dan. 9:23.   [61] Dan. 9:25-27.

minute explanation of these seventy weeks, even when the reckoning was to be commenced. The time, therefore, from which these days were to be counted, was the decree to restore and to build Jerusalem. If we can ascertain when this decree was issued, we have the definite certainty when to begin the numbering.

THE MEANING OF THE DAYS.

35. It should be borne in mind that these seventy weeks, or four hundred ninety days, are part of the twenty-three hundred days. [62] This, therefore, being true, the beginning of the four hundred ninety days marks also the commencement of the twenty-three hundred, because the former are cut off from the latter.

36. When the angel gave to Daniel the vision in the eighth chapter, he revealed it to him in metaphors; hence the reason for the angel's giving him the explanation in the latter part of the same chapter. This being true of the first part of the vision, it must be equally true of the last part; therefore, these days are metaphors; or, when speaking of prophecy, we use the term *symbols*. It will then be necessary to understand the meaning of these symbolic days, even as it was necessary for Daniel to understand the meaning of the ram, the he goat, etc.

THE SYMBOL EXPLAINED.

37. The Bible makes this point very clear; and a lucid definition is given of a prophetic day. In the thirteenth and fourteenth chapters of Numbers, we have the account of the twelve spies going to search the promised land, and their reports,—the evil report of the ten, the good report of the two. After spending the entire night in weeping,[63] the people desired and hoped that they might die in the wilderness rather than go into such a country, where there seemed so many obstacles. The Lord answered their request, and informed them they should certainly die in the wilderness. A part of His sentence reads as follows:

[62] Dan. 8:14.   [63] Num. 14:1.

"After the number of the days in the which ye searched the land, even forty days, *each day for a year*, shall ye bear your iniquities, even forty years, and ye shall know My breach of promise." [64]

38. The Prophet Ezekiel, in a vision given to him concerning a period of time, gives this description of the divine explanation :

" Lie thou also upon thy left side, and lay the iniquity of the house of Israel upon it : according to the number of the days that thou shalt lie upon it, thou shalt bear their iniquity. For I have laid upon thee the years of their iniquity, according to the number of the days, . . . *I have appointed thee each day for a year*." [65]

TWO OR THREE WITNESSES.

39. We are told that out of the mouth of two or three witnesses shall every word be established.[66] Here then we have two witnesses to testify that a day in the Bible, when used as a metaphor, or symbol, represents a year. Therefore the twenty-three hundred days [67] would represent twenty-three hundred years. The seventy weeks, or four hundred ninety days, would represent four hundred ninety years. (*f*)

THE GOING FORTH OF THE DECREE.

40. Having everything clear before us thus far, we are now prepared to consider the going forth of the commandment, or, in other words, the location of the period. There were three different edicts issued concerning the restoration of the temple, and its completed services ; [68] but the work of the decree was not fulfilled till the one issued by Artaxerxes.[69] (*g*) This being true, we learn that the time to commence the reckoning of this period is the year 457 B. C.[70] In the fall (*h*) of this year the seventy weeks and the twenty-three hundred days began to be counted.

41. The angel, however, divides the seventy weeks into three distinct periods :

[64] Num. 14: 34.   [65] Eze. 4: 4–6.
[66] Num. 35: 30; Deut. 17: 6; 19: 15; Matt. 18: 16; John 8: 17.   [67] Dan. 8: 14.
[68] Ezra 6: 14, margin.   [69] Ezra 7: 11–21.
[70] Ezra 7: 1, 8, 9, chronology in the margin.

1. The seven weeks, or forty-nine prophetic days, or years, were for the building of the wall of the city.[71]

2. The sixty-two weeks, after the seven, were to reach to the Messiah, the Prince.[72]

3. The one week,—during this time the Messiah was to be cut off, and the sacrifices and offerings were to cease.[73] See accompanying diagram.

THE TIME DEFINITELY LOCATED.

42. Beginning then with the fall of B. C. 457, the first part, seven weeks or forty-nine years, would end in the fall of 408 B. C. This was the time when the wall of the city was completed. From the fall of B. C. 408, adding 62 weeks or 434 years, would bring us to the fall of A. D. 27; or adding 49 to the 434, would bring the same result, A. D. 27. At this time the Messiah, the Prince, was to come. *Who is the Messiah, the Prince? And was this literally fulfilled?*

THE MESSIAH. A LITERAL FULFILLMENT.

43. The Messiah is none other than Jesus Christ. The word *Messiah* is a Hebrew word, משיח=*M-she-ach*, meaning *anointed*. This is explained in Ps. 2 : 2 : "Against the Lord, and against His Anointed." Hebrew, משיחו=*M-she-chi*, His Messiah. The same word which in the Hebrew means *Messiah*, is in the Greek, called, *Christos, anointed*.

44. When Andrew found the Savior, he wanted his brother Simon to meet Him; hence he said to him:

" We have found the Messias, which is, being interpreted, the Christ." Margin, "Anointed." [74]

45. When the woman at the well talked with the Savior, she said to Him:

"I know that Messias cometh, which is called Christ." [75]

Thus we see that the Messiah, the Christ, the Anointed One, is none other than Jesus.[76] But when was He anointed?

[71] Dan. 9 : 25.　　[72] Dan. 9 : 25, 26.　　[73] Dan. 9 : 27.　　[74] John 1 : 41.
[75] John 4 : 25.　　　　　　　　[76] John 1 : 42.

" Unto two thousand and three hundred days ; then shall the sanctuary be cleansed."   Dan. 8:14.

1 Day = 1 Year.   Num. 14:34; Eze. 4:6.

2300 Days = 2300 Years.

Cut off 70 wks. or 490 days = 490 years.

1810 yrs.

B.C. 7 wks. = 49 ds.
457.   7

62 wks. = 434 ds.
62

1 wk. = 7 ds.   A.D.
1   33,

Jan. 1, 457.   Oct.

Dec. 31, 33.   Oct., 34.

Oct. 7 wks.   —   62 wks.   —   69 wks.   Oct.   To Messiah.
457. 49 yrs.   434 yrs.   483 yrs.   A.D. 27.
B.C. 408.

April

Oct. ½ wk. = 3½ ds.   ½ wk. = 3½ ds.   Oct.
A.D. 27. 3½ yrs.   3½ yrs. A.D. 34.
A. D. 31.

A. D.
34.

2300 Years.

Oct.   70 wks.
B.C. 457.   490 yrs.

1810 yrs.

October,
A.D. 1844.

EXPLANATION OF THE VISION OF THE DAYS.

When did He become the Messiah? With what was He anointed?

"And it came to pass in those days, that Jesus came from Nazareth of Galilee, and was *baptized of John in Jordan.* And straightway coming up out of the water, He saw the heavens opened, and the Spirit like a dove descending upon Him. And there came a voice from heaven, saying, Thou art My beloved Son, in whom I am well pleased." [77]

This was at His baptism.

"And the Holy Ghost descended in a bodily shape like a dove upon Him, and a voice from heaven, which said, . . ." [78]

"How God *anointed Jesus of Nazareth* with the Holy Ghost and with power: . . ." [79]

46. Thus we see it is certain that the Messiah, the Prince,[80] is none other than Jesus Christ, who became the Anointed [81] of God, when He was baptized with the Holy Ghost and with power.

47. But the query might arise, "*Was this literally fulfilled in the fall of A.D. 27 ?*—Yes, most decidedly; for by consulting the chronology of an Oxford Bible at Mark 1, where the baptism is spoken of,[82] we find the year given A. D. 27. And proofs from other chronologists might be adduced which give the same results. Thus we see that *exactly* sixty-nine prophetic weeks, or four hundred eighty-three literal years from the fall of B. C. 457, Jesus Christ, the Messiah, became the great Prince, Savior, and Anointed of God. We can then appreciate the meaning of that text in Mark, mentioned in the fourth paragraph of this chapter:

"*The time is fulfilled, and the kingdom of God is at hand.*" [83]

THE JEWS COULD HAVE KNOWN THIS.

48. Yes, the Jews might have known all through the centuries when to expect the Messiah. They might have known the very year He was to come, the very month He was to appear;

77 Mark 1: 9-11.   78 Luke 3: 22.   79 Acts 10: 38.   80 Acts 3: 15; 3: 31.
81 Heb. 1: 8, 9.   82 See Mark 1: 10, margin; Luke 3: 21, margin.
83 Mark 1: 15.

and when He told them "the time is at hand," He sought to arrest their attention to the prophecy of Daniel concerning Himself; for this is the *only scripture* that has the definite time connected with the coming of the Messiah. How full of meaning then those words of the Savior:

"If thou hadst known, even thou, at least in this thy day, the things which belong unto thy peace! but now they are hid from thine eyes, . . . because *thou knewest not the time of thy visitation.*" [84]

49. No doubt this was what Luke had reference to when speaking of Paul's discussing the Bible with the Jews in the synagogue:

"And Paul, as his manner was, went in unto them, and three Sabbath days *reasoned with them out of the scriptures,* opening and alleging that . . . this Jesus, whom I preach unto you, is Christ." [85]

50. There are many scriptures [86] which have a slight bearing on this subject, all of which confirm what the Jews might have known concerning this wonderful prophecy relating to Christ.

"And He came to Nazareth, . . . and, as His custom was, He went into the synagogue on the Sabbath day, and stood up for to read. And there was delivered unto Him the book of the prophet Esaias. And when He had opened the book, He found the place where it was written, 'The Spirit of the Lord is upon Me, because He hath *anointed* Me to preach the gospel to the poor'; . . . And He began to say unto them, *This day* is this scripture fulfilled in your ears. And all bare Him witness, and wondered at the gracious words which proceeded out of His mouth. . . ." [87]

"But when the *fullness of the time* was come, God sent forth His Son, made of a woman, made under the law." [88]

51. Other scriptures might be cited which show how accurate and precise the Lord is, in having His word fulfilled. [89] Whether men are prepared to believe or receive it, [90] the word of the Lord is accomplishing its mission. What a blessed thing

[84] Luke 19: 42, 44.   [85] Acts 17: 2, 3.   [86] Acts 9: 22; 18: 5, 28, etc.
[87] Luke 4: 16–22.   [88] Gal. 4: 4.   [89] Isa. 55: 11.   [90] Eze. 2: 7.

it would have been to the Jews had they only been ready for Him, by having understood this most remarkable prophecy. May there not be a lesson for the church of to-day? Might it not be well to ponder and listen?

THE SEVENTIETH WEEK.

52. Having now followed the angel to the appearance of the Messiah, Gabriel said, Messiah would confirm the covenant with many for one week,[91] but in the midst of the week He would be cut off, as a result of which there would be a cessation of the sacrifices and offerings.[92]

53. When the Savior began to preach, His work was wholly among the Jews.[93] When He ordained the twelve, and sent them forth, and afterward the seventy, they were all commissioned to go to the lost sheep of the house of Israel.[94] He labored among them just *three and a half years*, then He was crucified. After His ascension, the Apostles carried on the work; and from the time of the crucifixion till the persecution of the church at Jerusalem,[95] when many were scattered abroad, some going to Samaria there to preach the gospel,[96] was just three and a half years. This completed the seventieth week. At the close of this prophetic week, or the four hundred ninetieth year, the Jews, as a nation, entirely rejected the gospel, and climaxed their national sin by stoning Stephen, while the glory of God shone in his face.[97] Then for the first time the gospel was preached to others outside of the Jews.[98] Paul, the great apostle to the Gentiles, was converted.[99] The seventy weeks had ended; Israel, as a nation, as a separate people, was cut off.[100] This brings us to the year A. D. 34, in the fall. See chronology in margin at Acts 8, also diagram.

GOD'S DIVINE TIMEPIECE.

54. Here, then, we see the tracings of the finger of God.

[91] Dan. 9: 27.   [92] Dan. 9: 26, 27.   [93] Matt. 15: 24.   [94] Matt. 10: 5, 6; Luke 10: 1.
[95] Acts 8: 1.   [96] Acts 8: 4, 5.   [97] Acts 6: 15; 7: 56-60.
[98] Acts 8: 5; Acts 11: 20.   [99] Acts 9: 5, 6.   [100] Matt. 21: 43; Rom. 9: 25, 26.

Here we observe how the Lord keeps the great clock of time in the best of condition. When the hour has arrived for any momentous event to be fulfilled, though it may have been predicted thousands of years before, instantly the alarm rings, the sound goes forth, the work is done.

THE FAITHFUL FULFILLMENT.

55. We will now return and briefly reiterate those eight events, mentioned in paragraph twenty-three of this chapter, and see how they were all literally and faithfully fulfilled.

(*a*) By the Jews rejecting the gospel, the Savior told them that the kingdom of God would be taken from them and given to another people who would bring forth the fruits thereof.[101] And the Gentiles, who formerly were not a people, had now become the people of God.[102]

(*b*) The day after Jesus rode triumphantly into Jerusalem, when the palm branches were strewed all along the way,[103] as He descended the Mount of Olives, He said that their house, the temple,—the sacred place of God's worship,—had become desolate, and was forever forsaken.[104] And the next day He told the disciples that the time would come when not a stone would be left upon another that should not be thrown down.[105]

(*c*) When the Jews clamored for the blood of Christ, they said they were willing to have His blood upon them and upon their children, only let Him be crucified.[106] The Savior, knowing they would do this, told them that all the righteous blood which had ever been shed in the world, beginning with the blood of Abel, would be required of them. They would drink to the dregs the cup of suffering.[107] They filled up the cup of their sins, when they crucified the Lord of glory, and stoned Stephen to death.

(*d*) When Christ hung on the cross, and cried, " It is finished," the vail of the temple was rent in twain, from top to

---

[101] Matt. 21:43.   [102] 1 Pet. 2:10.   [103] Matt. 21:4-9.   [104] Luke 19:37, 41, 43, 44.
[105] Matt. 24:1, 2; Mark 13:1, 2.   [106] Matt. 27:25.
[107] Matt. 23:34, 35; 21:38-41; Luke 23:29, 30.

bottom;[108] thus showing that sin offerings had forever ceased; because He, the great Sin Offering, was the fulfillment of them all.

(*e*) By His death He brought forgiveness of sins. He made the atonement[109] for the Jews and for the world. The forgiveness of sins came only through Him.[110]

(*f*) He was the righteousness of God.[111] He was the first and only person who could look the world, the flesh, and the devil in the face, and challenge them to convince Him of any sin.[112] Through His righteous life He brought righteousness to every man. He is the righteousness of God; and by faith in His blood,[113] and in His righteous life, all can share the same gift.

(*g*) His baptism, the length of time He preached, the rending of the vail of the temple, the warning to the disciples of the destruction of Jerusalem, and quoting Daniel to that effect,[114]—all went to prove that the vision was of God; it was established during this period; and the Prophet Daniel *was the messenger* who gave it to men by the hand of the angel.

(*h*) When Christ left this earth and went to heaven, He entered upon His ministry, not in the holy places made with hands, but in heaven itself, now to appear in the presence of God for us.[115] As long as the temple service was conducted, the work in the holy places in the heavenly sanctuary was not carried on;[116] but when the house was forsaken of its Lord, and the type was fulfilled in the antitype, then the holy places in the heavenly were anointed for the work of the Heavenly Priest, even Jesus Christ.[117]

THE REST OF THE DAYS.

56. Having found that the seventy weeks ended in A. D. 34, the question naturally arises, " When would the entire period of

108 John 19:30; Luke 23:45; Mark 15:38.   109 Rom. 5:11.   110 Acts 13:38; 3:26.
111 1 John 2:1; 1 Cor. 1:30.   112 John 8:46; 14:30; 16.33.   113 Rom, 3:24-27.
114 Matt. 24:15; Mark 13:14; Luke 21:20. compare Dan. 9:27.
115 Heb. 9:24, 8.   116 Heb. 9:9.   117 Heb. 8:1, 2.

20

the twenty-three hundred days terminate?" This is a simple proposition. Deducting 490 from 2300, we have a balance of 1810. The 490 terminating in the fall of A. D. 34, adding the balance of 1810, would give the ending of the entire period of 2300 days in the fall of 1844. See diagram. Then the angel said, the sanctuary should be cleansed. [118]

LOSS TO THE ANCIENT PEOPLE.

57. We have already seen what the Jewish people lost in not studying that period, in not being prepared to receive Christ at His first advent. Amid the multitude of their teachings and traditions, they neglected the *great themes of study*, the prophecies of the word of God; hence were unprepared for the event. They were looking for a kingdom brilliant with the luster of power, and dazzling with the brightness of outward glory; but this they did not receive, because the kingdom which Christ was to set up then, would be located in the hearts of men; [119] and the glory of their power would be heavenly. They lost all, power, statehood, glory.

WHAT THE CHURCH NOW MIGHT KNOW.

58. Church of the living God to-day! should there not be an arousing on the part of men and women, who live this side of the middle of the nineteenth century, to ascertain what is involved in the cleansing of the sanctuary? (*i*) Is it not possible that the time of visitation to the church of God to-day has come, even as it came to the Jews in days of old? The result of their neglect was sad and fatal; like causes produce similar results. Whatsoever was written aforetime was written for our learning, [120] that we, upon whom the ends of the world are come, [121] should take heed. Watch, take heed. [122] " But of the times and the seasons, brethren, ye have no need that I write unto you." [123]

[118] Dan. 8:14. [119] Luke 17:20, 21. [120] Rom. 15:4.
[121] 1 Cor. 10:11. [122] Luke 12:37, 38; Mark 13:35-37.
[123] 1 Thes. 5:1.

EXPLANATORY NOTES.

Paragraph 15.

(*a*) The word *days* in this verse should be translated, *evening, morning*. This is the correct rendering. The Hebrew is בקר ערב=*E-rev Vo-ker*=literally, *evening, morning*. These words are precisely the same as translated in Gen. 1:5, 8, 13, etc., *evening* and *morning*. It is important to bear this in mind for future consideration of this vision.

Paragraph 20.

(*b*) See explanatory note on chapter fourteen, paragraph 15 (b). The evening sacrifice was offered about the same time. This was the same time the incense was burned. Ex. 30:7, 8; Luke 1:9, 19. It was also the hour of prayer. This is no doubt why Peter and John were on their way to the temple at this hour. Acts 3:1. See also Acts 10:3.

Paragraph 23.

(*c*) The word *determined* does not make clear the thought in the text. The word in the Hebrew is נחתך=*Nech-tach*, literally, *to cut off short*. The root word is חתך, which means *to cut quickly, to decree*. One of the ablest Jewish commentators, makes this comment on the word, *Nech-tach:* "These years are decreed ones, in the sense of being cut off." And the word he uses here for cutting off is כרת=*ko-rath*, one of the most forcible words of this definition in the Hebrew. This thought will make more clear the exposition of this whole period.

Paragraph 28.

(*d*) This word *Cha-par* is used in Exodus and Leviticus, denoting atonement. See Ex. 29:36, 37; 32:30; Lev. 4:20, 26, 31, etc.

Paragraph 30.

(*e*) Leeser, the translator of the Old Testament from the Hebrew, says in his explanatory notes, that this expression, "seal up," means that prophecy and visions should be confirmed through the glorious fulfillment. And this is exactly what happened. The prophecy and the vision was "confirmed," because it found its "glorious fulfillment" in Jesus the Messiah, who was the One that fulfilled all things. See Luke 24:44.

Paragraph 39.

(*f*) Having given the reader a clear demonstration from the word of God that a day in prophecy represents a year, and therefore the 2300 days represent so many years, we will now call attention to the fact that the Hebrew teaches that same truth in a very direct way. Thus we shall have two witnesses from another view that this is the word of God.

The Hebrew words, translated *seventy weeks*, are *Sho-voo-im Shiv-im*=

שָׁבְעִים שִׁבְעִים, which by *all* Jewish translators are rendered "*Sib-tsik Shmee-tos*," or seventy *Shmee-tos*. But a *Shmee-tau* is a period of seven years. This is recognized by Jews everywhere. Therefore a literal translation from the Hebrew would be, seventy times the period of seven years, or four hundred ninety years. In his translation of the Old Testament, explanatory note, forty-seven, Leeser says on Daniel 9:24: "Ancient Jewish writers thought that the second temple stood four hundred twenty years, which, with the seventy years of the Babylonian captivity, make four hundred ninety years." While their application of the time is incorrect and erroneous, it expresses the view of ancient Hebrew writers, showing their understanding of the seventy weeks.

Paragraph 40.

(*g*) That the time to begin the counting of this period is the decree of Artaxerxes, and not of the others, will be evident from the conclusions reached in the body of the chapter, to which the reader is referred.

(*h*) The Bible method of reckoning months is different from that followed by the nations of earth. The first month, Nisan, occurs from the latter part of March to the latter part of April. It took them several months to reach Jerusalem, and to be accepted of the lieutenants and governors across the river. This would bring the time of the year, when the decree became effective, about the fall, or the seventh Jewish month. See Ezra 7:8, 9, 21; 8:36.

Paragraph 58.

(*i*) See chapter fifteen, paragraphs 20–38.

CHAPTER XVIII.

The Yoke of Bondage.

"Stand fast therefore in the liberty wherewith Christ hath made us free, and be not entangled again with the yoke of bondage." Gal. 5:1.

CHRIST'S CONTINUOUS LABORS.

JESUS labored unceasingly, and in every way, to have the people see that He was the Christ, the Son of the living God; that He had come to fulfill the prophecies predicted of the Messiah, and that He came at the very time when the Anointed of God was to appear. He used every object, every method, every illustration, which heart could devise; nevertheless the people seemed obdurate. On one occasion after He labored arduously to make clear to them that He was the Sent of God, and some of them actually believed on Him, He said:

"If ye continue in My word, then are ye My disciples indeed; and ye shall know the truth, *and the truth shall make you free.* They answered Him, We be Abraham's seed, and were never in bondage to any man; how sayest Thou, Ye shall be made free?"[1]

WHAT WAS THE BONDAGE?

2. This reply of theirs, and the conversation which followed, naturally suggests to one's mind a few expressions which we frequently meet with in the experience of Christ and the Jews, and also in the writings of the Apostles—"The yoke of bondage," "The burden grievous to be borne," etc.[2] What is meant by this yoke of bondage? What was this to which the people had been so long slaves, and from which they needed freedom? Various positions have been, and still are held relative to this matter, which will be given some consideration.

[1] John 8:31-33.   [2] Matt. 23:4; Acts 15:10; Gal. 2:4; 2 Pet. 2:19.

[309]

THE LAW OF GOD.

3. It has been and is still maintained that this yoke of bondage is the law of God, the decalogue, the ten commandments. This law it is claimed was difficult for the Jews to keep, and was a burden so unbearable that Christ and the Apostles overthrew it, by their teaching and by their conduct. To the candid, thoughtful person it will be clear at a glance that this position is without foundation.

4. It has already been shown in a previous chapter that this law is the reflection of God's own character, and contains the same attributes which exist in Christ. Moreover it is this law that defines sin;[3] for this law Christ died;[4] for this law He shed His blood; and this law is the very foundation of the government of God.[5]

5. By a careful examination of the precepts of this law it will be further seen that there is *not one single precept that could be removed or overthrown*, without destroying the very foundations of religion, of society, of government. The Jews recognized this, and for this reason the rabbis did all in their power to make this " hedge " around it so as to be sure that it could not be trampled upon.

THE FIRST TWO COMMANDS.

6. Which of these ten could be removed, and yet the blood of Christ be efficacious for the sins of men? Certainly not the first,[6] for this would sanction polytheism; and the greatest curses that ever came to this world were due to the worship of more than the one God.[7] Surely this command could not be laid aside. The blood of Jesus could not save men, if they continued and persisted in the worship of many gods.

7. This is also true of the second commandment. One of the great causes why the ten tribes went into Assyria,[8] and the

---

[3] 1 John 3 :4; Jas. 2: 9–11.　　[4] 1 John 3 : 4, 5.　　[5] Ps. 103 : 19–21.　　[6] Ex. 20: 1–3.
[7] Lev. 26:1; Deut. 6:14; Jer. 25:4–7; 35:15.　　[8] 2 Kings 17: 8–11.

Jews into Babylonian captivity for seventy years, was their image worship, and their bowing down to the Asherah. [9] More than one thousand million people to-day are in the darkness of heathenism and idolatry because of the violation of this second commandment. These people certainly need the gospel of Christ, the blood of Jesus.

8. Because of the dreadful idolatry of the fathers, the Jews sought to make rigorous laws that their posterity should never repeat such an experience, and thus receive the same treatment.

THIRD AND FOURTH COMMANDMENTS.

9. The third commandment strikes at the very foundation of one of the most terrible curses of modern times. The Savior told the Jews of its binding obligation; and commanded them not to swear at all. [10] But if the observance of this precept was a yoke, then why should the Savior place so much emphasis upon its observance?

10. The fourth commandment is recognized as one of the greatest essentials to the welfare of the human race. Everywhere people recognize the importance of the observance of the day of rest; and to abolish this command, or in the *least degree to alter it*, would be to encourage anarchy or lawlessness. The Sabbath which was made known to Israel at Sinai [11] was the one that was first given at creation; [12] was said by the Savior to have been made for man; [13] is to be as perpetual as eternity. [14] To do away with this precept, to consider the Sabbath of the Lord, the seventh day, a yoke of bondage, is to take away one of the greatest blessings of God to men, and to accuse the Son of God or His successors of overturning it. [15]

THE FIFTH AND SIXTH COMMANDMENTS.

11. The fifth commandment is the basis of all family relationship. The happiness of the home, the family, the commu-

9 Jer. 7:30; 2 Chron. 33:4–7; 36:14–17.   10 Matt. 5:34; Jas.5:12.
11 Neh. 9:13, 14.   12 Gen. 2:2, 3.   13 Mark 2:27, 28.   14 Isa. 66:22, 23.
15 Rom. 3:31; Acts 26:22.

nity, the society, the state, the nation, the world, depends upon the faithful observance of this precept. We are told that it is the first commandment which has a promise attached to it. [16] Surely there could be no yoke in the observance of this precept.

12. The sixth commandment is an extremely essential one. If this were any part of the yoke which needed to be overthrown; if the teaching of this as a faithful guide were to bind men with heavy burdens, then all the persecution, the martyrdom, the murder for nearly two millenniums, would be perfectly justifiable. The murders, the homicides, the matricides, the cruel killing during the Christian era would all be perfectly righteous, if this were done away. But Christ exalted this precept in the eyes of the Jews; and broadened its significance. [17]

THE LAST FOUR COMMANDMENTS.

13. This is also true of the seventh, the eighth, the ninth, the tenth. Every one of these is absolutely essential; and the more closely, through the power of Christ, the person observes every one of these precepts, the more peace, joy, love, happiness and power he will enjoy. [18] It must therefore be evident that this decalogue, the law of God, the ten commandments, cannot be the yoke of bondage, or the grievous burden. It is the law of liberty; [19] the law of freedom in Christ. [20]

THE LAWS OF CEREMONIES AND FESTIVALS.

14. It is also believed that the *ceremonial law is the yoke of bondage.* The abundant laws which were given to the people by Moses became so burdensome that the people could not bear them; therefore, this must be the yoke of bondage which was abolished. It is claimed that there are many scriptures which show conclusively that this is verily so.

15. But it may be well to inquire " Which of the ceremonies that God gave the people, in and of themselves, were a yoke?" It should be remembered that the charge Christ preferred

---

[16] Eph. 6:1, 2.   [17] Matt. 5:21, 22; 1 John 3:12.   [18] Ps. 119:97, 165; Rom. 7:22.
[19] James 1:25; 2:12.   [20] Rom. 8:2, 3.

against the scribes and lawyers was that *they* "lade men with burdens grievous to be borne;" [21] and that *they themselves* would not touch them with one of their fingers. The Apostles said, too, that this burden was so great that neither they nor their fathers could endure it. [22] Yet the Savior plainly told the people :

" The scribes and the Pharisees sit in Moses' seat : all therefore whatsoever they bid you observe, that observe and do; but do not ye after *their works :* for they say, and do not." [23]

LESSONS FROM THE FESTIVALS.

16. In paragraph one of this chapter, we find that the Savior told the Jews that He had come to make them free,—to free them from that very yoke of bondage. Which ceremony of itself was a bondage? Was it the Passover?—This plainly was a prophecy of the Messiah. [24] Was it the Pentecost ?—This was clearly a beautiful lesson concerning the first-firuits of His work. Was it the Feast of Tabernacles?—This was a forcible teaching concerning Christ, and His final work of redemption. Was it the New Year or the Day of Atonement?—These were to be reminders to the people of the great work of Christ's atonement, and their need of preparation for this work. Was it circumcision?—This the Lord said was to be the sign of an everlasting covenant between Abraham and His posterity. [25] Not that there was any virtue in the cutting away of the flesh ; [26] not that there was any special help to salvation in the carrying of it out; but in itself it had a great lesson, and it was this lesson that the Lord designed to have the people learn. [27] What then was this yoke of bondage? What was it?

THE FESTIVALS AND CIRCUMCISION.

17. It might, however, be said that all these things,—the festivals and circumcision,—were done away at the crucifixion ; and the Apostles plainly taught that these things were of no

[21] Luke 11: 46; Matt. 23: 2-4.   [22] Acts 15: 10.   [23] Matt. 23: 2, 3.   [24] 1 Cor. 5: 7.   [25] Gen. 17: 9-14.   [26] 1 Cor. 7: 19.   [27] Deut. 10: 16; 30: 6; 4: 4; Lev. 26: 41; Jer. 6: 10; 9: 26.

more service, Christ having abolished them at His cross. [28]
Very true; Christ did do away with them when He died.   But
why?—Because they were of no more service; the shadow had
met the object; type had been fulfilled in the antitype; the
greater glory had swallowed up the lesser.   It should be remembered, however, that nearly eight hundred years prior to this
time, a prediction was made that the time would come when
these things should cease; [29] when these things should be done
away; when they would be of no further service.   True,
this had a partial fulfillment at the Babylonian captivity; but
the prophecy itself looked forward to the time when all these
things should be of no value.

18. However, Jesus recognized the righteousness of circumcision, [30] for He was circumcised. [31]   Jesus recognized the
lawfulness of the observing of the feasts, [32] for He Himself took
part in them all.   The question might then arise, " Were these
to be perpetuated after Christ's crucifixion? "—No, indeed; for
the simple reason that they would be of no further use.
Having been a means to a great end, when the Object came, [33]
the means or illustrations were no longer needed. [34] (*a*) But
they in themselves were no yoke.   For if all these things were
to represent Christ, they in themselves could not have been a
bondage.   These things were designed of God to be great
blessings; were to teach great truths; were to illustrate great
principles.   As Moses said:

"And *the Lord commanded us to do all these statutes*, to fear the Lord
our God, for our good always, that He might preserve us alive, as it is at
this day." [35]

RABBINICAL LAWS AND USAGES MADE MEN SLAVES.

19. Still the question remains open, " What is this yoke of
bondage," from which Christ came to free men, and which
could not be borne by the ancestors of the Apostles?   The

---

[28] Eph. 2: 14, 15; Col. 2: 14.   [29] Hosea 2: 10, 11.   [30] John 7: 22, 23.
[31] Luke 2: 21.   [32] John 2: 13.   [33] Rom. 10: 4.   [34] Heb. 8: 13.
[35] Deut. 6: 24.

answer is very simple, when we understand the laws and usages at the time of Christ, and the terror which they struck to the hearts of the people if they failed to observe them. When we understand the nature of some of these, and the penalties attached to them, then we can appreciate the saying of Christ and of the Apostles, and also understand that the freedom which Christ came to give was freedom from human fear and from human slavishness. All this was sin. [36] And what was true of the condition of people in Christ's day at His first advent, is equally applicable at any other period of church history.

LAWS TOUCHING THE SABBATH.

20. Perhaps in nothing was this bondage of human servitude more apparent than in the rabbinical laws of the Sabbath. There was not a moment, from the afternoon before the Sabbath, till the close of Sabbath, but what there was some law which bound the man either to do or not to do. He must not take a needle of thread or a piece of cloth with him any time Friday afternoon, for fear he might carry it with him on the Sabbath. To do this he would bear a burden on the Sabbath. Hence he must lose a half day's labor on this day.

21. He must know every point of the Sabbatic laws concerning the toilet. For instance, when he first awakes, he must be sure not to touch his eyes with the tips of his fingers before he washes, because of the evil spirits which have been resting there during the night. If he should do so, he might be blind, or meet with some other calamity. When he washes, he must be sure to remember that he only washes certain parts of him, and this not with soap. For to wash with soap is unnecessary labor, and would be a violation of the Sabbath. He must be sure not to eat a particle of food before he goes to synagogue service; for this would not be a delight to the Lord, but simply carrying out his own delight. He must

[36] John 8: 33: 34.

be sure to empty his pockets of everything, even to a pocket-handkerchief, for this would be an unnecessary burden.

22. He must know just what kinds of knots may be tied and which are not permissible; for should he fall and injure one of his limbs if he tied his shoe-strings with the wrong kind of a knot, he would feel that this was because he violated the Sabbath.

23. He must be sure that he have no occasion to do any letter writing of any kind on the Sabbath, not even writing two letters of the alphabet together, if by so doing it would form a word which was intelligible. He must be very careful that he know the proper distance of a Sabbath day's journey; for should he get over the line, he would be subject to *Ma-koth Mar-doth*, the flogging of rebellion.

SEVERITY OF RABBINICAL LAWS.

24. In fact he must know the thirty-nine general divisions of laws touching the Sabbath, their sub-divisions, their sections and sub-sections, their headings and their appendices, their smallest minutia and detail. Should any of these be unobserved, and one of the rabbis discover it, he would be subject either to punishment, excommunication, or to be placed under the ban, which would mean loss of livelihood, and the enduring of other hardships.

25. Should he, however, be on a journey during the Sabbath, or having started on a journey, find it impossible to return before the Sabbath begins, he must remember just what to do with his mule, his loose money, his pocket-book, his Gentile servant, and everything else that concerns his Sabbath observance. For if everything were not punctiliously observed, whatever happened to him that day or for some time afterward, he would be told it was no doubt due to his having failed properly to keep the Sabbath. Thus scores, hundreds, yes, even thousands, of laws were made and enforced by the rabbis; and

all must be observed as sacredly and as rigidly as the very law of God itself.

SCRIBES ENFORCE THEIR LAWS.

26. We have a forcible illustration of the making and enforcing of laws by the rabbis, in the second holy day of the festivals, and its observances. For instance:

" These are the six days on which the Scripture has forbidden the doing of work. The first and seventh day of the Passover; the first and the last of the Feast of Tabernacles; the day of the Feast of Pentecost; and the first day of the seventh month. All these are called holy days. The sabbatism of all is alike."—" *Laws of the Holy Days.*"

" But to us who observe two days what is unlawful on the first day is also unlawful on the second day; and he who disregards the latter, is to be excommunicated."—" *The Ways of Life.*"

"Though the second holy day is of the *words of the scribes only*, everything which is considered unlawful on the first, is not permitted on the second. And every one who profanes the second holy day, even though it be the New Year's, whether it be a matter relating to the Sabbath, or to work, or by going beyond the limit of the Sabbath, he is to be excommunicated, or to be beaten with the flogging of rebellion, providing he be not a Talmudist."—" *Laws of the Holy Days.*"

27. We can thus see the force of the Savior's statement, when He said that the scribes placed burdens upon the poor people, which they themselves would not touch with their finger.

" Everything that is unlawful on the Sabbath, either because it has the appearance of work, or because it leads to work, . . . is unlawful on a holy day."—" *Laws of the Holy Days.*"

EFFECT OF THESE LAWS ON THE PEOPLE.

28. Well could the Savior say of the scribes and Pharisees, that they made void the commandment of God, in order to observe their tradition. [37] The catalogue might be enlarged, in citations of the Sabbatic and other laws; (*b*) but sufficient has been given to show what a burden these were upon the people. It made life rigorous; it bound them with cruel bondage; it took away its joy and pleasure; it enslaved the minds as well

[37] Matt. 15:6; Mark 7:7,13.

as the bodies of men. There was many a man who believed in Jesus, but did not dare to confess Him for fear of excommunication. [38] And for a man to be excommunicated meant almost death. Did they only appreciate the meaning of the Savior's words of freedom, and accept Him, they would certainly have been made free men. They thought and believed that the only way salvation and righteousness could come to them was by the punctilious observance of the thousand and one rabbinical sayings of the scribes.

THE LAWS OF DIVORCE.

29. God intended that the marriage law should be regarded as very sacred; [39] and Christ's own appearance at a wedding in Cana, placed much meaning upon this sacred institution. [40] But like every other grand truth which the Lord gave the people, the rabbis sought to pervert its true meaning, and frame it according to their own ideas, by which they could hold the people. Thus we find them, when Christ was here, seeking to entrap Him on this very question of divorce. [41]

30. The law was plain, the original law, as given in Genesis; [42] also the laws on divorce as given by Moses. [43] Were it not for the sinfulness of their hearts, there never would have been any need for divorce laws; [44] but because of their sinful and lustful practices, the Lord gave certain commands whose transgression was ground for a divorce. But even these were distorted by the rabbis; and were it not for the teachings of the Savior this very institution would have been completely buried beneath the mass of rubbish of the rabbinical tradition.[45]

THE TRUE TEACHING OF MOSES.

31. They came to Christ and asked Him whether it were lawful for a man to divorce his wife for every cause? Even the law of Moses was plain on this question; that was in the bounds of true marriage relationship. If they had only read it

---

[38] John 12: 42; 19: 38; 9: 22.   [39] Heb. 13: 4.   [40] John 2: 2.   [41] Matt. 19: 3.
[42] Gen. 2: 24, 25.   [43] Deut. 24: 1.   [44] Matt. 19: 8.   [45] Matt. 5: 27, 28, 31, 32

in the light of the Holy Spirit, they would have clearly discerned how far the permission extended. Instead of this the rabbis had enumerated scores, yes, hundreds, of prohibitions, and sought to have them come in under the law of divorce. So for this reason, no doubt, the scribes came to the Savior to see what He would say. *They said* that a man could divorce his wife, if she made broth for her husband that did not exactly suit his taste. If it contained either too much salt or was too hot when served, this was a sufficient ground for a divorce. This was the school of Hillel the Great (?).

SYNOPSIS OF LAWS ON DIVORCE.

It a man should meet his wife in the street, and see her with hair unbraided, this was sufficient to secure a divorce.

If a woman were spinning in the street or court-yard, and not in the house, the place where she ought to be, the man had sufficient ground for a divorce.

If a woman should speak very loud to her husband, especially in a rebuking manner, and the conversation should be overheard by some of the neighbors, the man could very easily secure a divorce.

If a man should meet a woman that pleased him more than his present wife, he had sufficient ground for a divorce.

If a woman became deaf or dumb, or had some other impediment befall her, except insanity, he could secure a divorce. If she became insane, he could marry if he chose, and place the first wife where he could support her in some institution. However, this was not obligatory. So with very slight provocation the sacred ties of the family relation could easily be destroyed. Thus the poor people were literally slaves to the whims and caprices of the zealous Pharisees; and the truth of the word of God had become polluted.[46]

CHRIST'S GREAT DESIRE.

32. The Savior, seeing their condition, longed to change

[46] Rom. 2: 22-24.

and improve it; He longed to make them free from such bondage; He longed to throw off the yoke which bound their
hearts and consciences to the altar of rabbinical power. "How
often would I have gathered thy children,"[47] He cried. The
power of the Spirit of Christ would free them from all this slavishness, and make them as free from all these things as Christ
Himself was free.

33. It must therefore be apparent what the yoke of bondage
really was. We can see why the Apostles and the early church
had no desire to be bound down by those traditions any longer.
They were impressed by the Spirit of Christ that when the Son
made them free, they were indeed free.[48] It must be admitted,
however, that it took even some of the Apostles quite a little
while to cut loose from these traditions and prejudices. Even
Peter, to whom the vision was given, showing him that there
was no difference among classes of men, fell back into some of
these Jewish customs again, and caused dissension in the Christian church.[49]

THE CONFERENCE AT JERUSALEM.

34. When the discussion arose at Antioch concerning the
work which the Judaizing Pharisees were doing, the Apostles
felt that some definite action must be taken.[50] The teaching
had been spreading that circumcision and the observance of the
law of Moses must be kept in order for men to be saved.[51] But
to keep circumcision and the law of Moses implied all the rites,
and forms, and ceremonies, and traditions that went with them.
Yet, the mere observance of circumcision and of the law of
Moses, in itself, was meaningless;[52] for we find that after
this strong discussion at the general conference at Jerusalem,
and the question had been decided,[53] even then Paul had
Timothy circumcised.[54]

47 Matt. 23:37.   48 John 17:23; 2 Cor. 3:17.   49 Gal. 2:11–13.
50 Act. 15:1, 2; Gal. 2:4, 5.   51 Acts. 15:5.
52 1 Cor. 7:9.   53 Acts 15:22–31.
54 Acts 16:3.

FESTIVALS AND CIRCUMCISION ARE NOTHING.

35. He knew that circumcision was nothing, and uncircumcision was nothing; but the keeping of the commandments of God that was everything. He wanted to be at certain places, at the time of Pentecost.[55] Paul knew that in these things there was no salvation; salvation came only in Jesus Christ. These men, however, wanted the people to observe these traditions and ordinances as a matter of salvation. If this were admitted, then it would be but a little while before there would have been no need of a Christ; for the people would go back to the old method of getting righteousness by works, by carrying out these injunctions of the rabbis.[56]

CEREMONIES SERVED THEIR PURPOSE.

36. Christ, however, came to free men from all these laws;[57] from all this slavishness of human fear. His freedom, however, did not cast aside the law of God,[58] did not even say there were not some lessons to be learned from the feasts and festivals. These, however, ran out by limitation, for in Christ we find their fulfillment. Consequently, as a natural result, they were nailed to the cross; they were taken out of the way. The bondage and servitude of the people, however, was in these man-made traditions—hundreds and thousands in number. It was from these that Christ gave freedom; from the sins and evil that there were in these, and those things that went with them.

THE LESSONS FOR THE PRESENT DAY.

37. When we see the laxity of the marriage relation at the present time, and how easily people secure separation of the sacred marriage tie, one is reminded of the precepts of the rabbis, and the unhappiness those laws brought to the people. The Christ, however, that made men free in those days, has the power to do the same for humanity at the present time.

[55] Acts 20:16; 1 Cor. 16:8.　　[56] Gal. 4:8–10.
[57] Eph. 2:14, 15; Col. 2:18, 20–23.　　[58] Rom. 3:31.

21

38. When we see how people are becoming bound by man-made institutions of the present time, how great then is the need to have Jesus Christ truly revealed. And as we see the growing tendency of enforced religious legislation, and the desire of many to compel others to observe rigorous religious laws, how clearly we discern that the professed church of Christ is following in the footsteps of the Jewish church. Should not the church, then, learn the divine lessons, and take heed? "Ye shall know the truth, and the truth shall make you free." [59] "Come unto Me. . . . Learn of Me. . . . My yoke is easy, and My burden is light." [60]

[59] John 8:32. [60] Matt. 11:28-30.

EXPLANATORY NOTES,

Paragraph 18.

(*a*) In speaking of the fulfillment of the types, in the Lord Jesus, one writer has thus beautifully expressed it:

"The Savior typified in the rites and ceremonies of the Jewish law is the very same that is revealed in the gospel. The clouds that enveloped His divine form have rolled back; the mists and shades have disappeared; and Jesus, the world's Redeemer, stands revealed."—"*Patriarchs and Prophets,*" *page 373.*

Paragraph 28.

(*b*) For other laws on various themes, see appendix.

CHAPTER XIX.

The Value and Inspiration of the Scriptures.

"And that from a child thou hast known the holy scriptures, which are able to make thee wise unto salvation through faith which is in Christ Jesus. All scripture is given by inspiration of God, and is profitable for doctrine, for reproof, for correction, for instruction in righteousness: that the man of God may be perfect, throughly furnished unto all good works." 2 Tim. 3 : 15–17.

THE PRESENT REGARD FOR THE BIBLE.

SINCE it has been the desire of the author in these pages to call attention to the causes of the condition of the Jews, which led them away from the simple truths of the Bible, and therefore their failure to see Jesus as the Christ; and by this means to have the reader understand what must necessarily be the results to the church of Christ, and to the people everywhere to-day, if they fail to heed these valuable lessons,—it would seem most fitting to close this work with a few thoughts on the value and inspiration of the Scriptures. It must be clear to every thinking person that the Bible is not prized nor appreciated to-day by the professed followers of Christ as it should be; its value is not correctly estimated; its truths are not as highly regarded as they ought to be; and their relation to the individual and to the church is not as clearly understood as it must be, in order to know and to understand what God requires.

2. We read that Christ was not only a stumbling-block to Israel at His first advent, but He would be a stumbling-block to *both* the houses of Israel.[1] Should not the Israel of God to-day,[2] the church of Christ, know just how she is steer-

[1] Isa. 8: 14.   [2] Gal. 6: 16.

THE HOLY SCRIPTURES.

ing, what are her bearings, and to what she is anchored? Is it to the word of the living God, or to the traditions of men?

DO NOT KNOW THE BIBLE.

3. When Christ came to earth He said to the Jews:

" Ye know not the scriptures, neither the power of God." [3]

This did not indicate that they were ignorant of the Bible; neither did it mean that they had not read the Bible; nor did it mean that they were not familiar with its teachings. There were men at that time who knew every book, every chapter, every sentence, and every word from Genesis to Malachi. They were thoroughly conversant with the wording of the Scripture; [4] but the great difficulty with them was they understood it only in the light of the interpretation, explanation, and construction placed upon the Bible by the teachers and rabbis.

4. When the priests and rabbis were asked by Herod where Christ was to be born, they turned to the Scripture very readily, and said, in Bethlehem of Judea. [5] And why?—Because the prophet said so. [6] But the difficulty was that at the very time they were reading this Scripture that very Messiah was lying close by them, but they did not appreciate the fact that He was the One in whom this prophecy was being fulfilled. " He came unto His own, and His own received Him not." [7]

WHY THE BIBLE IS NOT UNDERSTOOD.

5. The reason they did not know was because they did not rightly divide the word of truth. [8] Because many of the rulers of the Pharisees did not believe on Him, [9] it was taken for granted that the Scriptures could not apply to Him. As a result they were ensnared, entrapped, led away, by following the teachings of men. [10]

6. Is there not a striking parallel to-day with many of the professed religious people? They know not the Scriptures,

[3] Mark 12: 24.　　[4] Rom. 2: 18-20.　　[5] Matt. 2: 5.
[6] Matt. 2: 6, compare Micah 5: 2.　　[7] John 1: 11.　　[8] 2 Tim. 2: 15.
[9] John 7: 46-48.　　[10] Rom. 11: 8-10.

neither the power of God. Not that they do not have Bibles; not that they cannot read the Bibles; not that they are not acquainted with what the Bible says; but so much of the teaching of the Scriptures is believed according to the explanations and traditions of men. Human ideas are erected as standards for the interpretation of God's word; and men follow as they are led. If matters thus continue, we must expect similar results will follow, unless the people of the present time will awaken to their opportunities and responsibilities, even as did the disciples of Jesus,[11] and personally read the word of God, know what it teaches, and then with the courage of their convictions, follow wherever Jesus leads in the teachings of His blessed Word.

WHAT IS THE BIBLE? VARIOUS OPINIONS.

7. It might be well right at this juncture to pause and inquire, "What is the Bible?" We very well know there are scores, yes hundreds, of current opinions as to what the Bible is, and how it should be regarded. Scarcely any two agree. It is held by some educators and theologians that the Bible is a good book, but not much better than many other books. It is said by others that the Bible is inspired, but so are the works of many men. It is claimed by still others that there are many errors in the Bible, as there are in other books. It is also claimed that the Bible must be judged by the science of the day, as modern science is the test of all truth. As a result it is maintained that the Bible is not wholly in agreement with science, as it does not stand the test of truth on many scientific phenomena. So after all, we return to the query, "What is the Bible?" Have we any definite knowledge? Can we be positive what it is? Have we absolute certainty?

8. Yes, there is certainty, positive proof, absolute authority, as to what the Bible is; and the answer comes directly and distinctly:

[11] Acts 1: 15, 16, 20.

"It is the word of the living God;"[12] and "the word of God is quick [living], and powerful, and sharper than any two-edged sword, piercing even to the dividing asunder of soul and spirit, and of the joints and marrow, and is a discerner of the thoughts and intents of the heart."[13]

THE SWEETNESS OF THE BIBLE WHEN UNDERSTOOD.

9. It is not the purpose of the author to enter into any discussion to prove that the Scripture is the inspired word of God; neither does he wish to prove its inspiration from any logical or scientific standpoint, This the Lord is able to do Himself, by His own blessed Spirit; for it is written that the word which proceeds from the mouth of God shall not return unto Him void; it shall accomplish all that He wishes.[14] The one great desire of the writer is to call the attention of the reader to the value and inspiration of the whole Bible as the word of God, especially those scriptures which are so much neglected, and which are considered of so little value. When a proper estimate is placed on these great and neglected scriptures, then the Bible will be much more appreciated; the word of the Lord will be sweet as the honey and the honey-comb;[15] men and women will then want to eat the words of the living God,[16] which they will find will be to their souls like the heavenly manna.[17]

10. Very few people who really believe the Bible to be the word of God ever think of doubting the New Testament, though we find to-day the tendency growing to discredit even some portions of this. But so large a number of professed religious people to-day, seem to have the idea that the Scriptures of the Old Testament, the writings of Moses and the prophets, were very well in their time, and served their purpose; but are very little needed in the church of Christ to-day. It is thought that not much in them is really desirable, and only few of them can be understood. As a result they do not receive the study and consideration which they ought to have.

[12] 1 Thes. 2:13.   [13] Heb. 4:12.   [14] Isa. 55:10, 11.
[15] Ps. 19:9, 10.   [16] Jer, 15:16.   [17] John 6:34, 35, 63.

MOSES AND THE PROPHETS.

11. It is to Moses and the prophets,[18] the Scriptures of truth,[19] that the attention needs to be directed, for in these is found a solution of the value of the Bible as the word of God. In fact the very foundation of all the truth of the gospel of Christianity is based on Moses and the prophets; and if these are not believed then the foundations of the gospel are discredited.

12. A fact most remarkable yet lamentable is the general tendency to cast discredit on these sacred volumes, whereas Christ used them as proof and demonstration of His mission and authority. If this authority can once more be reinstated in the minds of men, the same effect will be seen in the lives of the devotees as was demonstrated when these truths were believed and preached. Science, philosophy, scholarship, literary culture, and intellectual pursuits, seem to conspire against these precious and sacred volumes: nevertheless the foundation of God standeth sure.[20]

13. Yes, Moses and the prophets are the inspired records of God,[21] proofs of the authenticity of the word of God, and bases for the fulfillment of God's blessed truth.[22]

WHAT IS INSPIRATION?

14. The question will naturally arise, however, as to what is inspiration? The answer is given as follows:

" Knowing this first, that no prophecy of the scripture is of any private interpretation. For the prophecy came not at any time by the will of man: but holy men of God spake *as they were moved by the Holy Ghost.*[23]

The Bible defines inspiration as the moving of the Holy Ghost upon the hearts of men; the Holy Spirit doing the breathing and speaking, (*a*) while having these men under its control. It is true there were times when men who spake under the inspiration of God said things they would rather not

---

[18] Luke 24: 26, 44; 16: 29, 31.   [19] Dan. 10: 21.   [20] 2 Tim. 2: 19.
[21] John 5: 46, 47.   [22] Luke 16: 31.   [23] 2 Pet. 1: 20, 21.

have said, because by so doing they were losers of wealth and influence; but they realized they were mouth-pieces for God, and were obliged to say only those things which God placed in their mouths. This was especially true of the Prophet Balaam who was called to curse Israel for the King of Moab. The king promised him a large sum of money if he would only come and curse the people. [24] He was told by the Lord not to go. [25] He finally insisted upon going; then he was granted permission. The Lord, however, told Him only to speak what he should be told. [26] Being brought to a certain place by the king, he went and asked God what to speak. On returning he said:

" How shall I curse whom God hath not cursed? or how shall I defy whom the Lord hath not defied?" [27]

The king then remonstrated with the prophet for blessing the people instead of cursing them, to which Balaam replied:

" Must I not take heed to speak that which the Lord hath put in my mouth?" [28]

15. Several times the king endeavored to have Balaam curse the people; and as many times the Lord placed words in his mouth, which he spake in blessing. [29] He could say only that which the Lord told him. This is inspiration. God speaking through men; God the speaker, the man the medium of communication. Thus the inspiration of the word of God is simply God talking to and through men. Oh, that men could but realize what it means to listen to God speaking to them. [30]

ALL SCRIPTURE INSPIRED.

16. In view of this definition of inspiration the Apostle Paul makes this statement:

" *All scripture is given by inspiration of God*, and is profitable for doctrine, for reproof, for correction, for instruction in righteousness; that

---

[24] Num. 22: 4-8.   [25] Num. 22: 12.   [26] Num. 22: 18-20.   [27] Num. 23: 8.
[28] Num. 33: 12.   [29] Num. 23: 16, 18-20; 24: 2-9, 10-13.
[30] 1 Sam. 3: 9, 10; Ps. 85: 8.

THE BIBLE WAS VALUED WHEN PROHIBITED.

the man of God may be perfect, throughly furnished unto all good works." [31]

Thus we are told by this inspired man of God that *all Scripture* is given by the breath of God; every part of it is inspired, all has been written by men, whom God selected. This of course does not imply that whatever is found in the Scriptures was directly spoken to the people by the Lord through His servants; as for instance the lie of Satan to Eve. [32] The serpent spoke to Eve; but God told Moses to write the conversation, and He told Him just what the statement was. And the same with other things; God told the men to write those things which others may have said, and the inspiration of God told the writers what to insert and what to omit.

17. Can it be demonstrated, therefore, that every one of the books we now have, known as the Old Testament, are really the inspired words of God, and were written by the men who are regarded as their authors? As proof that it can we will let Christ, the Author of truth, [33]—the fulfillment of Moses and the prophets,—and the Apostles, the chosen men of God, reply. May it be that by a proper understanding of these facts we shall better appreciate the value and inspiration of the blessed Scriptures, which were not only breathed into the lives of the men who wrote them, but may also be inhaled into the life of every man, who will receive them absolutely as they are, the living words of the living God. [34]

THE BOOK OF GENESIS.

18. Perhaps there is no book in all the Bible that is less regarded as really inspired and literally true than the first book of the Bible. It is twisted, distorted, explained away, philosophized, criticized, and generally disregarded. [35] It is said that one person wrote the first chapter, while some one else wrote the second and perhaps the third. (*b*) Then it is claimed that it is rather indefinite who wrote the fourth and fifth chapters,

---

[31] 2 Tim. 3:16, 17.   [32] Gen. 3:1-4; John 8:44.   [33] John 14:6.
[34] 1 Pet. 1:23, 25.   [35] Col. 2:8; 1 Tim. 6:20.

and those following; whereas many of the characters in the book are regarded as myths. Thus speaketh man. But what do Christ and the inspired men of God say concerning it?

(*a*) Christ's testimony :

"Do not think that I will accuse you unto the Father; there is one that accuseth you, even Moses, in whom ye trust. For had ye believed Moses, ye would have believed Me: for he wrote of Me. But if ye *believe not His writings*, how shall ye believe My words ? " [36]

"They have Moses and the prophets; let them hear them. . . . If they hear not Moses and the prophets, neither will they be persuaded, though one rose from the dead." [37]

"And beginning at Moses and all the prophets, He expounded unto them in all the scriptures the things concerning Himself." [38]

"These are the words which I spake unto you, while I was yet with you, that all things must be fulfilled, which were written in the law of Moses, and in the prophets, and in the psalms, concerning Me." [39]

WRITINGS OF MOSES NECESSARY TO BELIEF IN CHRIST.

19. It is thus evident that Jesus believed in Moses; He believed that Moses was inspired, that the writings of Moses referred to Himself. He believed and knew that Moses did write those things. The Savior, moreover, said that a basis of faith in Him as the Christ, the Anointed of God, were the writings of Moses. If they did not believe what Moses wrote, they could not believe His words. This being true, if people do not know what Moses wrote, how can they be prepared to believe what Jesus taught? The one is the basis for the other. If the Jews had only believed the writings of Moses, they would certainly have believed in Jesus. True, they claimed to believe in Moses, and went as far as to profess they were Moses' disciples; [40] but their faith in Moses was governed by their rabbinical traditions, instead of their personal faith and knowledge of the prophet's teaching. The church of to-day should bear that fact in mind; if the professed church desires to grow in faith and in the grace of Jesus Christ, [41] let her ascertain what Moses taught concerning the Lord.

[36] John 5 : 45–47.   [37] Luke 16 : 29, 31.   [38] Luke 24 : 27.
[39] Luke 24 : 44.   [40] John 9 : 29.   [41] 2 Pet. 3 : 18.

20. Did Christ then believe in the book of Genesis? We are all aware that it is recognized that the Jews at the time of Christ believed that Moses wrote that book; in fact there never has been known any learned Jewish rabbi or teacher, all through the centuries and millenniums of the past, that ever questioned the authenticity of Genesis, or cast discredit upon it, as not having been written by Moses. It was always so recognized, and even is to-day by the orthodox Jews.

21. Christ quoted from the second chapter of Genesis, to prove the marriage relation.[42] He quoted from the sixth chapter to show the wickedness of the last days.[43] He quoted Abraham on several occasions,[44] thus showing His faith in a number of other chapters in Genesis. He quoted from the nineteenth chapter to show what will transpire just prior to his second coming.[45] Many other instances do we find in the teachings of Christ Himself, where He freely used and quoted from the first book of the Bible. It was of value to Him; He believed in it; He relied upon it; He closely followed it. His strength and power lay in receiving and believing it, and adhering closely to its teachings.

THE APOSTLES BELIEVED IT INSPIRED.

(*b*) Matthew believed in it; for the very first sentence in his gospel refers to Abraham,[46] whose life's record is contained in Genesis.

(*c*) Mark believed in it; for He refers to that book, as the sayings of Jesus, in His writings.[47]

(*d*) Luke believed in it; for He quotes from it freely,[48] and also mentions a number of places where Jesus spoke of it.

(*e*) John accepted it, as the inspired word of God.

(*f*) Paul believed in it, and took many a sermon, filled with

---

[42] Matt. 19:3-6, compare Gen. 2:23, 24   [43] Luke 17:26, compare Gen. 6:5, 12, 13.
[44] Matt. 8:11; 22:32; Luke 13:16; 16:22, etc.; 19:9; John 8:37, 39, etc.
[45] Luke 17:28, 29, 32, see Gen. 19.   [46] Matt. 1:1.   [47] Mark 10:7, 8.
[48] Luke 1:59; 2:21, etc., compare Gen. 17:12, etc.

the power of God, from the writings of the first book of the Bible. [49]   Thus we find that all the inspired writers believed in that book, and believed that Moses wrote it.

22. Paul quotes from the first chapter, [50] the second chapter, [51] the third chapter, [52] the fourth chapter, [53] the fifth chapter; [54] in fact nearly every chapter of the book is quoted by the different writers of the New Testament, as well as by the Savior Himself.   Thus we can see the importance the Savior and the Apostles attached to the first book of the Bible. There is a reason for this, and the prince of evil is aware of it.

DESTROYING THE HOUSE: AN ILLUSTRATION.

23. If a man wished to destroy the house of an enemy, he would not begin by pulling out the nails, loosening the boards, or even removing the shingles.   But the quickest and most effective way to destroy the house would be by loosening the foundation of the building.   If he succeeded in accomplishing this, he is positive that the entire structure will soon go.

24. Thus it is with the work of God.   The house of God, which is the church of the living God, [55] is built upon the foundations of the Apostles and prophets, with Jesus as the cornerstone; [56] but the subsoil truth is the book of Genesis.   If the basis can only be shaken; if men can only lose faith in the absolute inspiration of this book; if men can be led to believe that this book is not the word of God, the devil knows he has not a hard task to overthrow the superstructure of the building. But we are told that the foundation of God standeth sure. [57] The Lord inspired the book.   He created the world in six days, (c) [58] days of twenty-four hours each, the same kind of a day that we have at the present time.   All the book is God breathed; hence the book received into the heart of the believer will give to him power, life, and energy which only the Author of it can bestow.

[49] Acts 13: 17.   [50] 2 Cor. 4: 6, compare Gen. 1: 3, etc.
[51] 1 Cor. 15: 45, compare Gen. 2; 7.   [52] 2 Cor. 11: 3, compare Gen. 3: 1-5.
[53] Heb. 11: 4, compare Gen. 4: 4, etc.   [54] Col. 3: 10, compare Gen. 5; 1.
[55] 1 Tim. 3: 15.   [56] Eph. 2: 20.   [57] 2 Tim. 2: 19.   [58] Gen. 2: 1-3; Ex. 20: 8-11.

THE BOOK OF EXODUS.

25. Is the second book of the Pentateuch the inspired word of God ? and have we authority that this book was written by Moses ? We might quote much on this point ; but a few witnesses must suffice.

(*a*) The Savior's evidence :

"And as touching the dead, that they rise : have ye not read in *the book of Moses*, how in the bush God spake unto him, saying, I am the God of Abraham, and the God of Isaac, and the God of Jacob?" [59]

The Master states plainly that *Moses wrote this book;* and if the third chapter of Exodus is read, the very words which are quoted here will be found. So this book is both inspired, and has for its author that faithful man of God, Moses.

(*b*) Paul's testimony :

"And not as Moses, which put a vail over his face, that the children of Israel could not steadfastly look to the end of that which is abolished." [60]

"Who serve unto the example and shadow of heavenly things, as Moses was admonished of God when he was about to make the tabernacle ; for, See, saith He, that thou make all things according to the pattern shewed thee in the mount." [61]

(*c*) Stephen's testimony :

"The same dealt subtilly with our kindred ; and evil-entreated our fathers, so that they cast out their young children, to the end they might not live. In which time Moses was born, and was exceeding fair, and nourished up in his father's house three months : . . . And Moses was learned in all the wisdom of the Egyptians, and was mighty in words and in deeds . . ." "This is he [that is, Moses] who received the lively oracles to give unto us." [62]

We have at least three witnesses, and more can be produced, inspired with the Holy Ghost, that testify to the truthfulness of Exodus, and Moses as its author.

THE BOOK OF LEVITICUS.

26. How few people there are who seem much interested in

[59] Mark 12:26, compare Ex. 3:6.   [60] 2 Cor. 3:13, compare Ex. 34:29, 30, 33, 34.   [61] Heb. 8:5, compare Ex. 25:40.   [62] Acts 7:19-38.

336 PRACTICAL LESSONS.

this volume of the book; [63] and yet this is one of the best and most blessed of all the lively oracles. [64] In fact the book of Hebrews never could have been written, were it not for Leviticus; for the whole plan of God's atonement for the world is vividly portrayed in this book.

CHRIST AND THE APOSTLES BELIEVED IT.

27. Yes, and Moses wrote it. Since Moses wrote it, it is evident it must have been written before his death. But he died before the children of Israel crossed the Jordan to enter the promised land. Therefore this book of Leviticus must have been written before the people reached the land of Canaan. We find that there seems to be a growing tendency in these latter days toward advocating that this book was written after the people were settled in Canaan. (d) We give one testimony which must be considered prime authority to show that this was not so, but that it was written by Moses.

28. Christ's testimony:

" When He was come down from the mountain, great multitudes followed Him. And, behold, there came a leper and worshiped Him, saying, Lord, if Thou wilt, Thou canst make me clean. And Jesus put forth His hand, and touched him, saying, I will; be thou clean. And immediately his leprosy was cleansed. And Jesus saith unto him, See thou tell no man; but go thy way, show thyself to the priest, and offer the gift that *Moses commanded*, for a testimony unto them." [65]

Here the Messiah, the Messenger of God, the only begotten of the Father, who always dwelt in the bosom of the Almighty, tells us Himself that the command concerning the law of leprosy was given by Moses. The record of these laws we find in Leviticus.

Luke's testimony:

29. The evangelist Luke in writing the account of the Savior's birth and dedication to the Lord, plainly states that Mary complied with certain laws of purification, which were

---

63 Ps. 40: 7; Heb. 10: 7.   64 Acts 7:38.
65 Matt. 8: 1-4, compare Lev. 14.

commanded by Moses. These laws we also find in the book of Leviticus. [66]

Paul's testimony :

30. As was previously mentioned, Paul, the author of the book of Hebrews, wrote that book largely as a result of the book of Leviticus. He freely quotes from the book, and gives many passages; [67] and clearly demonstrates from that third book of Moses the everlasting priesthood of the Lord Jesus. [68] Thus we have at least three witnesses concerning this volume, and more might be given.

THE BOOK OF NUMBERS.

31. The word which is translated into the English, *Numbers*, in the Hebrew is במדבר=*B-mid-bor=wilderness*. And it scarcely needs to be mentioned that Moses was the leader of the children of Israel all through the wilderness. He was with them from the beginning of their experience to the very time they were about to pass over. Who then was qualified as well as was he, to write the account of the dealings of God with the people. Many are the testimonies given by the inspired Apostles which conclusively show that this book is the testimony of the Lord. We can give but few.

32. Christ's testimony :

" And as Moses lifted up the serpent in the wilderness, even so must the Son of man be lifted up: that whosoever believeth in Him should not perish, but have eternal life." [69]

The account of the lifting up of the serpent we find in the book of Numbers. [70] This was done because of the murmurings of the people. Thus in this lesson from the book of Numbers we find an illustration of the work of Jesus, the Healer, the Messiah.

33. Matthew's testimony :

" Now when Jesus was born in Bethlehem of Judea in the days of

[66] Luke 2: 22–24, compare Lev. 12: 6–8.　　[67] Heb. 9.　　[68] Heb. 7.
[69] John 3: 14, 15.　　[70] Num. 21: 7–9.

22

Herod the king, behold, there came wise men from the east to Jerusalem, saying, Where is He that is born, King of the Jews? for we have seen His star in the east, and are come to worship Him." [71]

The prophecy of this *Star* was given by direct inspiration to Balaam the prophet, mentioned in paragraph fourteen of this chapter.   The prophecy is as follows :

"I shall see Him, but not now: I shall behold Him, but not nigh: there shall come a *Star* out of Jacob, and a Scepter shall rise out of Israel, and shall smite the corners of Moab, and destroy all the children of Sheth." [72]

34. Paul's evidence :

The Apostle Paul gives repeated testimonies from the book of Numbers. [73]   Most of the chapters of the book are quoted, several verses together sometimes; [74] but the faith of the apostle in this book was unbounded, and from its contents the Holy Ghost inspired him to select material to write the gospel of Jesus, the Son of God.

THE BOOK OF DEUTERONOMY.

35. We now come to the fifth and last book of the Pentateuch.   The word *Deuteronomy*, comes from the Hebrew word, דברים-*D-vo-rim*, which means *repetition*.   This is exactly what the book does.   It repeats the whole history of the dealings of God with the Israelites from the time of their passage through the Red Sea, till the time Moses was called of God to lay down his life.   The book itself, if it were only read, would clearly show that God spoke its contents, and Moses wrote the words.   We find, however, several statements from this book quoted as evidence for the belief of the Apostles in Jesus as the Christ.   The Savior Himself recognized that Moses was its author.

36. Christ's testimony :

" They say unto Him, Why did Moses then command to give a writing of divorcement, and to put her away? He saith unto them, Moses

[1] Matt. 2: 1, 2.   [72] Num. 24: 17.   [73] Acts 13: 18, compare Num. 14: 28, 29, 33, 34.   [74] 1 Cor. 10: 1-10.

On the Way to Emmaus.

because of the hardness of your hearts suffered you to put away your wives: but from the beginning it was not so." [75]

"The same day came to Him the Sadducees, which say that there is no resurrection, and asked Him, saying, Master, Moses said, If a man die, having no children, his brother shall marry his wife, and raise up seed unto his brother." [76]

37. In neither of these cases do we find the Savior denying that Moses was authority for the statements. He knew as well as did the Jews that Moses wrote them; and He repeatedly urged the people to believe and read His writings.

38. Peter and Stephen, men filled with the Holy Ghost, quoted from this book before the multitudes,[77] as their proof that Jesus is the Christ, and the great Prophet which God predicted should come. This truth we know cut the hearts of the Sanhedrin and many of the Jewish leaders,[78] thus demonstrating that these writings had power, and were essential to prove Jesus as the Christ.

THE ENTIRE PENTATEUCH.

39. Thus we have clearly shown that the whole of the Pentateuch, the five books of Moses, was written by inspiration of God, by the mighty man Moses. Every book was necessary; every book had a mission; every book had salvation; every book was directed by the Holy Spirit; every book taught Christ.[79]

40. When Christ had risen from the dead and walked with the disciples on their way to Emmaus, He called their attention to those things in Moses which concerned Himself. Moses, He said, wrote these things. Moses told that they would happen. Moses showed you all about My life and work. The disciples afterward admitted that their hearts burned within them, as the Scriptures were opened to them by the way.[80] If

---

[75] Matt. 19:7, 8, compare Deut. 24:1.   [76] Matt. 22:23, 24.
[77] Acts 3:22; 7:37; Deut. 18:18.   [78] Acts 7:54.
[79] Gen. 3:15; 49:10; Ex. 3:6, 14, compare John 8:58; Lev. 16:8, compare John 1:29; Num. 24:17, compare Matt. 2:2; Deut. 18:18, compare Acts 3:22, 23.
[80] Luke 24:32.

that was done with the writings of Moses once, and was repeated by the Apostles later, will not the same results naturally and necessarily follow, if Moses is taught again? If the people can but see that Jesus, the Christ, the Messiah, the Anointed of God is in Moses' writings, will not then these blessed Scriptures impart new life, light, and power to every soul?

THE CREATION.

41. Moses said that God made this world in six days, of twenty-four hours each in duration.[81] God said when giving the law, amid the thunders of Sinai, that the reason why mankind should observe the seventh day as the Lord's own Sabbath, was because He did create the world in six literal days.[82] Modern science seeks to overthrow that fact; the truthfulness of the Mosaic account of creation is much questioned and doubted at the present time; and it is not difficult, therefore, to see the cause for the dearth of spiritual energy and spiritual life. If God could make a world, and had power to create it, why could He not as easily create it in the time He specified in the Word? He could make it in a moment if He so saw fit;[83] but He declares that He made it in six days; and the word of the Lord endureth for ever.

THE BOOK OF JOSHUA.

42. The writers of the New Testament frequently mention this book, some even quoting therefrom to demonstrate the truthfulness of the work of justification through Jesus Christ. Paul believed it was the inspired word of God,[84] and frequently quoted it. James, the brother of Jesus, believed it, and referred to it.[85] The experiences of the people as brought to view in this inspired testimony of God's word may be read with profit and interest by all who are looking for that rest in the heavenly Canaan, where the great Joshua, Jesus, will give them rest from all their enemies round about.

[81] Gen. 2:2, 3.   [82] Ex. 20:8–11.   [83] Ps. 33:6, 9.
[84] Heb. 4:8; 11:30.   [85] James 2:25.

THE BOOK OF JUDGES.

43. One of the most powerful sermons that the Apostle Paul ever delivered while he was filled with the Spirit of God, had in it references from this book of God.[86] Some of the grandest illustrations of faith in God, which go to make up the great cloud of witnesses [87] for the church and the people of God at the present time, are drawn from this book.[88]

THE BOOK OF RUTH.

44. The small books of the Bible are often passed lightly by, whereas we find them not only suggestive and helpful, but some of them contain much of the genealogy and life of Christ. It is particularly true of this book. That Jesus is the Son of David, from a genealogical standpoint, is taken bodily from the closing verses of the book of Ruth.[89] Matthew certainly believed it to be inspired, and realized it was of great value to him to prove to his Jewish brethren and to the entire church for all time, that Jesus was of the seed of David according to the flesh.[90] This same position was taken by Paul.[91] The blood relationship for the redemption of humanity, the reason why Jesus should be born of a woman and under the law in order to save the world, is all here contained.[92] It is helpful; it is important; its inspiration by the Spirit will give life to all who read and ponder its truths in the light of the Holy Spirit.

THE BOOKS OF SAMUEL.

45. Beginning with the Prophet Samuel, we have what is generally considered as the *first* [93] of the regular line of the prophets. Samuel was certainly called of God,[94] and wrote much by the mouth and Spirit of the Lord. That the books bearing his name are the inspired testimony of the Spirit of God, and an absolute necessity for the church, is evidenced by a number of statements from the inspired Apostles.

---

[86] Acts 13: 20.   [87] Heb. 12: 1.   [88] Heb. 11: 32.   [89] Ruth 4: 18-22.
[90] Matt. 1: 3-5, compare Ruth 4: 18-22.
[91] Acts 13: 22; Rom. 1: 3, compare Ruth 4: 22.
[92] see chap. 4, especially verse 14, margin.   [93] Acts 3: 24.   [94] 1 Sam. 3: 3-10.

PETER'S TESTIMONY.

46. Peter, in that memorable sermon he delivered the day the man was healed at the gate of the temple, called Beautiful, said :

"Yea, and all the prophets from Samuel and those that follow after, as many as have spoken, have likewise foretold of these days." [95]

From this testimony of Peter we learn that

1. Samuel predicted of the days of Christ's mission on earth, of Christ as the great Prophet like unto Moses, of the results which would come to those who rejected the Savior's words.

2. Samuel was not only a prophet of God, but that he was the first of the prophets, who next to Moses, spoke concerning Christ. That is to say, that not only is the book of Samuel the inspired word of God, but the very order in which it is placed is according to the plan of God. This shows us conclusively that Samuel was written under the direction of the Spirit of God, and the words of the book were absolutely essential to a better knowledge and understanding of Jesus Christ.

47. The great apostle to the Gentiles refers to this prophet, quotes from his writings, and cites several experiences from the books to illustrate the wonderful working of true faith in God.[96]

THE BOOKS OF KINGS.

48. There can be no question whatever concerning the inspiration of these books; for recent years have demonstrated repeatedly, that God has had witnesses buried beneath the ground for thousands of years which have been waiting to testify to their truthfulness. Recently they have been unearthed, and have been literally crying out that these books are true. The Savior said :

"If these should hold their peace, the stones would immediately cry out." [97]

[95] Acts 3:24.   [96] Acts 13:21; Heb. 11:32.   [97] Luke 19:40.

Men and women, who ought to have been giving the truths of the word of God to the world, have sought to conceal these truths, and to quiet the minds of the people; hence God has been raising these rocks to prove that His word is the truth,[98] and what the " volume of the book " records has the seal of divine inspiration.

49. The Savior quotes from these books;[99] the Apostles quote from them,[100] and use them as their authority for their teaching in the church of Christ.

THE BOOKS OF CHRONICLES.

50. The word *Chronicles* is derived from two Hebrew words, meaning literally, *the words of the days;* that is, these books are simply a repetition of the words and deeds which had been written from the creation to this time; and are placed in these volumes as a reassurance that what had been previously done and recorded was faithfully and truthfully done.

EZRA, NEHEMIAH, AND ESTHER.

51. These books were written by persons who lived near the same time, and they were all in Babylonian captivity. The Jews to this day are witnesses to their authenticity. The pre serving of the record of the birth of Christ was due largely to their work;[101] and the Angel Gabriel, who dwells in the very presence of God,[102] who announced the birth of Christ, is a witness to the authenticity of the words of these books; (*e*) and Luke had faith enough in the angel of God to record the incident. What wonderful witnesses God has given to the world, whereby men may know that the blessed Scriptures of truth were written by men whom God selected.

THE BOOK OF JOB.

52. Of this book, one of the most helpful, instructive, and

---

[98] John 17 :17.
[99] Matt. 12:42, compare 1 Kings 10:1; Luke 4:25, 26, compare 1 Kings 17:9, 10; Luke 4:27, compare 2 Kings 5:14.
[100] Jas. 5:17, 18.　　[101] Ezra 2:61, 62; 8:3; Neh. 7:5, 6.　　[102] Luke 1:19.

encouraging letters from the Lord to a needy and hungry world, laden with words of cheerfulness and helpfulness, very little is studied or even read at the present time. Its authenticity is questioned, and the person represented by its title is considered a fictitious character. Much of its teaching is considered untrue, if not impossible; thus doubt and indifference cause many to fail in receiving the very help which God designs this book to impart to men.

THE PERSONALITY OF JOB.

53. While much is said to-day against the existence of such a person, the word of the Lord plainly teaches that such a man actually did live, and the experiences and trials through which he passed were indeed true. One or two testimonials may be of help on the question:

" The word of the Lord came again to me, saying, Son of man, when the land sinneth against Me by trespassing grievously, then will I stretch out Mine hand upon it, and will break the staff of the bread thereof, and will send famine upon it, and will cut off man and beast from it: though these three men, Noah, Daniel, and *Job* were in it, they should deliver but their own souls by their righteousness, saith the Lord God." [103]

Here the Lord not only recognizes the personality of Job, but compares him with such men as Daniel and Noah, great and true men of God. In other places in this same chapter, they are again mentioned; while at the same time we are told that Ezekiel spoke by the word of the Lord.[104]

AN EXAMPLE OF PATIENCE.

54. The following is from James, the Lord's brother:

" Behold, we count them happy which endure. Ye have heard of the patience of *Job*, and have seen the end of the Lord; that the Lord is very pitiful, and of tender mercy." [105]

55. This man of God is held up as an example of Christian courage and patience for the men and women of to-day, and is regarded as one through whom God revealed His won-

[103] Eze. 14:12-14.   [104] Eze. 14:19, 20.   [105] James 5:11.

derful grace and mercy. Can the men and women of the present time not find much help, comfort, and grace, in the reading of this blessed book, and in knowing what his experiences were?

QUOTATIONS USED BY NEW TESTAMENT WRITERS.

56. The writings of the book are frequently referred to in the New Testament, and are used as God's authority in teaching men the way of life and salvation, and encouraging them to a better knowledge and understanding of the work of God.

57. That they have been used by the New Testament writers we have an abundance of proof, but perhaps a few citations will be sufficient:

" Be not deceived; God is not mocked: for whatsoever a man soweth, that shall he also reap. For he that soweth to his flesh shall of the flesh reap corruption; but he that soweth to the Spirit shall of the Spirit reap life everlasting." [106]

If the fourth and thirteenth chapters of Job were read, it would be clear where Paul got his basis for the remarks just quoted in the text.

58. Here is another:

" For the wisdom of this world is foolishness with God. *For it is written, He taketh the wise in their own craftiness.*" [107]

The apostle quotes this text from the fifth chapter of Job. Many more texts might be cited, but these must suffice.

59. Other of the New Testament writers have quotations from this book, the Savior Himself quoting from these writings.[108] They offer admonition, instruction, courage, and faith in God. Should then a book like this not be studied and pondered, that help might be received to find out more of the right ways of the Lord?

GREAT TREATISE ON SCIENCE.

60. While some scientists and theologians consider this work

[106] Gal. 6:7, 8, compare Job 4:8; 13:9. [107] 1 Cor. 3:19, compare Job 5:13.
[108] Matt. 24:28; Luke 17:37, compare Job 39:30.

as of little value, it is nevertheless a fact that this book contains some of the greatest scientific truths that the world has yet produced. If scientists would devote more thought and study to this blessed book, they would know more of the works of God than they now know, and would at the same time strengthen the weak in the word of God. Perhaps it may be placing the matter in a somewhat strong light; nevertheless history and facts demonstrate that scientific knowledge has been hindered in its progress thousands of years because of a lack of the knowledge of these great scientific truths as revealed in this and in other of the books of God.

THE EARTH'S REVOLUTION.

61. Take for instance the discovery of the revolution of the earth on its axis. When this thought was first given to the world, the learned and scholarly were rather skeptical, then shocked, then surprised; but after facts and demonstrations were presented, they believed. That this great mundane sphere hung in space only, and constantly revolved, seemed preposterous to believe. But if men had read the book of Job and studied its truths, they would have discovered that God inspired this truth to be written thousands of years ago; [109] and many of the great men of God knew this, since the time God had it written.

62. Just so with other astronomical truths, as the opaqueness of the moon, and the great empty space in the north.[110] All these God had caused to be written for our admonition upon whom the ends of the world are come,[111] that we might have comfort and hope in the Scriptures.[112]

THE BOOK OF PSALMS.

63. Very few people cast discredit on the Psalms, nevertheless their value and helpfulness are not appreciated as they might be. The Psalms were written by the Holy Ghost,[118] and

[109] Job. 26:7.   [110] Job 25:5; 26:7.   [111] 1 Cor. 10:11.   [112] Rom. 15:4.
[113] Mark 12:36; Luke 20:42; 2 Sam. 23:1, 2; Acts 1:16.

the very numbering of them is of God.[114] Jesus showed that His life and death were foretold in them; [115] and all things which happened in His eventful life were portrayed in Moses, in the prophets, and in the Psalms. The writers of the New Testament all use them as the Scriptures of truth which must be fulfilled, and which cannot be broken.[116] Neither time nor space would permit the quoting of many of them in the text; but there are very few Psalms written but what are quoted in the New Testament.

THE WRITINGS OF SOLOMON.

64. In the inspired writings of the wise man are found some of the most precious truths concerning Jesus Christ.[117] Some most glorious and divine principles have blessed every believer who has received them; and they are spoken of by the inspired Apostles as the very truths which the church and the world need,[118] in order to know of the great and essential truths necessary to a better knowledge of God and of Jesus Christ, whom rightly to know is eternal life.[119]

THE REST OF THE PROPHETS,

65. Thus each book of the Old Testament might be considered separately; their writings shown to be freely quoted in the New; and *all* would be found inspired of God for the church of to-day, as well as for the Jews of old. Pentecost, with its mighty power, was brought about by the Spirit, as a fulfillment of the prophecy of Joel,[120] and the prophecy of the sixteenth Psalm; [121] the great revivals in the early Christian church were brought about through the teachings of the prophets and their prophecies. [122] We not only find that every book is given by

---

[114] Acts 13:33; Ps. 2:7.   [115] Luke 24:44.   [116] John 19:36; Ps. 34:20.
[117] Prov. 8:22-32.
[118] Prov. 2:6, compare James 1:5, etc.; Prov. 3:7, compare Rom. 12:16; Prov. 3:27, compare Rom. 13:7; Prov. 3:34, compare Jas. 4:6; 1 Pet. 5:5.
[119] John 17:3.
[120] Acts 2:14-21; Joel 2:28-32, compare Luke 24:49; Acts 1:4.
[121] Acts 2:25-28, compare Ps. 16:8-11.
[122] Acts 3:17-21; Acts 8:27-37; Acts 18:24-28, etc.

inspiration of God, but many of the expressions in the different chapters are brought out individually and alone. Were it not for Isaiah, what could John the Baptist have done in preaching the first advent of Christ? [123] Were it not for Hosea, how could the Apostles give the Gentiles hope as being part of the true Israel of God? [124] Were it not for the book of Amos, how could the Apostles at that first conference which gathered at Jerusalem [125] have decided the great question which came before them? [126]

CHRIST'S WORK PROVED FROM THE PROPHETS.

66. Were it not for Zechariah, how could the Savior have ridden through Jerusalem triumphantly, as the fulfilling of the Scripture? [127] Were it not for Daniel, how could Jesus have proved that He was the Christ, in direct fulfillment of the prophetic time when the Messiah ought to appear? [128] And were it not for the book of Daniel, what would the early disciples have done to save themselves from being slaughtered in that awful destruction of the temple and of the city of Jerusalem in A. D. 70? [129] Yes, and if the writings of this prophecy were more studied at the present time, how much better the church of God would be prepared for the solemn and stirring events the world has yet to see? [130]

GOD'S GREAT ADMONITION.

67. The one great admonition of God, through Jesus Christ, and through His holy prophets and inspired Apostles, has been for men to believe the word of the living God, [131] to search the Scriptures, [132] to know what the prophets and Moses have written, [133] to teach none other things save what Moses and the prophets did say should come, [134] and to preach, believe,

[123] Matt. 3:1-3, compare Isa. 40:3, 4.
[124] Rom. 9: 25, 26; 1 Pet. 2: 10, compare Hosea 1: 10; 2:23.
[125] Acts 15:2.   [126] Acts 15: 13-18, compare Amos 8: 11, 12.
[127] Matt. 21: 4, 5, compare Zech. 9: 9.   [128] Mark 1: 15, compare Dan. 9: 25, 26
[129] Matt. 24: 15, 16, compare Dan. 9:26, 27, last part in each verse.
[130] 2 Pet. 1: 19.   [131] John 8: 31; 12:47-50; 2 Chron. 20: 20; 1 Thes. 2: 13.
[132] John 5: 39; 2 Tim. 3:15.   [133] Luke 10:26, 27.   [134] Acts 20: 27; 26: 22

and teach, the word of the living God. [185]   God admonished the
Jews prior to, and at the time of, Christ's coming, to search the
word of God as for hid treasure; [186] there they would find the
Pearl-of great price, [187] and the truths of salvation.   The Word
would keep them from the errors and snares of the evil one. [188]
This counsel the people rejected; [189] this they refused to do; [140]
the result is apparent to all. [141]

THE TESTIMONY TO THE CHURCH OF GOD.

68. What was true of the people of God at the time of our
Lord's first advent is true with equal, if not with greater, force
at the present time.   The writings of Moses, the prophets, the
Psalms, the Scriptures, need to be studied, to be searched, to be
diligently sought after.   In them is salvation from sin, [142] the
power of the Holy Ghost, [148] the knowledge of God to the
human heart.   They are eternal life; [144] they are the salt of the
earth ; they are the light to the world. [145]   The Old Testament
is God's great treasure-house of truth, in which is locked up the
riches of the wisdom and of the knowledge of God's plans
and purposes for every human soul.   In Moses and the prophets
are found nuggets of the most precious divine truth, which the
heavenly Merchantman is seeking to freely bestow upon all
who desire these gems of heavenly light.

69. The New Testament is God's key which, by the power
of the Holy Spirit, unlocks the treasures of the Old Testament, and enables the searcher to discover rich mines of
light, grace, and salvation.   When these blessed truths are
freed from the rubbish of tradition and of human philosophy, [146]
and are cleansed by the power of God's Holy Spirit, then the
searcher, who receives these inspired testimonies as the breath-
ings of God's own Spirit, will indeed shine as a star in the

[135] 2 Tim. 3: 1, 2; Jas. 1: 21.   [136] Matt. 13: 52.   [137] Matt. 13: 45, 46.
[138] 2 Thes. 2: 10-13.   [139] Luke 19: 14.   [140] Acts 3: 14.   [141] Luke 21: 22.
[142] 2 Tim. 3: 15.   [143] 2 Pet. 1: 20, 21.   [144] John 6: 63.
[145] Ps. 119: 105.   [146] Col. 2: 8.

firmament of glory,[147] and as a diadem in the glorious crown [148] of Jesus Christ.

> " Great God with wonder and with praise,
>   On all Thy works I look ;
> But still Thy wisdom, power, and grace,
>   Shine brightest in Thy Book.
>
> Lord, make me understand Thy law,
>   Show what my faults have been,
> And from Thy gospel let me draw
>   Forgiveness for my sin.
>
> Here are my choicest treasures hid,
>   Here my best comfort lies ;
> Here my desires are satisfied,
>   And here my hopes arise."
>
> —*Isaac Watts.*

[147] Dan. 12:3.   [148] Isa. 62:3.

EXPLANATORY NOTES.

Paragraph 14.

(*a*) A very forcible illustration of the condition of people when under the direct inspiration of God is seen in the Prophet Daniel. He spoke and moved, yet he did not breathe. God breathed for him, and in him. What he said was God-breathed. Dan. 10:7, 16–18.

Paragraph 18.

(*b*) Within a number of years there has arisen a tendency among scholars and critics to claim that the first and second chapters of Genesis must have been written by different persons. The specific reason given is that the term *God*, in the first chapter, is *E-lo-him ;* whereas the element used in the second chapter for Lord is *Je-ho-vah.* Hence these two chapters have been regarded as the *E-lo-histic* and *Je-ho-vistic.* This view of these two chapters has been growing with marked rapidity, so that it has come to be accepted as *lux et veritas.*

But the author must take exception to this view, for these reasons :

1. It is a perversion of the truth.

2. It is misinterpreting the Scripture.

3. It is doing for the church to-day, exactly what the Jewish rabbis did for the Jews anciently,—hiding Jesus Christ from their sight.

4. Because by a proper understanding of the relation of these two chapters, and the three chapters following, we have one of the grandest proofs of the preexistence of Christ, and His association with the Father, as co-Creator. In the first chapter the only term used for God is *E-lo-him*, literally *Gods*. This has been fully considered in paragragh thirteen, chapter nine. This is why the first chapter is known as the *E-lo-histic* view of God.

In the second chapter of Genesis the term *Lord* is introduced; this in the Hebrew is *Jehovah*. See paragraph twenty-one, chapter nine. Therefore the second chapter of Genesis is known as the *Je-ho-vistic* view of God. But one thing has been overlooked in the second chapter of Genesis, and that is that the word *Lord=Jehovah* is never once mentioned, unless it is used in conjunction with *E-lo-him*, except in the first three verses, which rightfully are part of the first chapter. If this fact has not been overlooked, it is scarcely ever mentioned.

That this is a fact can be demonstrated by the reading of the following texts : Gen. 2 : 4, 5, 7, 8, 9, 15, 16, 18, 19, 21, 22. These are all the verses in which the term *Lord*, or *Jehovah*, is used; and never once unless in connection with *E-lo-him*. This of itself would indicate that the writer of the second chapter knew something of the opinion of the writer of the first chapter. It would clearly show furthermore, that *the same person wrote both;* only in the second chapter another term is applied to God, in addition to the one given in the first chapter.

But when we come to the third chapter we find the terms, *E-lo-him* and *Jehovah*, both used. Some of the time *E-lo-him* is used alone; at other times it is used with *Je-ho-vah*. See verses 1, 3, 5, when *E-lo-him* is used alone; verses 1, 8, 9; 13, 14, 21, 22, 23, where *Jehovah* is used in conjunction with *E-lo-him*.

Then in chapter four we find the term *Jehovah* is used alone, and *E-lo-him* used by itself. See verses 1, 25. This is also true of chapters 5; 6; etc. See chapters 5 : 1, 29; 6 : 2, 3. This certainly proves beyond the shadow of a doubt that one and the same writer penned all these chapters; but he wanted to show what was involved in the *E-lo-him* and in the *Jehovah*.

Now we have already shown that *E-lo-him* refers to the Father and the Son. See paragraph thirteen, chapter nine, of this book. It has also been demonstrated that *Jehovah* is a term applied to the Son. See paragraph twenty-one, chapter nine. Then why do we have the *E-lo-him* and *Jehovah* brought into the Scriptures in the manner Moses presented them ? No doubt, because God wanted the human race to understand that there existed a plurality in the God-head, Gen. 3 : 22; and that the *Jehovah* was always with the *E-lo-him*, as equal with Him, partner with Him, very part of Him. And this *Jehovah* is the Christ.

Therefore the current teaching of the first two chapters is certainly hiding Jesus Christ from the minds of people to-day; and naturally will cause the light of the gospel to go out in darkness. But the word of the Lord endureth forever. Isa. 40:8; 1 Pet. 1:25.

Paragraph 24.

(*c*) The reason which God gives that He is the true and the living God is that He is the Creator of the heavens and the earth. Jer. 10:10-13. But He says He created the heavens and the earth in six days. Gen. 2:1-3; Ex. 20:8-11. If, therefore, the idea which is gaining ground so rapidly that God did not create the world in six literal days, continues to prevail, it is easy to see how people will lose faith in God, in Jesus, and in the Bible. But let God be true, even if every man speaks to the contrary. Rom. 3:4.

Paragraph 27.

(*d*) It is claimed by some that the book of Leviticus could not have been penned by Moses, because it was not written until after the people entered into the promised land. But by reading the twenty-third chapter of Leviticus it is evident that the laws were given before they entered the land, as the commands were to be carried out after they reached Canaan. Moses never entered Canaan; he died in Mount Nebo. Deut. 34:5, 6.

Paragraph 51.

(*e*) The reader is referred to chapter six, paragraph sixteen, of this work; also, chapter seventeen, paragraph forty.

FINIS.

APPENDIX.

ADDITIONAL LAWS TOUCHING THE SABBATH.—(*Synoptical.*)

(*a.*) THE LIGHTING OF LAMPS.

1. There are at least eight sections devoted to the kinds of material which may be used to light lamps on the Sabbath, and which may not be used. They may not be lighted with moss which grows on cedars, or with undressed flax, or with sea-weed, or with pitch, or with tallow, or with sacred oil. They may be lighted with the dregs of pitch, with all kinds of oils, such as nut oil, seed oil, fish oil, naptha. Some of the rabbis, however, would not permit the use of these. Others would permit some, and refuse certain others.

2. A person must not take an egg, and bore a hole in it, and put oil therein, that it might drop into a lamp to keep it burning; but if, when the lamp was made, the regular feeder of a lamp was an egg shell with a hole in it, this was permissible; for the rabbis claimed it was but one vessel.

3. It was not permitted to put oil into a dish and set it beside a lamp, and set the wick into the oil to draw the oil to the lamp; this would be contrary to the law.

4. If a lamp was lighted before the Sabbath it was allowed to burn all through the Sabbath, but it must not be extinguished. It might go out of itself. But if the person wished it to burn all through the Sabbath, he would be allowed to fill it, as long as it was burning; this was not considered exactly to be work, it was regarded a matter of necessity.

5. A person was allowed to extinguish a lamp on the Sabbath, if he thought he were going to be robbed, or to be attacked by an evil spirit, or that an invalid might be disturbed in his sleep; but if it were to save his oil, wick, or lamp, he must not extinguish it under any circumstances, for then he would be guilty of Sabbath breaking.

(*b.*) THE LAWS OF COOKING.

6. Food may not be placed in a double range just prior to the Sabbath, if it is heated with ordinary wood, or with olive kernels. But if it is heated with brush-wood or stubble, food may be cooked. The school of Shammi claimed that only water might be heated by such

a stove, and not food; but the school of Hillel claimed that both might.

7. An egg must not be placed close enough to hot water on Sabbath to be affected by the heat; neither must an egg be placed in hot sand on the Sabbath, because this, too, might cook an egg.

8. Many laws are made wherein guile is used. Putting food in a certain relative position to heat is lawful; putting the same kind of food in another position, as related to heat, is unlawful. These laws were very burdensome. The above laws, with many others on this topic, are found in tractate " Sabbath," and tractate " Youm Tov," or Holy Days.

ADDITIONAL LAWS CONCERNING DIVORCE.—(*Synoptical.*)

9. If a person should bring a divorce to the wife of another man, and this messenger should say this divorce was written in my presence, then the divorce is lawful, and the husband and wife are dissolved from the marital law.

10. If the divorce were written in the Holy Land, in Palestine, he need not say that it was even written in his presence; the very fact that he had a divorce, and brought it to the woman from this place, was of itself sufficient. But if the woman should raise an objection as to its legality, then two witnesses must prove they were there at the time it was drawn up; then the divorce was legal.

11. The testimony of a Gentile or Samaritan is not to be accepted in any Israelitish court under any circumstances, except for a case of divorce. Under these circumstances the testimony of either of these classes is approved and is lawful.

12. The securing of a divorce depended almost altogether with the man. If he wanted a divorce he could get it. If he sent this divorce to his wife, it was lawful; if he recalled it, it was unlawful. If the divorce were already to be put into the hands of the woman, and he said he did not wish it so to be, then they were still husband and wife; but the moment the divorce was handled by her, the bond of union was dissolved.

13. If a woman made a vow, and her husband wished to absolve her from it, if she refused, he could divorce her. And when such a person is once divorced, he must not take her back.

14. If a man hears an evil report of his wife, he need not have any further testimony as to her character; he can secure a divorce at any time.

15. If it were rumored in a town that a woman once had been a divorced woman, before she married the man to whom she is wife, she can be considered a divorced woman.

16. In the treatise " Gittin," Divorce, are to be found these and many other laws; all of which show how lax the law of marriage had become in

the days of the Savior; and how that a man could "put away his wife for every cause."

LAWS ON WASHING OF THE HANDS.—*(Synoptical.)*

17. The laws of the washing of hands are the last code but one of the Mishna. One scholarly rabbi of modern times has this to say concerning these laws: "*These regulations rest entirely on the authority of tradition*, as no commandment of the Pentateuch is quoted or adduced in their support by the Mishna."

18. Nevertheless, when the hands are washed the person is obliged to offer the following prayer:

"Blessed art thou, O Lord our God, King of the universe, who hath sanctified us in His commandments, and hath commanded us concerning the washing of the hands."

Thus the people are made to believe that this law, while given by men, has the authority of God back of it. The rabbis themselves claim that the institution of this ordinance is from themselves; this we find in the New Testament as well as in the Mishna. Thus the traditions of men were made to appear as the commandments of God. Mark 7:3, 4, 8, 9, 13.

19. The first thing necessary in the washing of the hands must be the water. Four things must be attended to: 1. The right kind of water; that is, it must be lawful for this service. 2. There must be just enough for both the hands, which was about a quart; no more, no less. 3. The vessel from which the water is to be poured must be of a certain kind. 4. The person who does the pouring must have sufficient force back of him that the water shall flow properly, proportionately, and according to the time. Of course each one of these four definitions has a great many explanations as to the kind of water that was lawful, and which was not allowed. The kind of water which was used for manufacturing purposes was not allowed. It was therefore necessary to define the kinds of water which were non-permissible for manufacturing purposes, etc.

20. It was the same with the other three divisions. The same measurements for a quart were not regarded in everything, hence a proper knowledge of measurements must be gained.

21. Then there were certain restrictions as to the water, even though it were permissible for washing of hands. If it were used by those who were troubled with certain impediments, it was not lawful. The kinds of impediments are treated in another section of the Mishna, known as "The Laws of Ablutions."

22. It was also necessary to know just how far the hands must be washed, or the fists dipped. Then it must be known how much salt the

bread would contain which was to be eaten after the hands were washed; also the kind of salt which was expected to go into it. Matt. 15 : 10–12, 16–20; Mark 7 : 14–22.

23. If his hands touched a certain object after he washed but before he dried them and said the blessing, they were unclean; if he touched certain other things before he wiped them and said the blessing, they were lawful.

24. If he washed the hands, and spoke to some one before he dried them and said the blessing, they were unclean; he must wash them again.

25. The most strict accuracy must be considered in the washing of the hands, and in the proper observance of all these laws. Severe penalties were attached if these laws were not implicitly obeyed.

26. It is related in the treatise "Berachoth," or Blessing, that a prominent man who despised this law of the washing of hands, was excommunicated. When he died, the tribunal sent a number of men, and placed upon his coffin a heap of stones, as a memorial to the people that whoever despised these laws of the wise men, and did not wash their hands, would be stoned to death, in addition to being considered an outcast among Israel.

27. It is not at all surprising then that the Pharisees came to Jesus in surprise and asked Him why He and His disciples disregarded the laws of the scribes and Pharisees by not washing the hands. Jesus, however, came to make men free; and for this reason He answered them as He did. Matt. 15; Mark 7. "If the Son, therefore, shall make you free, ye shall be free indeed." John 8 : 36.

Hebrew Words.

Below is a literal transference of such Hebrew terms as are not translated in the body of the work:

Page 121, Explanatory Note (*a*), line five : Beth-din-Ha-go-dol.

Page 137, line one : El.

Page 137, line two : E-lo-him.

Page 137, paragragh three, line six : E-lo-him.

Page 137, paragraph three, line eight : Va-yo-mer E-lo-him Na-a-sa A-dam B-tsal-ma-nu Kid-mu-sa-nu Va-jir-du.

Page 138, paragragh twenty-one, line ten : E-a-yea.

Page 138, paragraph twenty-one, line sixteen : Na-oom Ye-ho-vah La-do-ni Shave Le-me-ne.

Page 138, paragraph twenty-one, line twenty-two : O-no-chi O-no-chi Ye-ho-vah Va-ain Me-bal-o-da Mo-she-a.

Page 139, line two : Va-ho-you La-vo-sor E-chod.

Page 139, line eight : Kach Eth Bin-cho Eth Yo-chid-cho.

Page 170, paragraph nine, line nine : Va-hish-ba-tem.

Page 170, paragraph nine, line ten : Shab-bath.

Page 208, line two : Ama-tha-im.

Page 209, paragraph twenty-nine, line seven : Lif-na Ye-ho-vah.

Page 227, paragraph twenty-three, line eight : Hif-ge-a.

Page 236, paragraph twenty-two, line two : Shab-ba-thon.

Page 245, paragraph fifteen, line seven : Ba-an Ha-ar-bo-yim.

Analytical Table of Contents.

CHAPTER I.

CHAPTER II.

CHAPTER III.

CHAPTER IV.

CHAPTER V.

CHAPTER XI.

CHAPTER XIII.

The Priesthood and the Offerings.

CHAPTER XIV.

CHAPTER XV.

CHAPTER XVI.

CHAPTER XVII.

24

CHAPTER XVIII.

APPENDIX.

ADDITIONAL LAWS TOUCHING THE SABBATH.

ILLUSTRATIONS

Scriptural Index.

General Index.

Abolished, what was, by Christ, 137

Abraham, call of, 11; Christ refers to, 69

Admonition, God's great, 348

Alphabet, Hebrew, 96, 97

Altar, brazen, 203

Altar, golden, 193; heavenly, 193

Anointed, everything in Jewish economy, 14

Apostles, release of, from prison, 10

Ark, the, 172; objects placed in, 174, 175; meaning of, 175, 176; heavenly, 177, 178; God's law in heavenly, 178

Atonement, Day of, 254, 264; Jewish methods of, 265

Authority, Christ teaching with, 100

Babylon, why Jews went to, 22

Bath-kol, what the, was, 27, 34, 118

Beatitudes, the, 93, 94

Bethlehem, meaning of, 209

Bible, rabbis dissecting, 75; one great truth revealed in, 124; why, not understood, 325; people do not know, 325; various opinions of, 325

Birth, new, 107, 108

Blessed, Jesus the Son of the, 124, 125

Blessing, cup of, 243

Blood, deliverance only through, 232; Christ's, only, saves, 234, 263

Body, Christ's, not allowed to remain over night, 234; not a bone in, broken, 235

Bondage, yoke of, 309; what was the, 309; law not, 310–313; ceremonial law and festivals not yoke of, 312, 313

Bread of presence, 186; meaning of, 188; Hebrew definition of, 209

Breastplate, the, and its lesson, 217

Burdens, Pharisees made, 216

Candlestick, golden, 189; heavenly, 191; lesson from, 192

Cherub, fallen, 181, 182; proper expression of the word, 208

Cherubim, 179; heavenly, 181

Christ, teachings of, 65, 98; teachings of, opposed to rabbis, 66; the teacher of truth, 65, 70, 76; Pharisees fear, 66; the fulfillment of Scripture, 66; quoting Scripture, 67; ground of defense, 69; method of applying Scripture, 70; teachings of, strange to people, 95; prophets knew, 113; preexistence of, taught by Himself, 125; exalted position of, 126

Christians, Day of Atonement for, 267

Chronicles, books of the, 343

Church, lessons for the, from experience of Israel, 18, 119, 120, 265; dangers to, in following traditions, 120; gifts in the, 153; God's longing for, of today, 196; what, will gain in seeing Christ, 207; to study Levitical laws, 225; how, may get power, 281; God's testimony to, 349

Circumcised, only, to eat Passover, 236

Circumcision, lesson from, 313

Conversion, of Jews, 19; Nicodemus should have known, 114; David's experience in, 115; the Jews might have known, 115

Court, making of, 205

Creation, the, 340

Cubit, measurement of, 208

[388]

Cut off, meaning of words, in Hebrew, 307

Dedication, feast of, 276
Definition, law's, of sin, 155
Desire, Christ's great, 319.
Deuteronomy, book of, 338
Disobedience, results of, 5
Divorce, laws of, 318, 319
Door, open and shut, 198

Edersheim, 7, 63
Egypt, Israel's deliverance from, 12; a type of sin, 157; spiritual, 232
Elohim, exposition of, in Hebrew, 136, 137
Ephod, the, 214; lesson taught by, 216
Essenes, belief of, 41
Esther, book of, 343
Evenings, Christ died between the, 234
Exodus, book of, 335
Ezra, book of, 343

Fasts, 278, 280; of fourth, fifth, and seventh months, 278, 279, 280
Fathers, Ethics of the, 23
Feast of Pentecost, 248; another view of, 250; application of, 250
Festivals, why given, 228
Fire, offering of strange, 196

Galileans, belief of, 34, 35
Garment, virtue in, 80; fringes on, 80, 81: border on, 80; righteousness in, 83; material of, not to be mixed, 88
Geikie, 7
Gemara, formation of, 21
Genealogy, Israel faithfully kept record of, 14; Jesus', never questioned, 16; traditional, 19
Genesis, book of, 331–334
Ghetto, the, 9
Gnat, straining at a, 27
Goats, the two, 256
God, sparing mercy of, 152
Gospel, Abraham had, 110, 111; Israelites had, 111; law and, 169
Great Synagogue, institution of, 22

Harvest, gathering of, 276
Heaven, sanctuary in, 145, 146

Hebrews, why record of, preserved, 4
Herodians, 39, 40
Hillel, the great, (?) 27, 75; sayings of, 93
Holy place, furniture in, 200
Holy Spirit, people had, before Christ's advent, 116
Humanity, great need of, 136

Impurity, Christ defines, 100
Incense, heavenly altar of, 193
Inference, teaching by, 72
Inspiration, what is, 328
Inspired, all Scripture, 329
Interpretation, rules of, 28
Israel, faithless, 16; gave birth to Messiah, 16; failure of, 17; everything offered to, 122, 123

Jehovah, Hebrew rendering of, 138
Jerusalem, conference at, 320
Jesus, Helper, Savior, 11; why reviled by Jews, 30; ate with publicans, 37
Jews, a peculiar people, 9; customs of, 9; to reveal Messiah, 11; an object lesson, 11; a witness to integrity of the Bible, 18; sects of, 32; belief of, 32; what, might have known, 103; what the, lost in not seeing Christ, 135
Job, book of, 343; personality of, 343
Josephus, 46
Joshua, book of, 340
Jot and tittle, 96
Judgment, day of, 260
Judges, book of, 341

Kings, books of, 342
Knowledge, people lost, of God, 157

Laid, meaning of, in Hebrew, 227
Lamb, paschal, 29; when killed, 229; lesson from, 231; Christ, the Passover, 233
Laver, use of, 200, 201; rabbinical ideas of, 203
Law, fencing in the, 23, 92; oral and written, 24; Jesus teaching the, 92, 98; immutability of the, 96; Christ magnifying the, 101; difference between, of God, and

TEACH Services, Inc.
P U B L I S H I N G

We invite you to view the complete
selection of titles we publish at:
www.TEACHServices.com

We encourage you to write us
with your thoughts about this,
or any other book we publish at:
info@TEACHServices.com

TEACH Services' titles may be purchased in
bulk quantities for educational, fund-raising,
business, or promotional use.
bulksales@TEACHServices.com

Finally, if you are interested in seeing
your own book in print, please contact us at:
publishing@TEACHServices.com

We are happy to review your manuscript at no charge.